T0192633

Pro Visual Studio Team System Application Lifecycle Management

Joachim Rossberg

Apress®

Pro Visual Studio Team System Application Lifecycle Management

Copyright © 2008 by Joachim Rossberg

Softcover re-print of the Hardcover 1st edition 2008

ISBN-13: 978-1-4842-2042-9

ISBN-13 : 978-1-4302-1079-5 (eBook)

DOI 10.1007/978-1-4302-1079-5

9 8 7 6 5 4 3 2 1

Lead Editor: Tony Campbell
Technical Reviewers: Norman Guadagno, Dan Massey
Editorial Board: Clay Andres, Steve Anglin, Ewan Buckingham, Tony Campbell, Gary Cornell, Jonathan Gennick, Matthew Moodie, Joseph Ottinger, Jeffrey Pepper, Frank Pohlmann, Ben Renow-Clarke, Dominic Shakeshaft, Matt Wade, Tom Welsh
Project Manager: Beth Christmas
Copy Editor: Sharon Wilkey
Associate Production Director: Kari Brooks-Copony
Production Editor: Laura Esterman
Compositor: Patrick Cunningham
Proofreader: Linda Seifert
Indexer: Becky Hornyak
Cover Designer: Kurt Krames
Manufacturing Director: Tom Debolski

Distributed to the book trade worldwide by Springer-Verlag New York, Inc., 233 Spring Street, 6th Floor, New York, NY 10013. Phone 1-800-SPRINGER, fax 201-348-4505, e-mail orders-ny@springer-sbm.com, or visit http://www.springeronline.com.

For information on translations, please contact Apress directly at 2855 Telegraph Avenue, Suite 600, Berkeley, CA 94705. Phone 510-549-5930, fax 510-549-5939, e-mail info@apress.com, or visit http://www.apress.com.

Apress and friends of ED books may be purchased in bulk for academic, corporate, or promotional use. eBook versions and licenses are also available for most titles. For more information, reference our Special Bulk Sales–eBook Licensing web page at http://www.apress.com/info/bulksales.

Amelie: You swept me away when you entered my life. I love you.
Opus: I miss the furry, warm shape of your body on the keyboard.
I'll see you again sometime, I'm sure about that.
Karin: Thanks for all the support and for giving me such a wonderful daughter. Love you.
Gaston: Best (living) cat in the world. Thanks for staying away from the keyboard.

Contents at a Glance

Contents

Foreword

Developing software is hard—really hard. Even more so when you think about the fact that as an industry we do not typically examine software development in a holistic approach. That is, we don't ask ourselves questions such as "What are the business drivers for this project?" "What benefits will this project provide us?" and "How do we determine if the project is successful?" In many cases, the software development industry is concerned with simply developing the software.

Software failures cost companies billions (yes, that's not a typo—*billions* with a *b*) of dollars every year. Organizations can no longer afford to ignore these failures. They have to understand how software helps them reach their goals and how to prioritize investments in software. Organizations must also understand the difference between software that provides value and successful software projects (which may not be the same thing). Unfortunately, this has been a difficult transition.

I have worked with numerous customers who do not know the benefit of building a particular piece of software. Likewise, I have worked with numerous developers who did not understand the importance of the software they were building. Situations like these are unacceptable in the current marketplace. Everyone must understand the context in which applications are being built and the fact that the context can change during the development process. Companies that cannot respond to change effectively are no longer in business.

Application Lifecycle Management (ALM) is a relatively new term describing the overall process of prioritizing, developing, and managing software development projects to provide maximum benefit to the business organization. ALM principles have been around for a number of years now, but the focus on software development organizations is just starting to come around. The "What cool new thing can we build now?" philosophy that was so popular during the Internet boom (and subsequent bust) is now giving way to "What cool new thing can we build now *that will help improve our business*?" This is a fundamental shift and an acknowledgment that the role of IT organizations has to change.

To make this shift, you have to understand how your organization develops software right now. Do you have a governance process? Do you have a standard Software Development Lifecycle? Do you have a standard operations framework? And more important, how well do these things work together? Microsoft started the ALM assessment program as a way to help companies understand these three major areas of ALM. These assessments give companies insight into what they are doing that works well and what areas they need to target for improvement. It also enables companies to prioritize their improvements and introduce changes rapidly but in a controlled manner.

Up to this point, I haven't mentioned tools. Tools can certainly help organizations accomplish their jobs better—but without understanding the underlying process, tools only exacerbate the current situation. But how do you deal with a process that needs to change over time? You need a tool that can change with you. Microsoft Visual Studio Team System (VSTS) is the premier tool to help you manage your software development projects with an eye on the business. It brings the business perspective to the developers and enables the business to view important software project metrics. VSTS also provides you the necessary metrics to understand which areas need improvement and enable you to track that improvement over the course of numerous software development projects.

By combining the process of ALM with the technical capabilities of VSTS, most organizations can realize significant benefits with a carefully thought-out plan to improve the process. *Pro Visual Studio Team System Application Lifecycle Management* gives you the context and detailed understanding of how to use these tools to the benefit of your development team *and* your business.

Jeff Levinson
ALM practice lead, Northwest Cadence
Microsoft Team System MVP

About the Author

JOACHIM ROSSBERG is a project manager working and living in Sweden. These days he works for Know IT, one of Sweden's most renowned IT consulting firms, and he is also a member of the Visual Studio Team System Inner Circle program. Before working for Know IT, he was employed by Capgemini for several years, working with IT architecture, project management, and much more.

At Know IT, he works mainly as a project manager or scrum master (if you are unfamiliar with this term, Chapter 3 will tell you more about it). He is, together with his colleague in Stockholm, Jonas Samuelsson, responsible for Know IT's alliance with Microsoft, focusing mainly on Visual Studio Team System (VSTS).

Development processes are a favorite topic for Joachim, and he is a member of the Microsoft Customer Advisory Council for VSTS. He has cowritten two previous books with a colleague, Rickard Redler: *Designing Scalable .NET Applications* (Apress, 2003) and *Pro Scalable .NET 2.0 Application Designs* (Apress, 2005).

Before starting in the IT business in 1998, Joachim worked for 10 years as an assistant air-traffic controller in Halmstad, on the west coast of Sweden. He then earned a bachelors degree in psychology from the University of Gothenburg, including studies in criminology and pedagogy. Rather than join the academic research world, he started studying informatics and working for Capgemini.

On the personal side, Joachim was born in 1967 on the east coast of Sweden in a town called Kalmar. He lived in Halmstad, on the other side of Sweden, for 10 years while working there. Halmstad is also the town where he met his wife, Karin. In 1996, Joachim moved to Gothenburg a bit further up on the Swedish west coast (or best coast as the people there say) where he has lived ever since.

Karin and Joachim have a wonderful daughter, Amelie, born in 2007. They also have a cat called Gaston, who goes (on a leash) for long walks in the neighborhood. And yes, they do get the occasional stare from people. ☺ Opus, Joachim's cat and companion for 16 years who helped write Joachim's first two books for Apress by sleeping on the keyboard or monitor, passed away in 2006.

In Joachim's spare time, when he is not writing books, he listens to a lot of music. Some of his favorite artists are Arch Enemy, Neil Young, Bob Dylan, The Hives, Sahara Hotnights, Ulf Lundell, Bruce Springsteen, LCD Soundsystem, and Underworld. He also watches a lot of movies, an interest from his early working life as a cinema machinist. Joachim also tries to go to the gym and out for a jog a couple of times a week.

About the Technical Reviewers

NORMAN GUADAGNO is currently director of product marketing for Visual Studio Team System at Microsoft. In his previous role at Microsoft, he was responsible for the company's marketing efforts to the architect audience worldwide, including owning the Microsoft Strategic Architect Forum and the *Microsoft Architecture Journal.*

Norman has more than 10 years of experience in the software industry. Prior to Microsoft, he was VP of marketing at Qpass and VP of marketing and business development at Primus Knowledge Solutions. Earlier in his career, he was a senior director at Oracle on the Oracle Application Server team. Norman began his career as a usability engineer and in technical product management. He has a BA degree from the University of Rochester and an MA from Rice University. Norman and his family live and work in Redmond, Washington.

DAN MASSEY is a software architect in the Microsoft Visual Studio Team System group. Previously, he worked on Application Lifecycle Management (ALM) products at Borland and was a mentor at TogetherSoft. Dan began leading agile teams in 1999, starting with feature-driven development. Since then, Dan has managed agile delivery organizations and consulted on large-scale agile implementations using ICONIX, Extreme Programming, and Scrum. His areas of interest include agile architecture, domain modeling, SOA, and team-centric process improvement.

Acknowledgments

Sam Guckenheimer, Microsoft. Thanks for giving me valuable information and contacts at Microsoft.

Dan Massey, Microsoft. Dan, thanks for giving priceless input for the book. As a technical reviewer, you have been great. The book is so much better now after all your input.

Norman Guadagno, Microsoft. Norman, your feedback as a technical reviewer has been invaluable. Together with Dan, the two of you have improved the book very much.

Tony Campbell, Apress. Thanks for all the feedback, Tony. Having three technical reviewers scared me at first, but the improvements to the book were great.

Dag König, Microsoft. Dag, I missed giving you credit in my last book. I'm sorry about that. Thanks for the continuing support.

Jeff Levinson. Thanks for writing the foreword and giving feedback on my work.

Ewan Buckingham, Apress. Ewan, thanks for pushing me in deciding to write this book.

Ameya Bhatawdekar, Microsoft. Thanks for taking your time to discuss the Project Connector with me.

Andreas Nordenadler, Microsoft. Thanks for your support.

Colin Bird, Conchango. Thanks a lot.

Thomas Gustavsson, Know IT. Thanks for helping me out.

Mattias Olausson, Sweden. Thanks for helping me with some code samples and discussions.

Per Wallentin, Know IT. Thanks for all the support and the nice MacBook Air I have used to write this book.

Thanks to all the other people at Apress working on this book: Beth Christmas, Sharon Wilkey, Laura Esterman, and anyone else who was involved. It couldn't happen without you.

I'm sure I forgot someone in this list, but I thank everybody who has helped me and supported me along the line.

I also thank you, the reader, for purchasing this book. Without readers, there would be no books.

Introduction

At the end of 2006, Know IT was asked by Microsoft Sweden if we were interested in putting together a seminar tour introducing Visual Studio Team System (VSTS) in Sweden. This was too interesting for me to pass up, so a colleague and I set of to work. Microsoft gave us free rein in filling the seminars with topics, which was great because we then did not feel like we had to please them but instead could be realistic about the set of tool(s).

We were invited to visit important customers and talk about the benefits (and of course the concerns) of using VSTS in an enterprise. We traveled from the north of Sweden to the south and had a pretty interesting time. Some customers had already started adopting VSTS, but most of them were curious and had not taken the step yet.

During this tour, my interest in Application Lifecycle Management (ALM) started for real. I had of course heard the term before, but now I had to dive deep inside it to see what place VSTS had in all this. Before this, my focus had been mostly on the tool itself and never about where it fits in an organization. I was impressed by what I saw, and by what I felt such a tool could do in my own projects. I knew that the tool at that stage was not entirely ready for everything in ALM, but I felt it had great potential. And so far it has lived up to my expectations.

What This Book Will Cover

I will try to cover a great deal in this book. The primary focus of the book is to help organizations invest in IT projects that return business value to the customer. This can be done in many ways, and by investing in the Application Lifecycle Management process and tools supporting this process, I hope to give you my vision on this.

These are the chapters and a short overview of each.

Chapter 1

The first chapter focuses mainly on the IT project world of today. Far too many IT projects seem to fail or at least have significant overruns when it comes to time and budget. More important, many of them seem to not deliver the business value that the customer wants. And this is a very bad thing. You will look at some of the difficult questions that challenge IT organizations. What makes it so hard to calculate the outcome of an IT project? What are the challenges they face? Why don't IT systems align better with the business processes? Why don't IT projects seem to deliver the business value the customer wants? What can be done to eliminate these problems?

Chapter 2

In Chapter 2, we discuss what Application Lifecycle Management (ALM) really is. I define ALM so we will have a common ground to stand on for the rest of this book. You will also see how the ALM process can be supported by tools and what requirements we can have on such tools.

Chapter 3

All organizations have processes for how work is carried out. They could have a sales process, a procurement process, and so on. Chapter 3 focuses on the development process and gives a few examples of different popular processes, such as Microsoft Solutions Framework and Scrum.

Chapter 4

One of the biggest issues in IT development today is that there is a gap between the business and IT sides of many organizations. This chapter shows two topics that can help bridge this gap and that are important to address in the ALM process. The first is service-oriented architecture (SOA), which is a popular software system architecture intended to provide flexibility in our IT systems so we can better align these with the business process in the organization. This is extremely important for the ALM process to be successful.

The second topic is IT architecture and the roles of IT architects, big topics in ALM. Traditionally, an IT architect has a very technical position, holding deep technical knowledge. By redefining the architect role and extending it to cover business areas as well, we can make sure the IT systems really support the business and the business processes.

Chapter 5

I have seen many organizations implementing Visual Studio Team System (VSTS) over the last few years. Some of them have truly used the potential of the product while others have implemented only parts of it. Most companies I have seen, however, belong to the latter group and use mostly the VSTS version-control system.

By doing a thorough assessment of our ALM process (including the Software Development Lifecycle, or SDLC, process) by using a couple of tools from Microsoft, we can better see which parts of VSTS will help us most in improving our ALM process.

Chapter 6

Here you will see how to use VSTS to fulfill the ALM vision. In Chapter 6, I give an overview of what Visual Studio Team System is and what tools are included in it. This set of tools is Microsoft's answer to how we can improve our ALM process, including such things as a flexible development process foundation, collaboration platform, version-control system, development environment, work item workflow system, and much, much more.

After you read this chapter, I want you to have a good understanding of the benefits and concerns of using VSTS as an ALM tool.

Chapter 7

This chapter wraps everything up. Here you will see how to use VSTS to fulfill the ALM vision. You will have a look at customizations and deployments scenarios for VSTS, and how you can customize VSTS to achieve even better business value.

Chapter 8

The final chapter shows how I have used the ALM assessment I described in Chapter 5 to help organizations with their ALM process. I think this is extremely important to do before implementing any ALM tool in an organization. By assessing the ALM process, we can implement a process that will give business value to the organization. You will also see how to adopt the changes that an assessment has found necessary and implement these in the organization.

Who Should Read This Book

The main audiences for this book are IT managers and business managers with an IT interest as well as portfolio management decision makers. I aim to give project managers, scrum masters, and architects something to think about as well.

If you do not feel like you belong to these groups, don't hesitate to read this book anyway. I hope that I will have some treats for you as well. Developers, for example, can benefit from getting the bigger picture for their efforts. Where does your work fit into the ALM process? This is important to know because everybody involved in a development project is also an important participant in the ALM process.

CHAPTER 1

■ ■ ■

Why Do We Develop Business Software and Systems?

Information is available at our fingertips all the time if we want it these days. I remember the days back when I was a teenager. Music and movies were, and always will be, two of my top interests. This obsession started during my teens, and I chased rare records of my favorite artists and hard-to-find horror movies everywhere. When I found a rare vinyl pressing of a precious record from the United States, for instance, I was ecstatic. Not to mention my emotional turmoil when I managed to purchase a Japanese edition of the same record. Those days I wrote snail mail asking for record mail-order catalogs from all over the world, based on ads in magazines such as *Rolling Stone* or *Melody Maker*. After carefully considering what I wanted to purchase, I wrote down my purchase order, enclosed crisp bills, and sent a letter with my order inside. Then came the long wait for the package. And believe you me, this wait could be long indeed. These days I just go on the Internet, check some sites, and purchase what I want directly by using a credit card. The stock of many sites is so huge compared to what they were in my teens, and I can usually find what I want very quickly. In a few days the package comes, and I can start using the things I bought.

We communicate differently as well. Sites such as MySpace and Facebook have generated massive followers, not only by the early adopters of technology, but by our societies as a whole. MSN Messenger, mobile phones, Short Message Service (SMS), and other means of communication practically have exploded, at least in the parts of the world where the infrastructure for this is available.

Development teams in organizations also use new collaboration tools such as Visual Studio Team System, the focus of this book. *VSTS*, as it is generally called, is an Application Lifecycle Management (ALM) platform tying together a company's business side with its information technology (IT) side. *Application Lifecycle Management* itself is, briefly, the process an organization can use to care for an application or software system from its conception to its retirement. ALM is the glue that ties the development processes together and defines the efforts necessary to coordinate the process. You will see more about this in Chapter 2.

With the new opportunities organizations have to do business, much has changed in the world for us, including the reality for our companies. They now have to deal with a global environment presenting both opportunities and challenges. This means that business has changed and still is changing at a rapid pace. This is why we need to be clear on why we develop business systems and software.

I know that in my early days as a developer and system designer, I did not think about business value much, if at all. Those days I was much more interested in cool technology and clever ways of solving technical and logical problems. And I definitely was not alone in doing so.

During my university studies at the University of Gothenburg in Sweden, nothing was ever mentioned about this either. We learned C and C++, some Visual Basic for Applications (VBA), and perhaps Structured Query Language (SQL) and how to use our skills at writing code. Nobody said anything about *why* we should write that code or *why* we should learn SQL and all those other things. We never were taught the connection between the requirement of the software and the final value it should produce. This is an essential issue in development for an enterprise. We need to make sure that our development turns business requirements and business needs into business value. That is the whole point of business software.

I hope this attitude and focus has changed since then, but when I meet people fresh out of school, I often get the feeling that nothing much has happened. Sure, these recent graduates are very good at technology and programming, but they seem to lack a fundamental insight into why we write business software. So shouldn't the school put more emphasis on the reasons for the existence of business software? Wait! Don't answer yet. Read some more of this chapter before you do.

Understanding the Cornerstones of Business

First let's define the term *business*. What do we mean when we talk about this concept? After we agree on this, we can reach an understanding of what *business software* is so we don't talk about two different things here. When I discuss business in this book, I am talking about not only the commercial part of the company, but all the functions in the company. This means that business software is intended not only for e-commerce, but for all the things going on in an enterprise.

There are three cornerstones in business system development that are important:

- Processes

- Business rules

- Information

These three are dependent on each other. One of my coworkers makes an analogy with the human body. If the processes are the muscles of our company and the rules are the brain and nervous system, we can say that the information can be seen as the spine. Not one of them could be functioning without the other.

Processes

A company uses different *processes* to support its business. For developers, project managers, software designers, or people with other roles in a development project, it is so easy just to focus on the development process. We are often interested in development processes such as the Scrum process or the Extreme Programming (XP) process. The business people mostly focus on the business side of course, and have no interest in learning about the development process.

Processes in an enterprise are so much more than just development. A large company needs processes for procurement, sales, manufacturing and so on, and the development process is just one of them. The other processes are needed for the company to function and live on.

Obviously, business processes are valid not only for commercial companies but for all organizations, including those in the public sector. According to Sundblad & Sundblad, a typical company uses somewhere between 10 and 20 comprehensive and dominating processes to support its functions.[1]

SCRUM, XP, AND RUP

For those of you who don't have the full picture of what SCRUM, XP, or Rational Unified Process (RUP) are, I will cover them in Chapter 4. For now, it suffices to say that all three are development process models we can use for controlling our development efforts in projects.

Wikipedia (www.wikipedia.com) has the following short description of the three processes:

Scrum *is an iterative incremental process of software development commonly used with agile software development.*

Although Scrum was intended to be for management of software development projects, it can be used in running software maintenance teams, or as a program management approach.

Scrum is a process skeleton that includes a set of practices and predefined roles. The main roles in scrum are the scrum master, who maintains the processes and works similar to a project manager; the product owner, who represents the stakeholders; and the team, which includes the developers.

During each sprint, a 15–30 day period (length decided by the team), the team creates an increment of potential shippable (usable) software. The set of features that go into each sprint come from the product backlog, which is a prioritized set of high-level requirements of work to be done. What backlog items go into the sprint is determined during the sprint planning meeting. During this meeting, the product owner informs the team of the items in the product backlog that he wants completed. The team then determines how much of this they can commit to complete during the next sprint. During the sprint, no one is able to change the sprint backlog, which means that the requirements are frozen for a sprint.

Extreme Programming (XP) *is a software engineering methodology (and a form of agile software development) prescribing a set of daily stakeholder practices that embody and encourage particular XP values. Proponents believe that exercising these practices—traditional software engineering practices taken to so-called "extreme" levels—leads to a development process that is more responsive to customer needs ("agile") than traditional methods, while creating software of better quality.*

The Rational Unified Process (RUP) *is an iterative software development process framework created by the Rational Software Corporation, a division of IBM since 2003. RUP is not a single concrete prescriptive process, but rather an adaptable process framework, intended to be tailored by the development organizations and software project teams that will select the elements of the process that are appropriate for their needs.*

Business Rules

The second cornerstone is the *business rules* the organization needs in order for it to function well. The business rules tell us what we can and cannot do in the company. They also tell us what we *must* do. If we compare the processes to the muscles of our body, we can say the rules are equivalent to our brain and nervous system—that is, the things controlling our actions and deeds.

---

1. Sten Sundblad, "SOA and Business Processes," 2006, http://academy.2xsundblad.com.

Information

A third cornerstone of any company is its *information*, that is, information about the company and what is going on in it. For example, we can have all customer information, order information, product catalog, and so on here. Without access to relevant information at the correct time, the business will quite simply not function. Consider this example: it will be impossible for a company to sell any of its products if it has no information about which products it has or what price they sell for.

Understanding the Need for Business Software

So to get back to the question about business systems and software: the reason business software exists is to support the business. Business software should take the business needs and requirements and turn them into business value through the use of business software. Application Lifecycle Management is the process that can help us deliver this business value. And if we IT people do a poor job of building this kind of software or systems by having a broken ALM process, the business will obviously suffer.

This is the reason I think we need to have the question about why we develop business software and business systems in mind all the time (no, you do not have to think about it in your free time, even though your manager probably thinks so). We do not write software for an enterprise to fulfill our technological wishes alone; we write it to make the business run smoother and create more value (see Figure 1-1). This does not, however, make it less cool or interesting to learn new technology or write smarter code. These are important parts of any software or system, fortunately.

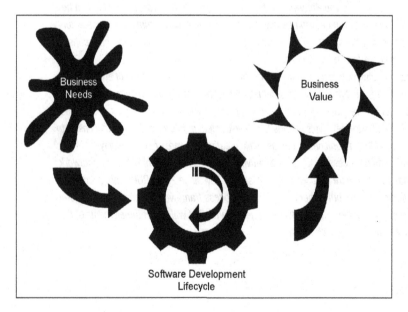

Figure 1-1. *The reason we write business software is to turn business needs and opportunities into business value.*

To furthermore stress the importance of the reason we write business software, we can take a look at a 2005 survey of department managers by IDC, a part of the International Data Group in Sweden.[2] In this survey, department managers were asked to indicate their most important IT priorities. Most of the managers—36.2 percent—wanted programs and services that were better integrated with the company's business processes. This was closely followed by a wish for better access to relevant information, at 35.2 percent. The third priority was better systems for cooperation and communication, with 31.6 percent.

These results definitely tell us that we IT people need to focus more on business value in the systems we develop. We will come back to other implications of this later in this chapter as well as in Chapter 3.

Today's Business Environment and the Problems We Face

With the new opportunities organizations have for business these days, much has changed in terms of the realities they face:

- Companies now have to deal with a global environment presenting both opportunities and challenges. A global way of doing business means competition can come from all sorts of places. Low-cost countries such as China and India can offer many of the same products and services as high-cost countries. This is a great challenge for development organizations all over the world. Consulting firms are opening development shops in low-cost countries, and other companies use these services they provide. An organization's internal development organization may also see their work move to these countries. So no matter where we work, this fact affects our jobs and us, and competition is fierce. In order for us to handle this situation, it is essential to have control over our ALM process. Through this process, we find the support for collaboration between the dispersed teams we see these days, which can give us the competitive edge we need to face competition from others. We need to automate and fine-tune the work process (read: ALM process) we use in our organizations so that we can face challenges, keep costs down, and win deals.

- This new reality has forced businesses to become more agile, ready to transform quickly to gain competitive advantages. This obviously affects the way we must architect and write business systems as well. In the ALM process, these topics are addressed and can help us achieve agility.

- Communication has also become more complex and different from before. Production of products and services is spread over the world, and gone are the days when an industrial plant supplied everything for a company. For us in IT, this means that software development has moved to countries such as India or China and we need to handle this somehow. This is quite a challenge. Just consider the potential communication problems in a company with offices or manufacturing spread across the globe—not to mention problems with time and cultural differences.

---

2. Sten Sundblad and Per Sundblad, "Business Improvements Through Better Software Architecture," January 2007, http://msdn.microsoft.com/en-us/library/bb266336.aspx.

As you can see, this means that business processes can (and do) change rapidly. Hence the supporting IT systems must also be ready for quick changes. If we do not have systems that allow this, business will suffer. This is one of the main reasons ALM tools such as Visual Studio Team System have emerged. Without an effective development process tied closely to the business side and supported by a set of tools, we will run into problems and risk being left behind by competitors already using such tools. And it is not only the ALM tools that are important; we need to consider the whole ALM process as well, including the way we run our development projects.

Project Health Today: Three Criteria for Success

What do we mean when we talk about project health? How can we measure this? Many surveys indicate the same criteria for success (or failure, if you are so inclined). Let's take a closer look. There is slight variation, but these three can be said to be the main criteria:

- Project delivered on time

- Project delivered on budget

- Project scope fulfilled

Let's discuss these three a bit. Is it reasonable to use these criteria to evaluate project success or failure? I am a bit skeptical and will explain why.

Projects Delivered on Time

In traditional project models, a lot of effort is put into time estimates based on the requirements specifications. This way of estimating was (and still is) great when estimating construction of buildings, roads, and other traditional engineering efforts. These are the projects that traditional project management wisdom comes from.

Such projects are far more static than most software development projects. The engineering discipline is also rigorous in its requirements management process, which helps a lot. You don't see as many changes to requirements during the process, and the ones that occur go through a comprehensive change request process. Many companies use CMMI to improve their process and thus be better at controlling projects. *CMMI*, which stands for *Capability Maturity Model Integration*, enables an organization to implement process improvement and show the level of maturity of a process.[3]

CMMI can be used to guide process improvement across a project, a division, or an entire organization. The model helps integrate traditionally separate organizational functions, set process improvement goals and priorities, provide guidance for quality processes, and provide a point of reference for appraising current processes.

Based on my experience at the Swedish Road Administration (SRA), where I have been for the past seven years, design risks when building a road, for instance, are pretty low, design costs are small, especially compared to building costs, and so on. Here you set the design (or architecture) early in the project based on pretty fixed requirements. From this, you can more easily divide the work into smaller pieces and spread them elegantly across your Gantt schema. This also means you can assign resources based on a pretty fixed schedule. Another

---

3.   Software Engineering Institute, "What Is CMMI," www.sei.cmu.edu/cmmi/general/index.html.

benefit is that project governance will be easier because you can check off completed tasks against your Gantt schema and have better control over when tasks are completed and if there is a delay or lack of resource during the process. On the other hand, if you fail an engineering project, lots of money has been wasted, and in the worst case, somebody has lost their life because of poor control of the process.

When it comes to more-complex buildings, such as a new tunnel the SRA built in Gothenburg and which was opened in 2006, things are a bit different. A tunnel of this magnitude was not something that the construction companies built everyday. This made it harder for the team to estimate time and money for the tunnel. In this case, the opening of the tunnel was held at almost the date estimated from the beginning. It differed by a couple of months as I recall, which must be considered well done because the whole project took more than five years to complete. The reason for this was that everything from risk management to change requests, and all construction-related tasks, were handled with rigorous processes.

I think that one thing that greatly differs between construction processes and software development processes is that construction workers know that if they make a mistake, somebody might get hurt or die. We in the software development industry tend not see that connection clearly, as long as we don't work with software for hospitals, or other such areas. This could be one reason that we haven't implemented better processes before.

In his book *Software Engineering with Microsoft Visual Studio Team System* (Addison-Wesley Professional, 2006), Sam Guckenheimer calls this way of breaking down the project into work tasks a *work-down approach* because it is easy to see this as a way of burning down a list of tasks. This method of managing projects, he argues, is great for projects with low risk, low variance, and a well-understood design. In the IT world, you can see that implementations of standard products could benefit from this model. In such projects, you can do some minor customizations of the product, and the development effort is pretty small, especially compared to the effort put into business analysis, testing, and so on.

When it comes to IT projects with a lot of development efforts, things change. The uncertainty in the projects increases because so many things can occur that we cannot know about from the beginning. This inherent uncertainty in complex IT projects makes it hard to estimate tasks in a correct way early on. Things happen along the way that throw aside earlier estimates.

Considering this, is it then realistic to measure a complex IT project against planned time? To really know how projects are doing, we might want to consider whether this is just one of the measurements we can use.

Projects Delivered on Budget

Much of the same reasoning in estimating the time of a project applies to estimating costs, because so much of the cost is tied to the people doing the work. But cost involves other factors as well. We have software costs, office costs, and other costs, but these are often easier to estimate than development costs, because they are fixed for the office we use for development. We can put a price tag on a developer, for example, based on that person's salary, the cost of leasing of a computer, and the cost for licenses needed. This can be done in advance, and we then know that one developer costs a certain amount of money each day. Development cost, on the other hand, is harder to determine because it is harder to estimate the complexity of the system beforehand. The changes we encounter are hard to estimate in advance and hence the cost is hard to estimate as well.

Project Scope Fulfilled

This is also a tricky criterion, because what does *scope fulfillment* really mean? Does it mean that all requirements set at the beginning of a project are fulfilled? Or does it mean that the system, when delivered, contains the things the end user wants?

Most surveys seem to take the traditional approach: requirements are set early and never change. But what about the problems we saw with complex projects earlier? Can we really know all the requirements from the start? Something that I think everybody who has participated in a software project can agree on is that requirements change during the course of the project, period!

It might very well be that all the requirements that we knew about from the start have been implemented, but things have changed so much during the project that the users still do not think the project has delivered any value. The project could be seen as successful because it has fulfilled its scope, but is it really successful if the users do not get a system they are satisfied with? Have we really delivered business value to our customer? That is what we really should have as a goal.

All through the development process, we need to identify the business value that we will deliver and make sure we do deliver it. The business value might not be obvious from the start of the project but should be focused on during the process. A good development process and ALM process can help us achieve this.

Let's now take a look at what factors influence project success.

Factors Influencing Projects and Their Success

As I have said, today's enterprises face a lot of new challenges. Let's go through some of these in more detail, starting with the most important one based on the surveys presented earlier but also on my own experience.

The Gap Between Business and IT

Let's start with the biggest issue, which I mentioned before, as you may recall. IT managers' top priority was better integration between the company's business processes and the supporting IT systems. There seems to be quite a gap between the IT side and the business side, making it difficult to deliver software and systems that really do support the business. IT managers may focus on security, scalability, or availability instead of on supporting the business processes. These are of course important as well, but not the only issues IT should focus on. Business managers, on the other hand, may have trouble explaining what they want from the systems. This gap poses a great threat not only for projects but also for the entire company. We will discuss this later in Chapter 3 because I think this is an important topic that needs to be solved somehow.

The Development Process

Let's continue with the development process. Can this affect success? Obviously, it can. I have seen organizations that have spent lots of effort, time, and money on developing a good process. These organizations have trained both project managers and participants in RUP, XP, or any other development model they chose, and you would think all was dandy. Still, projects seem to suffer quite a lot. One reason for this might be that when a project starts, it is hard to follow the process. RUP, for instance, is often said to be too extensive, with many documents to write and milestones to meet. Let's face it—even Ivar Jacobson himself seems to think this, considering his latest process development. If the process is seen as a problem or a burden, project members will find ways around it, and the money spent on training and planning will be wasted. The process may also be hard to implement because the tools have no way of supporting it. If we cannot integrate our development process into the tools we use to perform work, we most likely won't follow the process. Using the process must be easy, and the tools should make the process as transparent as it can be, so that we can focus on work but still follow the process.

When I travel around Sweden talking to organizations about VSTS and ALM, I usually ask what development process the organizations use. Often the answer is "the chaos model," or "the cowboy model," meaning they use a lot of ad hoc, often manual, efforts to keep it all going. Many say this is due to an inability to integrate their real development model into their tools, but others just had not given it a thought. These companies had hardly considered using any structure in work and if they had, the thoughts had often stayed in the heads of the developers (who quite often are the ones longing for a good process) or managers. Maybe a decision had been made to consider training staff in a model, but the company had never gotten around to it. No wonder these organizations experienced lots of failed or challenged projects.

Speaking of processes. I would say that not having a flexible development process (more on these processes in Chapter 4) most definitely will affect project success. Because business is sure to change during a development project, we need to be flexible in our process so that we can catch these changes and deliver business value in the end. I had a discussion with one of my customers about this some time ago. Most customers agree that there must be a way to make it easier to catch changes to requirements and make the system better reflect reality during the project. Otherwise, the perceived value of the project will suffer. But in this case, the IT manager was almost scared to even consider this. He argued that all requirements must be known at the start of the project and that they must remain static throughout the project. He thought the project would never reach an end otherwise. Not one single argument could break down his wall. He wanted to run his company's projects by using the Waterfall model as he always had. And still he kept wondering why projects so often ended badly.

Geographic Spread

With development spread across the globe and outsourced development, running projects can be very hard indeed. When development teams in a project are geographically separated, means of communication between them must exist and function seamlessly. For example, how can we share project status in an effective way, so that everybody can see how the project is going? How can we get a good, robust version control of source code and documents to function when we have long distances between teams? How can we catch changes to requirements when users, developers, and decision makers are separated?

The complexity in this takes its toll on both project managers and the projects themselves. Tools and processes must be in place supporting the project teams. Obviously, both time and cost can be severely negatively affected by this fact. If we do not catch requirements changes, fulfillment of project scope (or the perceived added value of the project) will most likely suffer as well, making the project one of the challenged, or in worst cases abandoned, in the statistics.

Synchronization of Tools

Numerous times I have seen situations where a developer (or other team member) must use several tools to get the job done. There is one tool for writing code, one for bug reporting, one for testing, one for version control, one for reports and statistics, and so on. I am sure you recognize this as well. The coordinating effort to keep all information in sync between these systems is immense. Not to mention the difficulties of implementing a development process in all of them, if this even is possible in all systems.

Resource Management

What about *Project Portfolio Management*, or *PPM*, as it is also known (see Figure 1-2)? Keeping track of all running projects and their resources can be a considerable problem for enterprises. The investments in applications and projects are enormous, both if you look at them from a financial perspective or from a human capital perspective. PPM helps organizations balance the costs and values of IT investments so they can achieve their business goals.[4]

Forrester says, "PPM provides a fact-based process for evaluating, prioritizing, and monitoring projects. PPM unites the process of strategic planning, resource and budget allocation, project selection and implementation, and post-project metrics."[5]

This basically says it all about what issues are covered by PPM.

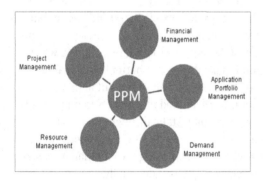

Figure 1-2. *ALM and PPM*

We can also see that a great portion of IT investments are focused on custom application development. If we cannot manage the resources we have at our disposal, the projects will most definitely suffer. We need to know, for example, that Steve will be available at the time he is needed in our project according to our project plan. If he is not, the schedule might have to change and the project most likely will be affected by both time and cost increases. To make matters worse, tasks depending on Steve's work might suffer as well. I would say this issue is one of my customers' top priorities now. A lot of the questions I get when speaking about VSTS implementations concern resource management integration with VSTS.

4. Kelly A. Shaw, "Application Lifecycle Management and PPM," June 2007, www.serena.com.
5. Craig Symons with Bobby Cameron, Laurie Orlov, Lauren Sessions, Forrester Research, "How IT Must Shape and Manage Demand," June 2006, www.forrester.com/Research/Document/Excerpt/0,7211,39660,00.html.

Project Size

Project size could also affect the outcome of the projects. This is perhaps no surprise, because complexity usually increases when project size increases. It is hard to manage a project that has many people involved or a long timeline. If you combine a large project size with geographically spread project teams or members, keeping it all from falling apart becomes harder, and it will be harder to foresee everything that can happen. This obviously does not mean that only the large size and geographic spread create these challenges; the combination of several risks in software development makes it hard to anticipate what might happen.

As you can see from all this, and everything you know for yourself, a lot of things can affect the outcome of projects. It is a complicated situation and because lots of money is involved, we have many considerations during the process.

What does research say about project success? When discussing this topic with coworkers, many have views and opinions, but not that many can reference research directly. They seem to argue on a gut feeling. So let's take a look at what the research indicates.

Project Success in Research

This section covers some of the research on project success over the years. You will see a well-known report from the Standish Group as well as some disagreement to this report. You will also see what the Swedish IDG has found and some research from ACM

The Standish Group

The Standish Group performs a survey on a regular basis on the performance of IT projects in the United States and Europe. The first report in 1994 was quite famous. It showed that many IT projects were cancelled or severely challenged. Since then, the Standish Group has performed the survey several times.

In 2006, the figures looked like this:[6]

- 46 percent of projects were challenged (53 percent In 1994).

- 19 percent of projects failed (31 percent in 1994).

- 35 percent were successful (16 percent in 1994).

Figure 1-3 presents these figures in graph form.

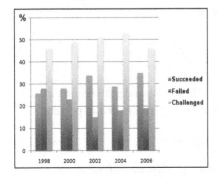

Figure 1-3. *The Standish report from 2008 shows figures from 1998 and forward.*

---

6. The Standish Group International, "Chaos Summary 2008."

The figures have improved a little over the years, but still 65 percent of all projects seem to be unsuccessful in some way. But to lump failed and challenged IT projects into the same bucket is not quite correct. Just because a project is challenged does not mean it has not added value to the company. A project might be late or overrun its budget but still deliver great value to the company, which might make it a well-received project anyway. Keep this in mind when you see figures like the preceding ones mentioned. A little perspective on the figures does not hurt.

Before we leave the Standish report, let's look at what it says about the reasons for project success. These are interesting no matter whether you believe in the actual success figures of projects or not. Here are the Standish Group's top ten reasons for project success:[7]

1. User involvement

2. Executive management support

3. Clear business objectives

4. Optimizing scope

5. Agile process

6. Project manager expertise

7. Financial management

8. Skilled resources

9. Formal methodology

10. Standard tools and infrastructure

Pretty interesting reasons, don't you think? Keep them in mind when you read about Visual Studio Team System later in the book (Chapter 6). We will also come back to some of them later in this chapter.

Robert Glass

The figures from the Standish Group have been challenged by other researchers. Robert C. Glass wrote an interesting article that questions where the data of the Standish report really comes from.[8] He also questions the methods used by the Standish Group.

Glass asks us to stand back and ask ourselves two things:

- Does the report represent reality?

- Is it supported by research findings?

Glass asks these questions because many other academic studies and guru reports in this area reference the Standish report from 1994. However, these other studies do not present

---

7. Deborah Hartmann, "Interview: Jim Johnson of the Standish Group," 2006, www.infoq.com/articles/Interview-Johnson-Standish-CHAOS.

8. Robert C. Glass, "The Standish Report: Does It Really Describe a Software Crisis?" August 2006, *Communications of the ACM*.

much new material to support the old findings, according to Glass. Another problem is that the Standish Group does not describe its research process or indicate where their data came from so that we can discuss its validity. This is of course a huge problem.

IDC

IDC recently published an article about the success (or perhaps failure) of Swedish IT projects. According to Sundblad & Sundblad, the article stated that as many as 82 percent of the IT projects were not finished to the customers' satisfaction.[9] This was the second time that this survey was carried out. The first time the survey was carried out in 2005, this figure was 72 percent, which means things have gotten worse. The survey has been carried out through the Swedish web site Projektplatsen.se on public as well as on private companies.

Thirty-four percent of the public IT managers stated that they did not get the features they wanted, and 20 percent of the private managers said the same thing. Forty percent of the IT projects in 2006 were delivered late, and the same number goes for projects running over budget. These figures were slightly lower than during the first survey.

Probable causes for these poor figures were believed to be the following:

- Internationalization of the business (more competition, to put it simply)

- The industry boom

- Higher demand for better efficiency in the public sector

The projects and customer satisfaction were evaluated on the following criteria (I will discuss the relevance of such criteria(s) later, so please bear with me a while more).

- Projects delivered on time

- Projects delivered on budget

- Competence of project provider

- Fulfillment of required functions

- Increase of efficiency

- Communication in the project

These figures are embarrassing and a poor grade for Swedish IT suppliers. What is even worse is that these figures seem to be similar internationally if we trust the Standish Group report.

Size and Volatility Survey

I want to address another survey before moving on. This survey claims that 67 percent of all projects are delivered close to budget, schedule, and scope expectations—quite the opposite of the preceding findings.[10] Of the 412 UK project managers in the study, they on average overshot budget by 13 percent, schedule by 20 percent, and underdelivered on scope by 7 percent. These figures are considerably lower than the Standish Group findings as well as the Swedish IDC findings.

---

9. Sundblad, "Business Improvement Through Better Software Architecture."

10. Chris Sauer, Andrew Gemino, and Blaize Horner Reich, " The Impact of Size and Volatility on IT Project Performance," November 2007, *Communications of the ACM.*

Table 1-1 shows the performance variance of the five types of projects defined in this study. Table 1-2 shows the size characteristics of these project types.

Table 1-1. *Performance Variance*

Performance Variance	Type 1: Abandoned Projects	Type 2: Budget Challenged	Type 3: Schedule Challenged	Type 4: Good Performers	Type 5: Star Performers
Schedule	n/a	+34%	+82%	+2%	+2%
Budget	n/a	+127%	+16%	+7%	+2%
Scope	n/a	–12%	–16%	–7%	+15%

Table 1-2. *Size Characteristics*

Size Characteristics	Type 1: Abandoned Projects	Type 2: Budget Challenged	Type 3: Schedule Challenged	Type 4: Good Performers	Type 5: Star Performers
Median budget	£1,000	£625	£500	£450	£2,000
Average budget	£24,232	£8,978	£12,513	£6,106	£12,119
Schedule	798	557	212	89	170
Budget	17.4	20.0	13.0	11.2	15.3
Scope	35.7	17.7	12.9	7.3	9.8

These figures are interesting, but the following findings are even more so. What the following three figures show is that size matters. Figure 1-4 shows that the size of the project directly affects the outcome. The more effort in terms of person-months we have in a project, the greater are the chances of failure or low performance.

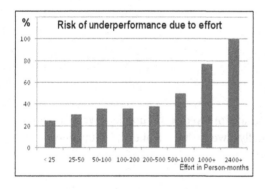

Figure 1-4. *Person-months*

Figure 1-5 shows that the duration of the project also impacts performance.

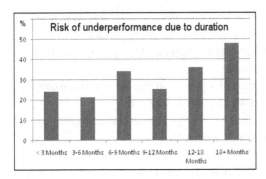

Figure 1-5. *Project length*

The longer the project, the greater the risk. Note that it seems like the greatest risk comes when the project duration reaches over 18 months.

Figure 1-6 illustrates the risk of project failure based on the size of the team.

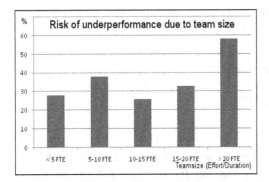

Figure 1-6. *Team size*

The risk seems to be the greatest when we have a team size of more than 20 people. Below that, we see that risk is pretty much the same.

To be counted as a low performer, the following three project categories applied:

- Abandoned

- Budget challenged

- Schedule challenged

These criteria are also found in the Swedish IDC survey presented earlier. The size and volatility survey further showed that changes to project targets affected the success rate as well. The more changes, the bigger the chance of being a low performer.

Conclusions

So what do all these figures tell us? Well, we can clearly see that projects are not carried out in the most optimal way. There are still too many challenged and abandoned projects in this day and age. No matter which survey we choose to believe, the figures are worrisome.

If our projects are not successful, the whole ALM process will suffer. The reason why we should take control of the ALM process is that we can deliver better projects; having an overall process helps us. And with this process comes a mindset focused on the application from its birth as a business need to the delivered business value.

Measuring project success or failure is complicated. We need to take this into consideration when we read surveys stating that this or that many projects succeed.

The importance of an overall ALM process is that it can help us control the project outcome better in the end, enabling us to deliver true business value.

The work-down paradigm mentioned earlier has a widely accepted *iron triangle* showing the relationship between time, resources, and functionality (Figure 1-7).[11]

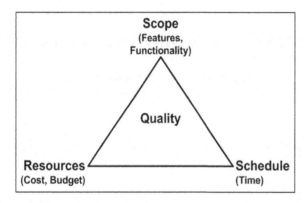

Figure 1-7. *The iron triangle*

In this we can see quality as a fourth dimension, giving us a tetrahedron. In this model, the relationship is fixed between the faces of the tetrahedron. If you stretch one, at least one other needs to be stretched. If more resources are needed, for example, you might need to stretch time as well, and so on. With complex projects, the scope usually changes unpredictably during the process and suddenly we might need to add more resources, which obviously affect the schedule.

We need to reflect on the results of surveys before we take them as the truth. This does not mean that the surveys I have referred to are without value. They definitely tell us something is wrong with the way we perform IT projects today. Why do so many IT projects fail? Have we not learned anything from the past years? The IT industry has been around for quite some time now, and we should have learned something along the way, shouldn't we?

Could it be because the problems we need to solve just keep getting harder and harder? Or is it so hard to estimate and plan for projects that we can only take an educated guess at the beginning of a project? If the latter is true, why do we still measure a project's success based on time, money, and requirements fulfillment? Maybe we should just shift our focus to business value instead? If the business value is greater than the cost of implementing the solution, time and money are usually of less importance.

11. Sam Guckenheimer and Juan Perez, *Software Engineering with Microsoft Visual Studio Team System* (Addison-Wesley Professional, 2006).

IT Budget Spending

In many companies that I have seen, the better part of the IT budget is usually spent on operations and maintenance and not on new development. The implications of this are that organizations have fewer possibilities to enhance their IT systems, and instead just spend the budget on keeping the systems alive. This could be a problem because the IT budget is needed to develop systems for meeting changes in the business processes.

Development vs. Operations

In 2006, the Corporate Executive Board (CEB) published the results of a survey concerning IT spending.[12] The survey found that of all IT spending in 2006, 30 percent related to IT system development. That might sound like a big part of the cake, but consider where the rest of the money is spent: 70 percent of an IT budget is spent on operations and maintenance (Figure 1-8).

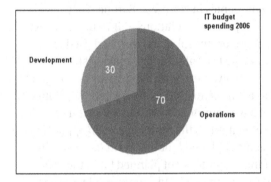

Figure 1-8. *IT spending in companies*

These figures are confirmed time after time in my discussions with customers. One of my coworkers told me that when he worked as an IT manager at a large Swedish car manufacturer, the figures applied as well.

Is it really rational to spend 70 percent on operations and maintenance? Wouldn't it be more interesting to try to switch these figures around? Imagine the possibilities of adding value to an organization with so much more money to spend on IT systems. And think about the cool new features we could try out when we might have a larger budget for testing new technologies. I say we can switch these figures around (see Figure 1-9) without increasing the total IT budget or lowering the quality of operations and maintenance. This is definitely not an impossible task, which I hope this book will show.

My friend from the car industry started this process in his part of the company. He never got to see the final result of his efforts before he left the company for a consulting business but he saw the figures turning—enough to make him even firmer in his opinion that it can be done. The key here is obviously to take control of your ALM process (see Chapter 2) by using a tool such as VSTS.

Before we get into a discussion about how to take control of our ALM process, let's look at some of the factors influencing this split of IT money.

---

12. Corporate Executive Board, "Application Budget, Staff, and Portfolio Benchmarks," 2006.

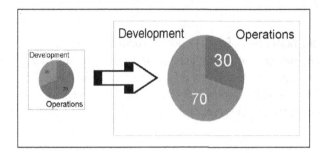

Figure 1-9. *Making the switch*

Factors Influencing IT Spending

I recently visited one of the biggest mail order companies in Northern Europe. They have managed to change their IT budget spending to 30 percent operations and 70 percent development. When I asked what was one of the most important solutions they had used to accomplish this, the IT manager said that they had just simply stopped making small changes or fixes to the existing systems. The cost involved in such changes was far too great, so only very important changes were allowed to be implemented. With greater traceability and automated unit testing, he said, they could have continued lowering operation costs.

One other cost driver for maintenance and operations is the retirement of an application or system. Raise your hand, everyone, who has actually planned for this event (okay, you in the back, you can take your hand down now). If this scenario is not planned for in the beginning of an application's lifecycle, great surprises can occur in its end. One example is from my friend, the car manufacturer. At times his business had to retire applications because the specific platform running the application became obsolete or a new version of the application was developed. Support for the platform might end because of newer platforms replacing it. On some occasions, my friend found that there was no way to migrate the historical data in the application(s). This scenario had not been planned for earlier and suddenly posed a great problem. The car company then had to negotiate an extended support contract with the platform vendor, which was way more expensive than it had been when the application was alive. It was quite ironic that they had to pay more for having access to historical data than they had when they actually used the system(s). One of the solutions to begin turning the figures around was to start planning for application retirement early in the lifecycle. The ALM process was changed so that, for example, data migration was planned for, making it unnecessary to keep applications slow cooking at a great cost.

I cannot cover all cost factors in this book, but I will mention some more key issues here. A big element causing increased operation costs is the way we have traditionally built our systems (and still do build them). Some years ago, client-server solutions dominated much of our IT environment. After that came multitier applications. These gave us great opportunities in writing business systems, with scalability and availability in mind, not only as standard Windows applications but also as web applications. My coworker Rickard Redler and I even wrote two books on this topic, *Designing Scalable .NET Applications* (Apress, 2003) and *Pro Scalable .NET 2.0 Application Designs* (Apress, 2005).

If we have only a few applications, this architecture works fine, but when new applications are added, it gets complex (see Figure 1-10).

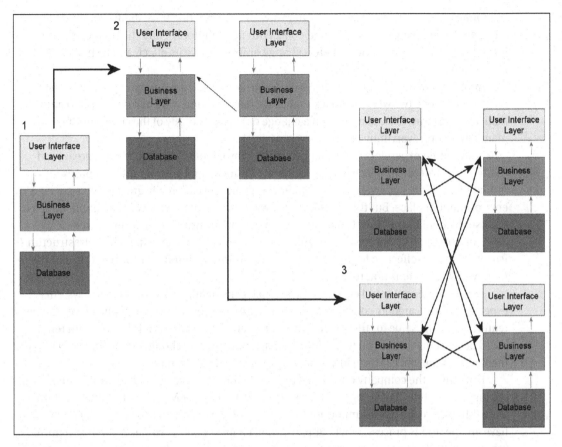

Figure 1-10. *A traditional multitier application design. When we have several applications trying to access each other's functions, problems may arise.*

Imagine what happens when a new application needs to access data from another. There are ways to solve this, as position 2 of this figure shows. We simply let the data layer of the new application access the business interface layer of the first. This way, we can reuse the logic that already existed and not spread database security and rights management around. If we have only a few applications, this works fine, but as you can see in position 3, things can get pretty complicated when only a few more new applications are introduced. Most large enterprises have perhaps hundreds of applications spread across the company's different locations. If there is no documentation task force in the company, there really is no way to have control over where the business logic is located.

In Chapter 4 we will discuss service-oriented architecture (SOA) a bit and see how we can be helped by that mindset. SOA has the potential, if implemented correctly, to help us align our business process with our business systems, making us adjust quickly to new competitive business strategies. SOA itself is a natural evolution from previous development architectures, where we have found that component-based development and traditional architecture just does not work for providing the flexibility we need these days.

Having an inflexible architecture is a great cost driver in maintenance (and of course in new projects). Imagine the nightmare of implementing a change request or bug fix in this environment. There really is no way to have control over where a change or fix will have its impact, so just a small change will need extensive testing on much more than just where the fix was implemented. This makes the cost of it much greater than it should need to be.

One way to avoid this is to have better ways of documenting traceability from the original requirement to accepted and delivered code. With the right tool(s) and the right work process, it would be much easier to find where a change or fix will have its effect, and testing could be minimized.

Another way to make the testing easier and hence less costly is to have good unit tests ready for the code (we will come back to this in Chapter 5) and ways of running them automatically. This way, it is easier to see if a change or a fix affects any of the code without manually testing everything else.

I have often experienced another problem at my clients. A company has a great (and costly) infrastructure in place with redundancy for most applications and databases. Availability is high, and everyone should be happy because it's really great to have such an environment in place. But think about it this way: is it really necessary for all applications to have such an infrastructure? Consider this: does a low-priority application not requiring 24/7 support or 99.999 percent availability need to run on such an expensive infrastructure? Isn't it more cost-effective to run those applications on a different platform and spend the money on the systems that really need it?

Furthermore, you could cut costs if you make considerations for the time the system is expected to live. Carefully consider the infrastructure needed for all new applications. Are the requirements the same for the system with a lifespan of two years as it is for one with ten? It could be, of course, based on its business impact, but a system should not be routinely implemented on a specific platform just because you always do it like that.

How about the company operations process? Is one in place or is ad hoc work done? I am talking Information Technology Infrastructure Library (ITIL) or Microsoft Operations Framework (MOF) here. It's just as important to have a good development process in place as it is to have an operations process. What happens when change requests come? When bug reports are entered? When new releases are introduced? Having a well-defined process in place could be a major factor in cutting operations costs. We will discuss this a bit more in Chapters 6 and 7 because it is an important topic.

With better traceability in our systems in place and tool(s) supporting it, I am certain that we could have a situation where we would not have to stop implementing small changes or features just to cut costs. If we can trace exactly where an update or bug fix will affect the system, we can make sure not to break anything else.

If we also consider our system architecture, we could create a better structured environment where we could more easily see how changes affect the system as well. Converting slowly but steadily to a SOA would be a good start.

Before we leave this chapter, I want to discuss the gap between IT and the business side again. If the business processes and the IT systems are not well aligned, there will be problems when processes change. This is a little bit like what we saw earlier with the application mess we can end up in. It is hard to say where we need to make changes to our systems when new processes need to be implemented or old ones change, if we do not know the structure of our systems. A lot of the costs involved in this process unavoidably end up in the operations budget.

Summary

An alarmingly large portion of IT projects delivered today are challenged or, in the worst case, abandoned. Many projects have overruns in terms of cost and time. Projects are also criticized for not delivering business value, and hence are not what the customer expects them to be in the end. One of the greatest risks is definitely the lack of integration between the business side and the IT side. This gap makes it harder to deliver what we should deliver in our project, which is business value. Having a development process that is ill-defined or not even used is another great risk. Furthermore, the lack of great ALM tools makes it harder to deliver as well, especially because we have more geographically dispersed development or project teams these days. Considering the amount of money spent on these projects, we can be certain lots of it is thrown away because of these challenges.

We can also be certain that much of our companies' IT budgets go into operations and maintenance, giving less money to develop better and more-efficient systems that give more value to the business. To the technology interested, this means less money and opportunity to try new cool techniques or tools, less testing of new technology, and so on. For the business, it means less opportunity to earn money and add value to the company. Either way you choose to see it, this model for IT budget spending is definitely a great problem.

The problems addressed in this chapter can be greatly improved by having control of our whole ALM process. This process, as you will see in the next chapter, focuses on taking the business needs and requirements, and turning them into business value for the organization. ALM does so by enforcing a process on how we work when developing software.

This book will show you how, with the use of a set of tools, Team Foundation Server (TFS) and Visual Studio Team System, we can take control of the ALM process. The result will be that we can reduce the impact of the problems presented in this chapter. We might not get all the way with the current versions of VSTS and TFS, but we can certainly come a long way. So follow me to the next chapter, where you will see what ALM really means.

CHAPTER 2

■■■

Application Lifecycle Management

Application Lifecycle Management. What do you think about when you hear that term? During the seminar tour I mentioned in the preface, we used to ask people what ALM was and if they cared about it. To my surprise, many people equated ALM with operations and maintenance. Maybe that was your answer as well? But think about it again. Application Lifecycle Management! Doesn't that include more than just operations? Yes, it does. ALM is the thread that ties the development lifecycle together. It involves all the steps necessary to coordinate the development lifecycle activities. Operations are just one part of the ALM process.

This chapter explains what ALM is so that you can understand how a tool such as Visual Studio Team System can help you improve this process.

Roles in the ALM Process

All development includes various steps that are performed by persons playing a specific role in the process. There are many different roles in the ALM process, and I define some of them in this section. (Please note that the process could include more roles, but I have tried to focus on the main ones.) Take a look at Figure 2-1, which illustrates ALM and some of its roles.

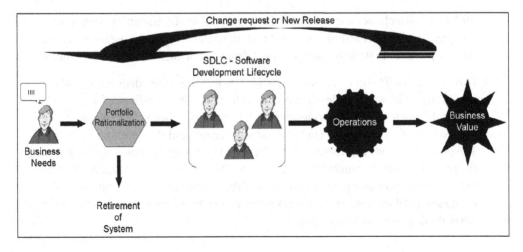

Figure 2-1. *The Application Lifecycle Management process and some of the roles in it*

It is essential to understand that all development is a team effort. The roles collaborate on projects in order to deliver business value to the organization. If we don't have this collaboration, the value of the system will be damaged. If we look at the development process one step up from the actual project level, it is also important to have collaboration between all roles involved in the ALM process, so that we perform this process in the most optimal way possible.

The roles in the ALM process include the following:

- *Business manager*: Somebody has to make a decision that a development activity is going to start. After initial analysis of the business needs, a business manager decides to start a project for the development of an application or system that will deliver the business value wanted. A business manager, for instance, will have to follow the approval process for the new suggested project, including portfolio rationalization, before a decision to go ahead is reached. Other people involved in this process are of course IT managers, because the IT staff will probably be involved in the project's development and deployment into the infrastructure.

- *Project manager*: The project manager is selected and sets off to work on the project after the decision to go ahead is made. In the best of worlds, this person continues leading the project all the way through, so that we have continuity in project management. It is the project manager who must make sure that smooth cooperation between the different roles exists.

- *PMO decision makers*: People from the project management office (PMO) are also involved in the planning because a new project might very well change or expand the company's portfolio.

- *Business analyst*: After requirements collection starts, the business analyst has much to do. A business analyst is responsible for analyzing the business needs and requirements of the stakeholders, to help identify business problems and propose solutions. Within the systems development lifecycle, the business analyst typically performs a collaborative function between the business side of an enterprise and the providers of services to the enterprise.

- *Architect*: The architect starts drawing the initial picture of the solution. I will not go into great detail here because Chapter 4 does that later. But briefly, the architect draws the blueprint of the system, and the system designers or engineers use this blueprint.

- *User Experience (UX) design team*: Hopefully UX design is a core deliverable and not something we leave to the developers to handle. UX design is sadly overlooked and should definitely have a status elevation. It is important to have close collaboration between the UX team (which could be just one person) and the development team. The best solution is obviously to have a UX expert in the development team all through the project, but that is sometimes not possible. The UX design is so important in making sure users can really perceive the value of the system. We can write the best of business logic if we want, but if the UX is not as well designed, the users will probably never think the system is any good.

- *Database administrators (DBAs)*: Almost every system or application uses a database in some way. The DBAs are the ones who can make our databases run like lightning with good up-time, so it is essential to use their expertise in any project involving a database. Be nice to them; they can give you lots of tips on how to make a smarter system.

- *Developers*: Developers, developers, developers as Microsoft CEO Steve Ballmer shouted in a famous video. And who can blame him? These are the people doing their magic to realize the system that we are building by using the architecture blueprint drawn from the requirements. These are the people who make the changes when the change requests come in.

- *Testers*: Testing is something we should consider from the first time we write down a requirement, and continue doing during the whole process. Testers and test leaders are important in this process. In Chapter 5, we will come back to this a bit more.

- *Operations and maintenance staff*: Here it is. When an application or system is finished, it is handed over to operations. The operations staff will take care of it until it retires. Don't forget to involve these people early in the process, at the point when the initial architecture is considered, and keep them in the project until all is done. They can give great input to what can and can't be done in the company infrastructure. So operations is just one part, but an important one, of ALM.

All project efforts are done as collaborative work. No role can act separately from any of the others if we are to succeed with any project. It is essential for everybody in a project to have a collaborative mindset and to have the business value as the primary focus at every phase of the project.

Table 2-1 lists some of the activities in the ALM process and the roles that perform those activities. Of course, a real project would have many more activities, but these are some top-level ones.

Table 2-1. *Mapping Roles to Activities in ALM*

Activity to Perform	Role of Person Who Performs Activity
Gather requirements and business needs	Business analyst Project manager
Decide to start project	Business manager(s) PMO decision maker(s) IT manager(s) Stakeholder(s)
Plan project execution	Project manager
Enable cooperation between all parties	Project manager Everybody
Make sure project delivers business value	Everybody
Set (initial) architecture of the new system or application	IT architect Infrastructure architect Business architect
Implement architecture	Developers Database administrators and developers

Continued

Table 2-1. *Continued*

Activity to Perform	Role of Person Who Performs Activity
Make sure system or application is thoroughly tested	Developers Testers Database developers Everybody
Perform data management	Database administrators and developers
Make sure user experience is considered	User Experience team Developers
Deploy project	Operations Architects Developers
Perform maintenance and operations	Operations Help desk Developers
Make decision on retirement of system or application	Business manager(s) PMO decision maker(s) IT Manager(s) Stakeholder(s)

Four Ways of Looking at Application Lifecycle Management

Application Lifecycle Management is the glue that ties all these roles and the activities they perform together. Let's take a look at four ways of looking at ALM (see Figure 2-2). I have chosen these four because I have seen this separation in so many of the organizations I have worked with or spoken to:

- *Software Development Lifecycle (SDLC) view*: This is perhaps the most common way of looking at ALM because development has "owned" this question for a long time. This could very well be an effect of the gap between the business side and the IT side in most organizations, and IT has taken the lead on this.

- *Service management or operations view*: Operations have also had (in my experience) an unfortunate separation from IT development. This has resulted in them having their own view of ALM and the problems in this area.

- *Application Portfolio Management (APM) view*: Again maybe because of the gap between business and IT, I have seen many organizations with a portfolio ALM strategy in which IT development is only one small part. From a business view, the focus has been on how to handle the portfolio itself and not on the whole ALM process.

- *Chief information officer (CIO) view (or the unified view)*: Fortunately, some organizations focus on the whole ALM process by including all three of the preceding views. This is the only way to take control over, and optimize, ALM. For a CIO, it is essential to have this view all the time; otherwise, development activities can easily get out of hand.

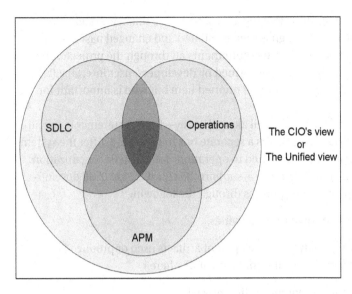

Figure 2-2. *The four views of the Application Lifecycle Management process*

The SDLC View

Let's take a look at ALM from an SDLC perspective first. In Figure 2-3, you can see the different phases of a typical development project. Keep in mind that this is just a simplified view for the sake of this discussion. I have also tried to fit in some of the different roles from the ALM process presented earlier.

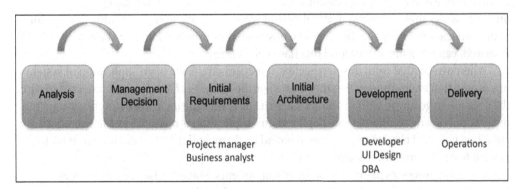

Figure 2-3. *A simplified view of a typical develoment project*

First somebody comes up with an idea based on an analysis of the business needs: "Hey, wouldn't it be great if we had a system that could help us do this (whatever the idea is)?" It could also be the other way around: the idea comes first, and the business value is evaluated based on the idea.

So an analysis is performed, costs are estimated, and hopefully a decision is made by IT and business management to start the project as an IT project. A project manager (PM) is selected to be responsible for the project and starts gathering requirements with the help of business analysts, PMO decision makers, and users or others affected. The PM also starts planning the project in as much detail as possible at this moment.

When that is done, the architect starts looking at how to realize the new system, and the initial design is chosen. The initial design is then evaluated and changed based on what happens in the project and what happens with requirements all through the project. After that, the development starts, including work performed by developers, user interface (UI) designers, and DBAs (and any other person not mentioned here but who is important for the project).

Testing is, at least for me, something we do all along the way—from requirements specification to delivered code—so I do not have this as a separate box in Figure 2-2. After the system has gone through acceptance testing, it is delivered to operations for use in the organization.

What ALM does in this development process is support the coordination of all development lifecycle activities from the preceding process through the following:[1]

- Enforcement of processes that span these activities.

- Management of relationships between development artifacts used or produced by these activities. (In other words, we talk about traceability here.)

- Reporting on progress of the development effort as a whole.

As you can see from this, ALM does not support a specific activity by itself. Its purpose is to keep all activities in sync. It does this just so we can focus on delivering systems that meet the needs and requirements of the business. By having an ALM process helping us synchronize our development activities, we can more easily see if any activity is underperforming and thus more easily take corrective actions.

The Service Management or Operations View

From a service management or operations view, we can look at ALM as follows: ALM "focuses on the activities that are involved with the deployment, operation, support, and optimization of the application. The main objective is to ensure that the application, once built and deployed, can meet the service level that has been defined for it."[2]

When we see ALM from this perspective, it focuses on the life of an application or system in a production environment. If in the SDLC view the lifecycle of the development started with the decision to go ahead with the project, here it starts with the deployment of the system into the production environment. Once deployed, the application is operated by the operations crew. Bug fixes and change requests are handled by them, and they also pat it on its back to make it feel good and run smoothly.

There are processes to help us maintain our systems. Microsoft has developed their Microsoft Operations Framework, or MOF as it is usually called, but there are others as well. One that immediately springs to mind is the IT Infrastructure Library (ITIL). But ITIL's perspective is dual. ITIL suggests that the relationship between application development and service management is very tight. ITIL focuses on ALM from both perspectives as it stresses that we need alignment between both of these views in every phase. So ITIL describes the six phases of ALM, as shown in Figure 2-4.[3]

---

1. Carey Schwaber, Forrester Research, "The Changing Face of Application Lifecycle Management," 2006, www.serena.com.

2. Office of Government Commerce, *ITIL Application Management* (TSO, 2002).

3. Office of Government Commerce, *ITIL Application Management*.

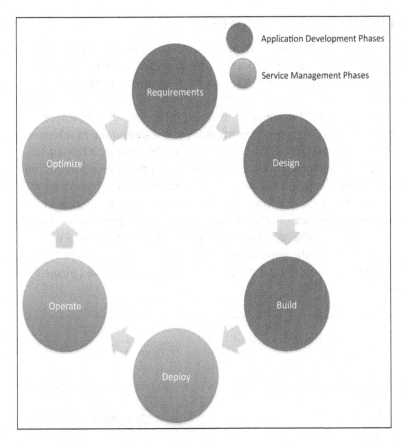

Figure 2-4. *The phases of ALM from an ITIL perspective. An application lifecycle encompasses both the application management and service management activities.*

This is a quite healthy way of looking at ALM in my opinion, because I think that both development and operations are two pieces of ALM, cooperating in order to manage the whole ALM process. Both pieces are also something that should be thought of when planning a development project from the beginning; we cannot have one without the other. If we take the Microsoft perspective to somewhat copy this thinking, we need to combine Microsoft Solutions Framework (MSF), which is Microsoft's development process (see Chapter 3), with MOF.

Table 2-2 shows how MSF and MOF map to ITIL's phases.

Table 2-2. *Comparing Microsoft MSF and MOF with ITIL*

MSF/MOF	ITIL
Envision	Requirements
Plan	Design
Build/Stabilize	Build
Deploy/Changing	Deploy
Operating/Supporting	Operate
Optimizing	Optimize

The Application Portfolio Management View

The third view we will look at is the APM view of ALM. In this view, we see the application as a product managed as part of a portfolio of products. We can say that APM is a subset of Project Portfolio Management (PPM), which we talked about in Chapter 1. Figure 2-5 describes this process.

This view comes from the Project Management Institute (PMI). Managing resources and the project these resources work on is very important for any organization. In this view, we can see that the product lifecycle starts with a business plan—the product is the application or system that is one part of the business plan. An idea for an application is turned into a project and carried out through the project phases, until it is turned over to operations as a finished product. When business requirements change or a new release (an upgrade in this figure) is required for some other reason, the project lifecycle starts again, and a new release is handed over to operations. After a while (maybe years), the system or application is discarded (this is called *divestment*, the opposite of investment). This view does not specifically speak about the operations part nor the development part but should be seen in the light of APM instead.

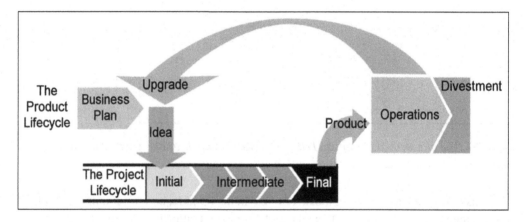

Figure 2-5. *The PMI view of ALM*

The Unified View

The final view is a unified view of ALM. In this view, we have made an effort to align all these views with the business. Here we do as the CIO would do: we focus on the business needs, not on separate views. This we do to improve the capacity and agility of the project from start to end. Figure 2-6 shows an overview of how these three views are included in the whole unified ALM aspect of a business.

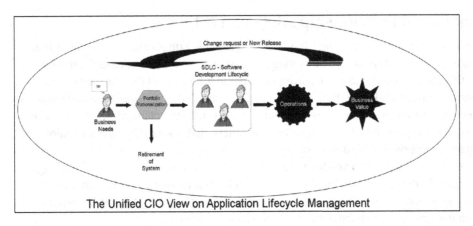

Figure 2-6. *The CIO's view takes into consideration all three views previously mentioned.*

Three Pillars of Application Lifecycle Management

Let's now look at some important pillars we find in ALM, independent of the view we take. Forrester Research defines three pillars in ALM,[4] as shown in Figure 2-7.

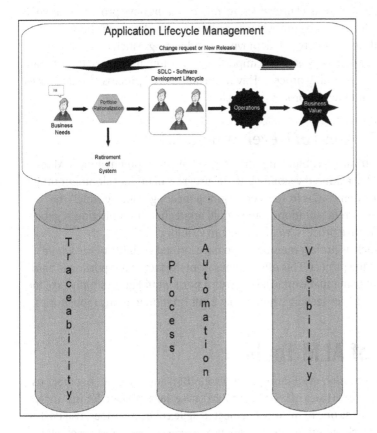

Figure 2-7. *The three pillars of ALM*

---

4.   Carey Schwaber, "The Changing Face of Application Lifecycle Management."

Traceability of Relationships Between Artifacts

As you may recall, my customer from Chapter 1 stopped doing upgrades on his systems that were running in production because the company had poor or even no traceability in its systems. To this client, it was far too expensive to do upgrades because of the unexpected effects even a small change could have. The company had no way of knowing which original requirements were implemented where in the applications. This customer claimed, and I have seen and heard this in discussions with many other customers, that traceability can be a major cost driver in any enterprise if not done correctly.

There must be a way of tracing the requirements all the way to delivered code—through architect models, design models, build scripts, unit tests, test cases, and so on—not only to make it easier to go back into the system when implementing bug fixes, but also to demonstrate that the system has delivered the things the business wanted.

Another reason for traceability is internal as well as external compliance with rules and regulations. If we develop applications for the medical industry, for example, we need to have compliance with FDA regulations. We also need to have traceability when change requests are coming in so that we know where we updated the system and in which version we performed the update.

Automation of High-Level Processes

The next pillar is automation of high-level processes. All organizations have processes, as you saw in Chapter 1. For example, there are approval processes to control hand-offs between the analysis and design or build steps, or between deployment and testing. Much of this is done manually in many projects, and ALM stresses the importance of automating these tasks for a more effective and less time-consuming process. Having an automated process also decreases the error rate compared to handling the process manually.

Visibility into the Progress of Development Efforts

The third and last pillar is providing visibility into the progress of development efforts. Many managers and stakeholders have limited visibility into the progress of our development projects. The visibility they have often comes from steering group meetings, during which the project manager reviews the current situation. Some would argue that this limitation is good, but if we want to have an effective process, we must ensure visibility.

Other interest groups such as project members also have limited visibility of the whole project despite being part of the project. This often comes from the fact that reporting is hard to do and often involves a lot of manual work. Daily status reports would quite simply take too much time and effort to produce, especially when we have information in many repositories.

A Brief History of ALM Tools

ALM is not a new process description even though Microsoft, IBM, and the other big dragons right now are pushing ALM to drive sales of VSTS or, in IBM's case, Jazz. We can, for instance, continue to use Excel sheets, or as one of my most dedicated agile colleagues does, use Post-it notes and a pad of paper to track requirements through use cases/scenarios, test cases, code, build, and so on to delivered code. It works, but this process takes a lot of time and requires much manual effort. With constant pressure to keep costs down, we need to make tracking requirements more effective.

It also happens that we as project members "simplify" the process by not reporting everything as much as we should. With a good tool, or set of tools, we can cut time (and thus costs) and effort, and still get the required traceability we want in our projects. The same goes for reporting and all those other activities we have. Tools can, in my opinion, help us be more effective, and also help us automate much of the ALM process right into the tool(s).

By having the process directly in our tools, it is much easier for the people involved to not miss any important step by simplifying anything. For instance, my agile friend I mentioned could definitely gain much from this, and he has now started looking into VSTS to see how that set of tools can help him and his teams be more productive. So process automation and the use of tools to support and simplify our daily jobs are great things.

Take a look at Figure 2-8. It shows the disciplines involved in the ALM process.[5]

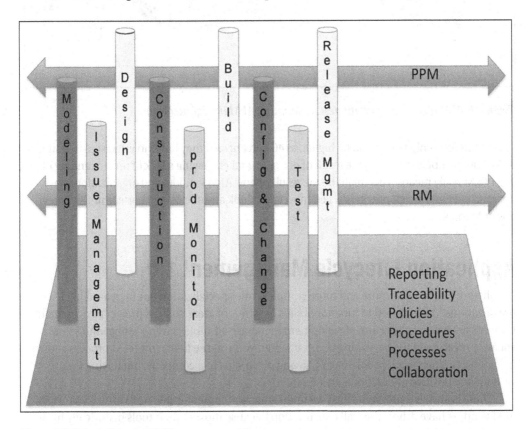

Figure 2-8. *Disciplines in ALM*

Imagine the Herculean task of keeping all those things in order manually. That would be impossible if we wanted to get something right and keep an eye on the status of projects. As we saw from the Standish Group in Chapter 1, projects seem to be going better because the number of failed projects is decreasing. Much of this progress is, according to Michael Azoff at

---

5. Serena Software, "Application Lifecycle Management for the Enterprise," April 2007, www.serena.com/solutions/alm-solutions/index.html.

the Butler Group, the result of some "major changes in software development: open source software projects; the Agile development movement; and advances in tooling, notably Application Lifecycle Management (ALM) tools."[6] So we can understand that finding tools to help us in the ALM process is important.

This has led to increasing awareness of the ALM process among enterprises (see Figure 2-9). This figure shows the interest in adopting ALM in organizations participating in the study.

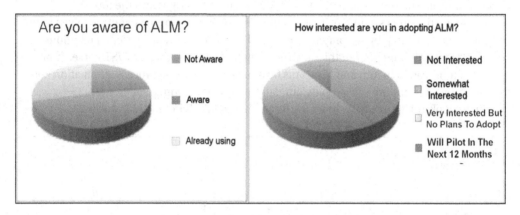

Figure 2-9. *ALM awareness and interest in adopting ALM in organizations*

So interest is high but could be higher, as 40 percent said they have no interest in adopting ALM. Forrester believes this is the result of decision-makers having a lack of understanding of what ALM really means. This might be the result of how ALM vendors and organizations have approached the concept previously. Let's now take a look at some of the shortcomings of previous ALM tools.

Application Lifecycle Management 1.0

As software has become more and more complex, role specialization has increased in IT organizations.[7] This has led to functional silos in different areas such as project management, business analysis, architecture, development, database administration, testing, and so on. As you may recall from the beginning of this chapter, you can see this in the ALM process shown in Figure 2-1. There is no problem with having these silos in a company, but having them without any positive interaction between them is.

There is always a problem when we build great and impenetrable walls around us. Most ALM vendors have driven the wall construction because most of their tools historically have been developed for particular silos. If we look at build management tools, they have supported the build silo (naturally) but have little or no interaction with test and validation tools—just to mention one area. This occurs despite the fact that interaction can give large synergies and have an obvious great potential. We need to synchronize the ALM process to make the discipline-centric processes a part of the overall process. This might sound obvious, but has just not happened until lately.

6. Michael Azoff, "Application Lifecycle Management Making a Difference," February 2007, Enterprise Networks and Services, OpinionWire.

7. "The Challenges of Software Change Management in Today's Siloed IT Organizations," a commissioned study conducted by Forrester Consulting on behalf of Serena Software, November 2006.

Instead of having complete integration between the disciplines and the tools they use, we have had point-to-point integration—for example, we could have a development tool slightly integrated with the testing tool (or probably the other way around). Each tool uses its own data repository, so traceability and reporting is hard to handle in such an environment as well (see Figure 2-10).

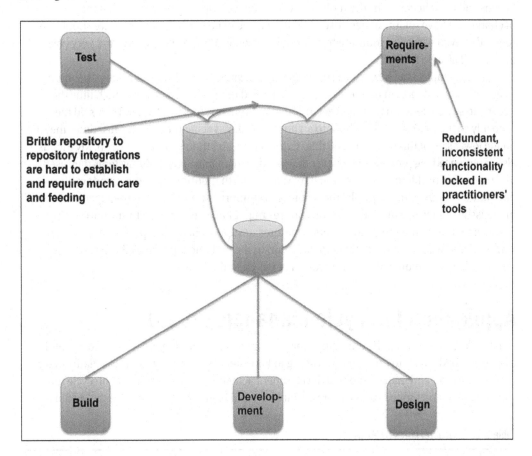

Figure 2-10. *ALM 1.0*

This point-to-point integration makes the ALM process fragile and quite expensive as well. Just imagine what happens when one tool is updated or replaced. Suddenly, the integration might break and new solutions have to be found to get it working again. This scenario can be reality if, for example, old functions in the updated or replaced tool are obsolete and the new one does not support backward compatibility. This can be hard to solve even with integration between just two tools. Imagine what happens if we have a more complex situation, including several more tools. I have seen projects using six or seven tools during development, and having so many tools has been a fragile solution when new versions have been released.

The tools have also been centered on one discipline. In real life, a project member working as a developer, for instance, quite often also acts as an architect or tester. Because the people in each of these disciplines have their own tools (or sets of tools), the project member must use several tools and switch between them. It could also be that the task system is separated from the rest of the tools, so to start working on a task, a developer must first retrieve the task from the task system—probably print it out, or copy and paste it, open the requirements system to check the requirement, look at the architecture in that system, and finally open the development tool to start working. Hopefully, the testing tools are integrated into the development tool; otherwise, yet another tool must be used. All this switching costs valuable time better put into solving the task.

Having multiple tools for each project member is obviously a great cost driver as well because all need licenses for the tools they use. Even with open source tools that may be free of charge, we have maintenance costs. Maintenance can be very expensive, so we should not forget this even when the tools are free. So such a scenario can be very costly and very complex. It will also be fragile.

As an example, I have two coworkers working at a large medical company in Gothenburg. They have a mix of tools in their everyday work. I asked them to estimate how much time they needed to switch between tools and get information from one tool to another. Their said they probably spend between half an hour to an hour each day syncing their work. Most times they are on the lower side of this scale, but still this is a lot of time and money in the long run. My friends also experienced big problems whenever they needed to upgrade any of the systems they used.

One other problem with traditional ALM tools worth mentioning is that vendors often have added features, for example, the test tool to support issue and defect management. And in the issue management system, some features might have been added to support testing. Because neither of the tools have enough features to support both disciplines, the users are confused and will not know which tool to go for. In the end, most purchase both just to be safe, and hence end up with the integration issues described earlier.

Application Lifecycle Management 2.0

So let's take a look at what the emerging tools and practices (including processes and methodologies) in ALM 2.0 try to do for us. According to Forrester, the emerging ALM "is a platform for the coordination and management of development activities, not a collection of lifecycle tools with locked-in and limited ALM features."[8] Table 2-3 and Figure 2-11 summarize these efforts.

Table 2-3. *Characteristics in ALM 2.0*

Characteristics	Benefit
Practitioner tools assembled out of plug-ins	Customers pay only for the features they need. Practitioners find the features they need faster.
Common services available across practitioner tools	Easier for vendor to deploy enhancements to shared features. Ensure correspondence of activities across practitioner tools.
Repository neutral	No need to migrate old assets. Better support for cross-platform development.
Use of open integration standards	Easier for customers and partners to build deeper integrations with third-party tools.
Microprocesses and macroprocesses governed byexternalized workflow	Processes are versionable assets. Processes can share common components.

---

8.   Carey Schwaber, "The Changing Face of Application Lifecycle Management."

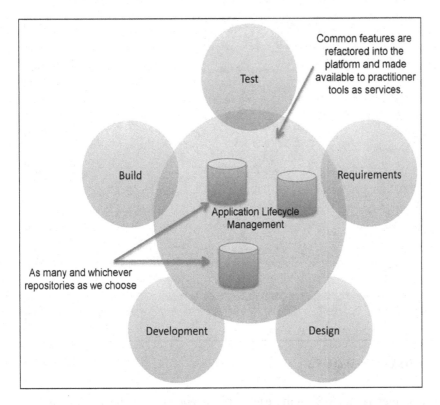

Figure 2-11. *ALM 2.0*

One of the first things we can see is a focus on plug-ins. This means that from one tool, we can add the features we need to perform the tasks we want. Without using several tools! If you have used Visual Studio, you have seen that it is quite straightforward to add new plug-ins into this development environment. Support for Windows Communication Foundation (WCF) and Windows Presentation Foundation (WPF), for example, was available as plug-ins long before their support was added as a part of Visual Studio 2008.

Having the plug-in option and making it easy for third-party vendors to write plug-ins for the tool greatly eases the integration problems discussed earlier. You can almost compare this to a smorgasbord, where you choose the things you want. So far this has mostly been adopted by development tool vendors such as IBM or Microsoft, but more are coming. Not much has happened outside of development tools so far but as you will see in Chapter 6, VSTS offers some nice features that definitely will help us a lot.

Teamprise, a third-party vendor, has developed a solution, giving access to the Team Foundation Server (TFS) in VSTS from a wide array of platforms, including Mac OS X (see Figure 2-12).

Another thing that will ease our development efforts is that vendors in ALM 2.0 are focusing more on identifying features that are common to multiple tools and integrating these into the ALM platform. We find things like the following among these features:

- Collaboration

- Workflow

- Security

- Reporting and analysis

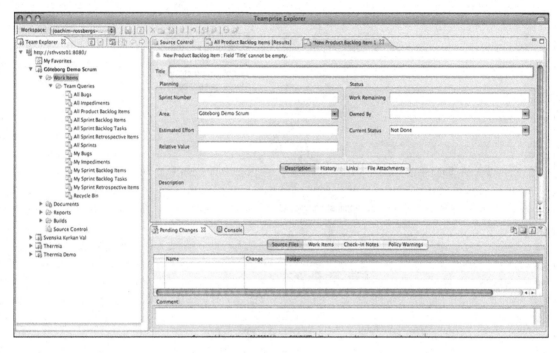

Figure 2-12. *Teamprise Team Explorer in Mac OS X*

You will see in Chapter 6 that VSTS has these features embedded out of the box. Microsoft uses Microsoft Office SharePoint Server/Windows SharePoint Services for collaboration among team members, for example. Active Directory is used for authentication and security. SQL Server obviously is the data repository giving us access to tools such as SQL Server Analysis Services for analytics and SQL Server Report Builder for reports. Here Microsoft has done a good job in giving us tools that will help us get the job done.

Forrester Research also mentions that ALM 2.0 should be repository neutral. They say that there should not be a single repository but many, so we are not required to use the storage solution that the vendor proposes. IBM, for example, has declared that their coming ALM solution will integrate with a wide variety of repositories, such as Concurrent Versions System (CVS) and Subversion, just to mention a few. This approach will remove the obstacle of gathering and synchronizing data, giving us easier access to progress reports, and so on. Microsoft uses an extensive set of web services and plug-ins to solve the same thing. They have one storage central (SQL Server), but by exposing functionality through the use of web services, they have made it fairly easy to connect to other tools as well.

An open and extensible ALM solution lets companies integrate their own repositories into the ALM tool. Both Microsoft and IBM have solutions, data warehouse adapters, that enable existing repositories to be tied into the ALM system. It is probable that a large organization that has already made investments in tools and repositories in the past doesn't want to change everything to a new ALM system; hence it is essential to have this option.

Any way we choose to solve the problem will work, giving us possibilities of having a well-connected and synchronized ALM platform.

Furthermore, ALM 2.0 focuses on being built on an open integration standard. As you know, Microsoft exposes VSTS and the TFS through web services. This way, we can support coming tools as long as they also use an open standard. By having it this way, third-party vendors have the option of writing tons of cool and productive tools for us.

Process support built into the ALM platform is another important feature. By this I mean having the automated support for the ALM process built right into the tool(s). We can, for instance, have the development process (RUP, Scrum, XP, Waterfall, and so on) automated in the tool, reminding us of each step in the process so that we don't miss creating and maintaining any deliverables or checkpoints. In the case of VSTS, you will see that this support includes having the document structure, including templates for all documents, available on the project web site, directly after having created a new VSTS project. We can also imagine a tool with built-in capabilities helping us in requirements gathering and specification, for instance—letting us add requirements and specs into the tool and have them transformed into tasks assigned to the correct role without having to do this manually.

An organization is not likely to discard a way of working just because the new ALM tool says it cannot import that specific process. A lot of money has often been invested in developing a process, and organizations are not likely to be interested in spending the same amount again learning a new one. A requirement of ALM 2.0 is the capability to store the process in a readable format such as XML. The benefits are that the process can be easily modified, version controlled, and reported upon. The ALM platform should then be able to import the process and execute the application development process descriptions in it. Microsoft uses XML to store the development process in VSTS. In the XML file the whole process is described, and many different process files can coexist. This means we can choose which process template we want to base our project on when creating a new project (see more in Chapter 6).

As you saw in Chapter 1, it is important for an enterprise to have control over its project portfolio to better allocate and control resources. So far, none of the ALM vendors have integrated this support into the ALM platform. The good thing is that having a standards-based platform makes integration with PPM tools a lot easier.

ALM and PPM

ALM and PPM can support each other quite well. Data from the ALM repository can be an excellent source of data for the PPM tool, and hence decisions can be based on the results of the PPM tool. This requires a working connection between the two, of course. Manual efforts by cutting and pasting information are not good enough because they are slow and error prone. A good integration between the two repositories gives project portfolio decision-makers access to accurate and timely data. This eases their decision-making process.

Gartner identifies five key activities in the PPM decision process that benefit from a working integration:[9]

- Review current projects and their status.

- Review the application portfolio impact on resources (which resources are available and when are they available, for instance).

- Present new capital requests. (Do we need to add more resources to a project?)

- Reprioritize the portfolio.

- Examine investments for effectiveness (basically reviewing the outcome of projects within six months of delivery).

---

9. Kelly A. Shaw, "Application Lifecycle Management and PPM."

We can see that a lot of data important for these activities can be found in the ALM repository.

Microsoft's solution to the ALM and PPM integration still has some room for improvement but works very well. The integration comes in the form of an add-on to VSTS called the Project Server connector. At the time of this writing, this connector is unsupported and available on CodePlex (www.codeplex.com/pstfsconnector), and the fact that it is unsupported inhibits some of my customers from trying it out. However, this connector will be built into coming versions of VSTS, making it a very good option for companies looking for this kind of support indeed.

Microsoft does offer the Microsoft Office Enterprise Project Management (EPM) solution. This is Microsoft's end-to-end collaborative project and portfolio environment. The aim of this solution is to help an organization gain visibility, insight, and control across all work, enhancing decision making, improving alignment with business strategy, maximizing resource utilization, and measuring and helping to increase operations efficiency. Whoa, lots of words, right? Taken straight from the Microsoft web site. I will not dive into the specifics of this solution here but I will tell you a little about its three parts.

First we have Microsoft Office Project Professional. If you are a project manager, chances are that you know this product already. If not, many of us have definitely seen the Gantt schema the project manager has produced. We can use Project Professional as a stand-alone product if we need it for only single projects. But the real value comes when we connect it to the second part of the Microsoft EPM solution: Microsoft Office Project Server. This server offers the possibilities of resource management, scheduling, reporting, and collaboration capabilities in the Microsoft EPM solution. We use Project Server to store project and resource information in a central repository.

The third part of Microsoft's EPM suite is Microsoft Office Project Portfolio Server. This is a management solution enabling organizations to get control of their product portfolios so that they best align with the company business strategies. Portfolio Server integrates with Project Server (see Figure 2-13) so we can have an end-to-end project portfolio management solution.

So far there is no problem with this set of tools. I have customers happy with the EPM solution from Microsoft. The problem is the integration between Project Server and TFS. Microsoft has an unsupported connector for this that should help us. There is nothing wrong with it per se, but it is unsupported as of now. I have asked Microsoft several times for references on anybody using this but still wait for their answer. Hopefully Microsoft will integrate this connector in coming versions of TFS, because many customers ask for this feature.

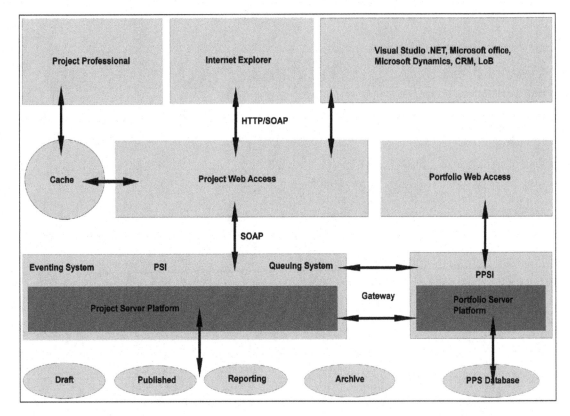

Figure 2-13. *The Microsoft EPM solution*

Summary

In this chapter, I have described an overview of what ALM 2.0 aims for and what it takes for the ALM platform to support ALM 2.0.

We know that traceability, automation of high-level processes, and visibility into development processes are three pillars of ALM. Other important key components are collaboration, workflow, security, reporting, analytics, being open standards based, being plug-in friendly, and much more, and they are focus areas of ALM. You have also seen that ALM is the coordination and synchronization of all development lifecycle activities.

The next chapter will focus on the development process itself. This is the core of all system development and project management. Personally, I find this topic very interesting. Follow me down that path for a while and hopefully you will share my interest (if you don't already).

CHAPTER 3

■■■

Development Processes and Frameworks

Over the years that I have worked in the IT business, I have come to adopt a mindset as to how I approach my job. This mindset has slowly but steadily grown on me, and I use it when I run projects for customers as well as when I have the role of being responsible for IT procurement. I cannot say I always succeed in following this mindset, but at least I try.

When I started reading about the agile movement a few years ago, I realized that the agile values were what I had been looking for. The agile community put words to the mindset I tried to follow in my daily work. The following excerpt from the Manifesto for Agile Software Development covers my mindset very well (http://agilemanifesto.org):

- Individuals and interactions over processes and tools

- Working software over comprehensive documentation

- Customer collaboration over contract negotiation

- Responding to change over following a plan

I like the idea of this thinking in the technical world of IT, and it has helped me in delivering better quality to my customers.

Before you start looking at the actual products that Visual Studio Team System consists of, I want to discuss the development processes or perhaps development frameworks. Unfortunately, this topic is pushed back a bit when many companies implement VSTS. Many seem to argue that one of the two process templates that Microsoft ships with VSTS is enough.

The two Microsoft Solution Framework (MSF) process templates that come out of the box with VSTS are two ways that Microsoft suggests we use to automate our ALM process. Consider, however, that Microsoft does not recommend using these without customization; they are provided as examples for implementing an ALM process in VSTS. So spend some time planning the process customization before implementing VSTS, and also keep in mind that you probably need to make ongoing adjustments to it.

A software development process can be said to be a structure imposed on the development of a software product—that is, a way of working that we should follow in order to successfully deliver an application or a system. You saw in Chapter 1 that the process was an important aspect of successful project completion, so I will dedicate this chapter to discussions of this topic.

Waterfall Model

Throughout the years, many development processes have come and gone. They all have tried to improve upon the former or have added a new aspect to development. The goal has probably been the same for all of them, even though the roads to that goal have varied.

One of the best known models has been around since 1970, when it was presented in an article by Winston W. Royce.[1] What is interesting about the model is that Royce presented it as an example of a flawed, nonworking model. Obviously, people did not bother with this fact and started using it as a way of running development projects anyway. The model I am referring to is of course the Waterfall model, even though Royce himself did not call it that.

The *Waterfall model* is a sequential process through which development is seen as a flow steadily moving downward, just like a waterfall, through its different phases. In Figure 3-1, you can see the phases of the model.

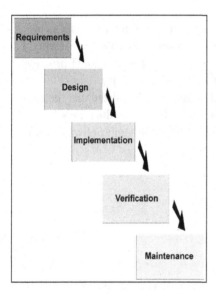

Figure 3-1. *The Waterfall development processes*

Royce wrote about seven phases in his original article:

- Requirements specification

- Design

- Construction (a.k.a. implementation)

- Integration

- Testing and debugging (a.k.a. validation)

- Installation

- Maintenance

---

1. Winston W. Royce, "Managing the Development of Large Software Systems," 1970, www.cs.umd.edu/class/spring2003/cmsc838p/Process/waterfall.pdf.

As you see in Figure 3-1, we usually speak of only five of these phases, because the model has evolved over the years. The thought is that the phases are carried out sequentially, and we never go back to what has been done. So when requirements specifications, for example, are done, they are virtually written in stone. After the spec is written, we move on to the next step, in this case the design phase, where we model our system and lay out the architecture. This effort can be seen as the blueprint of the system. In this phase, we transform the requirements into a design that we can give to the developers to turn into code.

When the blueprint is ready, we can move on to the next step, which is implementation. Now the coders do their magic, and the blueprint is transferred into code. At the end of this phase, individual software components are integrated and tested as a system. Different teams of developers might have developed the components, perhaps at different locations, which complicates things as well, because communication tends to be limited in such cases. As you can understand, we have an inherent problem here getting information about the available system to all involved. It is difficult for most project participants to get a clear and total picture of the system and how the components collaborate in the solution. If we test the system only after development is done, perhaps 12 months after coding begins, we might end up with lots of surprises. Just consider the immense rework needed if something is very wrong at this point. Many months of work might be going down the drain, and the project would surely be seen as a failure.

When the implementation phase is finished, we move on to testing the software. Hopefully, faults from earlier phases are found and removed in this part of the process. This might be the first time our customer or stakeholders see the final product. If, for example, more than a year has passed since the project began, much has surely happened to the requirements. But because we cannot go back to earlier phases, we are stuck with requirements that might actually be wrong. When testing is completed, we install the software and deliver it to maintenance.

What is important to remember here is that we do not move to the next phase until the former is completely finished. There is no jumping back and forth between them, and they cannot overlap.

The Waterfall model has been widely accepted and is used a lot—especially in the public sector, such as at the US Department of Defense, NASA, and many other large government agencies. This has been loosened a bit lately (fortunately), and more-agile methods such as Scrum are being implemented at these organizations as well.

The Waterfall model can be great when we know that nothing much will change during a project. Let's say that we are about to build a road. After gathering all requirements for the road, we can assume that they will not change much during the process. The same goes for the blueprints. Sure, some small things might change—placement of road signs and street-lights, for instance—but on the whole, the blueprint is pretty solid after it is approved. When we have such a project, the Waterfall model works very well.

Let's transform the road example to a development project. Implementing a standard product, such as an economy system, might be very static after the requirements are set, and the model could work well then. But even with such development efforts, things tend to change a lot anyway. According to Ken Schwaber of the Agile Alliance, and co-father of Scrum, about 35 percent of all requirements in a project change, which is a very high number and hence provides risk for the project.

Generally, one could say that the earlier we can find bugs, the easier and less expensive they are to fix. Steve McConnell estimates that "a requirements defect that is left undetected until construction or maintenance will cost 50 to 200 times as much to fix as it would have cost to fix at requirements time."[2] This is the reason why all phases in the Waterfall model must be 100 percent completed and absolutely correct before we move on to the next phase. The aim is to catch errors early to avoid problems and additional costs in the end.

Another cornerstone is documentation. Great focus is spent on documenting work. We need design documents, source code documents, and so on. Good documentation enables us to avoid problems if one of our team members falls off and nobody knows what that person has been doing. Much knowledge could be lost unless we have good documentation. If one person disappears, it should be relatively easy for the replacement to become familiar with the system and quickly become productive.

These are pretty solid arguments for the model, at least at first sight. But as you saw in Chapter 1, most development projects are more complex than implementing a standard system. This means that it is almost impossible to get one phase perfect before moving on to the next. Just to get all requirements correct is a tremendous task because the users/stakeholders probably won't be aware of exactly what they want unless they have a working prototype to investigate. Then, and only then, can they truly comment on it. It is also then that they will get a feeling of what is possible to accomplish with the software. If this awareness occurs late in the project, the changes to requirements they would want are hard to implement.

Another problem that we often run into is that during design, the architect or designers cannot know all the difficulties that could happen during implementation. Some areas can be hard to build or integrate that we were not aware of earlier. How do we handle that if we cannot go back to the design and change it after we have left it? Some requirements might also be contradictive, but this shows only during implementation. This will obviously be hard to solve as well without changing work done in earlier phases.

It seems like not even Royce really believed in the Waterfall model, as I said earlier. Instead, he was writing about how to change this model into an iterative one, with feedback from each phase affecting subsequent phases. It's strange that this fact has been virtually ignored and that the Waterfall model has been given so much attention through the years.

Spiral Model

Barry Boehm first defined the *Spiral model* in a 1988 article.[3] Although not the first model to discuss iterative development, it was in fact the first model to explain why the iteration matters.

When this model was designed, the iterations were typically six months to two years long. Each phase starts with a design goal and ends with the customer or stakeholder reviewing the progress so far. At each phase of a Spiral project, analysis and engineering efforts are applied, with a focus on the end goal of the project: the business value.

The steps in the Spiral model can be described as follows. Remember that this is a simplified view:

---

2. Steve McConnell, *Rapid Development: Taming Wild Software Schedules* (Microsoft Press, 1996).

3. Barry Boehm, "A Spiral Model of Software Development and Enhancement," 1988, www.cs.usu.edu/~supratik/CS%205370/r5061.pdf.

1. The *requirements are defined* in as much detail as possible. Interviews of a number of users representing all the external or internal users and other aspects of the existing system are often used at this stage.

2. A *preliminary design* is created for the new system.

3. Based on the preliminary design, a *first prototype* of the new system is created. Often this is a scaled-down system, showing an approximation of the characteristics of the final product.

4. A *second prototype* is evolved by a four-step procedure:

    Evaluating the first prototype in terms of its strengths, weaknesses, and risks

    Defining the requirements of the second prototype

    Planning and designing the second prototype

    Constructing and testing the second prototype

    If the customer thinks the risks are too great, the project can be aborted. Risk factors can be development cost overruns, miscalculation of operating cost, or any other factor that could, in the customer's judgment, result in a less-than-satisfactory final product.

5. The *existing prototype is evaluated* in the same manner as was the first prototype, and, if necessary, another prototype is developed from it according to the four-step procedure outlined in the preceding step.

6. These *steps are iterated* until the stakeholder is satisfied and convinced that the refined prototype represents the final product he or she wanted.

7. The *final system is constructed*, based on the approved prototype.

8. The *final system is extensively evaluated and tested*. Routine maintenance is carried out on a continuing basis to prevent large-scale failures and to minimize downtime.

It seems like the Spiral model is used on larger projects mostly. One example is the US military, which has adopted the Spiral model for its Future Combat Systems program (http://en.wikipedia.org/wiki/Future_Combat_Systems). However, I have never been a part of this kind of project, and neither have any of my coworkers, so it's hard to say if it scales that well.

Figure 3-2 shows the Spiral model.

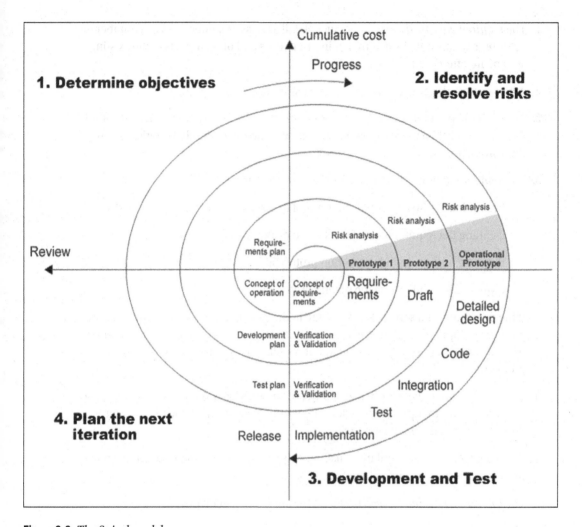

Figure 3-2. *The Spiral model*

Rational Unified Process (RUP)

During the 1980s, a team at Rational Software began looking into a new development model. Team members started this work by going back to the Spiral model created by Barry Boehm. Then they started to look into why software projects failed. What was the root cause of this in the past? Furthermore, they took a good look at software processes that were around at the time and how each of them tried to solve these causes of failure. Some of the causes they found were as follows:

- Ad hoc requirements management
- Complexity
- Ambiguous and imprecise communications

- Undetected inconsistencies in requirements, designs, and implementations

- Insufficient testing

- Subjective assessment of project status

- Uncontrolled change propagation

- Poor or insufficient automation

The team at Rational found that project failure most often was caused by a combination of several symptoms. They also concluded that every project that fails does so in its own unique way. After analyzing their results, they designed a collection of software best practices, which they named the *Rational Unified Process*, or *RUP* as we still say in daily life.

What is important to remember is that RUP is not a single, concrete, prescriptive process. It is an adaptable process framework intended to be adjusted by the organization and software team that will use it. The project team should choose the parts of the process they think are appropriate for the needs of that specific development task at hand.

The Principles of RUP

The Rational team based their framework on six key principles for business-driven development.[4]

- *Adapt the process*: The project or organization must, as I said, select the parts they need from the RUP framework. Things to consider here are, for example, how project governance, project size, and regulations affect the degree of formality that should be used. There are preconfigured process templates for small, medium, and large projects in RUP so that we can choose more easily. Most companies that I have seen usually adapt RUP in their own way. One of my former employers had several RUP adaptations based on different kinds of project types.

- *Balance stakeholder priorities*: RUP tries to take a shot at balancing out the business goals and stakeholder needs between the parties involved, because these often are conflicting.

- *Collaborate across teams*: As we all hopefully know, software engineering is a team process. We have various participants in a project, from stakeholders to developers. In Chapter 1, you saw that development these days is not often carried out at one location, but is geographically dispersed all over the world. This means that collaboration and communication between participants must be good, not only for requirements issues, but also for all aspects of the development process. Project status, test results, bug status, release management, design and architecture diagrams, and much more must be at hand for those who need it—and at the time they need it.

---

4. IBM staff, "Rational Unified Process: Best Practices for Software Development Teams," December 2003, www-128.ibm.com/developerworks/rational/library/253.html.

- *Demonstrate value iteratively.* One problem with the Waterfall model is that it does not allow us to go back a phase if we find things in one phase that throw things in earlier phases to the ground. By working iteratively, we deliver working software in increments. For each iteration, we collect feedback from everybody (including stakeholders) and use this as an input to the next iteration. This way, we can influence the development process and hence the business value while the project is being executed. By focusing strongly on iterative development and good risk management, RUP allows projects an iterative risk assessment process that is intended to ease the effort in delivering a successful project in the end.

- *Elevate the level of abstraction*: By elevating the abstraction level, RUP encourages the use of software patterns, a fourth-generation programming language (4GL), frameworks, reusable components, and so on. This approach hinders developers from going directly from the spec to writing their own custom-made code. This also means that we discuss architecture at a higher level than before. By using Unified Modeling Language (UML) or some built-in features of the development tool (see Chapter 6 for Visual Studio's architecture tools) in conjunction with a higher abstraction level, we elevate product architecture to a level where nontechnical stakeholders can better participate.

- *Focus continuously on quality.* Surprisingly, we do not focus on quality enough during many projects. I have had contractors at the Swedish Road Administration who definitely have not focused on quality in their projects. Instead, their primary goal was to make as much money as possible from the SRA (and from me as a taxpayer). This caused problems, as you would guess, because if we at the SRA did not keep an extra eye open, the projects would be unsuccessful. RUP encourages quality checks continuously through development. Automation of test scenarios, for example, helps us deal with an increasing number of tests caused by the iterative process and the practice of test-driven development.

The attentive reader (yes, I mean you!) has already noticed that if we take each starting character from these principles, we get the ABCs of RUP:

- *A*dapt the process

- *B*alance stakeholder priorities

- *C*ollaborate across teams

- *D*emonstrate value iteratively

- *E*levate the level of abstraction

- *F*ocus continuously on quality

The RUP Lifecycle

So what does the RUP lifecycle look like? Well, there are four major phases (see Figure 3-3). And no, we do not talk waterfall here. The phases are as follows:

- Inception
- Elaboration
- Construction
- Transition

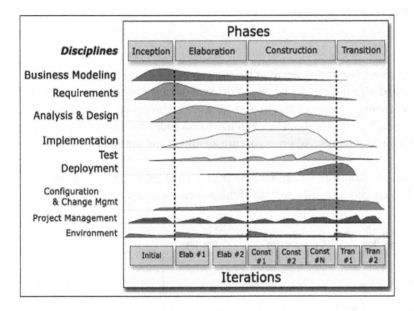

Figure 3-3. *The RUP development processes*

Inception Phase

As Figure 3-3 shows, the Inception phase has a strong focus on business modeling and requirements specifications. What is different from the Waterfall model is that we do not close these topics after the phase has ended. Instead, they are a constant part of all phases throughout the project. The Inception phase establishes a baseline so that we can compare actual expenditures to planned ones along the project. Before we move on to the next phase, we need to pass a milestone called the Lifecycle Objective Milestone (see Figure 3-4).

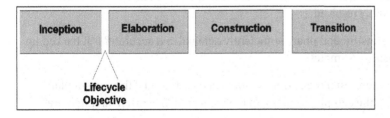

Figure 3-4. *The Lifecycle Objective Milestone*

To pass this milestone, the following criteria must be met:

- The stakeholder concurs on scope definition and cost/schedule estimates.

- The team agrees that the right set of requirements has been captured and that there is a shared understanding of these requirements.

- The team agrees that the cost/schedule estimates, priorities, risks, and development process are appropriate.

- All risks have been identified, and a mitigation strategy exists for each.

If we are not satisfied with the outcome of this milestone or the phase, we can choose to cancel the project or report this phase for redesign.

Elaboration Phase

During the Elaboration phase, we start to see what the project will look like. In Figure 3-3, you can see that analysis and design present the biggest effort here but must continue throughout the other phases. There are also other activities that we perform in this phase. We start to think about the implementation, how the code will be written, what to code, and so on. Most use cases are developed during elaboration, where actors are identified and the flow of use cases are thought out.

To pass the Lifecycle Architecture Milestone that finishes the Elaboration phase (see Figure 3-5), we should have completed 80 percent of the use-case models.

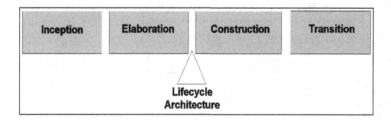

Figure 3-5. *The Lifecycle Architecture Milestone*

We should also have created a description of the architecture of our software. The risk list should have been written as well as a development plan for the entire project. These are the main criteria for passing the Lifecycle Architecture Milestone:

- Is the vision of the product stable?

- Is the architecture stable?

- Does the executable demonstration show that the major risk elements have been addressed and credibly resolved?

- Is the plan for the construction phase sufficiently detailed and accurate? Is it backed up with a credible basis of estimates?

- Do all stakeholders agree that the current vision can be achieved if the current plan is executed to develop the complete system, in the context of the current architecture?

- Is the actual resource expenditure vs. planned expenditure acceptable?

There are a few more criteria we must meet before we pass this milestone, but I will not go into them here. If we cannot pass the milestone, we can either cancel or redesign, just as in the preceding phase. When we continue to the next phase, project changes are more difficult to solve if we do not have a model that covers such events.

Construction Phase

Now we are ready for the Construction phase. This is where the coding starts as well as the implementation of our architecture. To make sure we catch changes of requirements, we do the development in iterations, each delivering a working prototype. We can show this to stakeholders and end users so that they have a chance to provide feedback. When going into this phase, the use cases have been prioritized and divided across the iteration. One good practice is to focus on the highest-risk use cases first, or at least as early as possible, so that we can catch their implications early. To end this phase, we must pass the Initial Operational Capability Milestone (see Figure 3-6) by answering the following questions:

- Is this product release stable and mature enough to be deployed in the user community?

- Are all stakeholders ready for the transition into the user community?

- Are the actual resource expenditures vs. planned expenditures still acceptable?

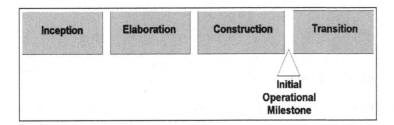

Figure 3-6. *The Initial Operational Capability Milestone*

Transition Phase

When we reach the last phase, the Transition phase, we have moved our system/software from the developers to the end users. This phase, as well as the Elaboration and Construction phases, can be performed iteratively. During transition, we train the end users and the operations department in their new system. We also do beta testing of the system to make sure we deliver what the end users and stakeholders expect. This means that we do not necessarily have the same expectations as when the project started, but expectations that have changed through the process.

If we do not meet either the end users' expectations or the quality level determined during the Inception phase, we do a new iteration of this phase. When we have met all objectives, the Product Release Milestone (see Figure 3-7) is reached and the development cycle ends. The following questions must be answered to pass the Product Release Milestone:

- Is the user satisfied?

- Are the actual resources expenditures vs. planned expenditures still acceptable?

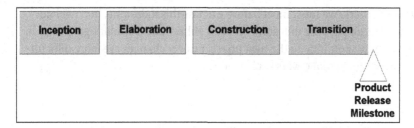

Figure 3-7. *The Product Release Milestone*

Disciplines

In RUP we speak about *disciplines*. There are nine disciplines in which we categorize our tasks in a software development project according to RUP. First we have the engineering disciplines:

- Business modeling

- Requirements

- Analysis and design

- Implementation

- Test

- Deployment

Then we have three supporting disciplines:

- Configuration and change management

- Project management

- Environment

Let's spend a few moments going over these in more detail. This is interesting especially when we compare this lineup to Scrum later in this chapter.

Business Modeling Discipline

The business modeling discipline is the first one out. The aim of this discipline is to establish a better understanding between business and software engineering. This is a welcome addition to performing better projects compared to the waterfall approach, because we already have seen that bridging the gap between these two is important. (In Chapter 4, you will learn about my own idea of how this could be done as well.) Business modeling explains how to describe a vision of the organization in which the system will be deployed. It also tells us how to use this vision as a basis when outlining the process as well as when selecting roles and responsibilities.

Requirements Discipline

The requirements discipline is responsible for gathering the requirements and using these to describe what the system is supposed to do, so that developers and stakeholders can agree on what to build.

Analysis and Design Discipline

This discipline takes the requirements and transforms these into a design of the system. An aim is to have a design that can be changed easily when functional requirements change, which they of course will during the project. The design model is an abstraction of what the source code will look like. We can call it a blueprint if we like, which shows us components, classes, subsystems, and so on, as we are used to. Having well-defined interfaces between components is another important task for this discipline. We also develop descriptions of how objects of the design collaborate to perform the use cases.

Implementation Discipline

The implementation discipline is responsible for taking the blueprint and converting it into executable code. We also find testing of developed components as units here. Components developed by individual teams are integrated into an executable system by this discipline. Focus is very much on component-based development, which is a way of developing that should encourage reuse of existing components. To be honest, I think this is a good idea in theory, but in real life I have seen very few good examples of component reuse. Sadly, I would say. Most times reuse is a developer using previously built snippets of code instead of components. It is a good effort to propagate components' reuse but in reality it seems like it is not working.

Test Discipline

There are several purposes of this discipline:

- Verification of interaction between objects

- Verification of all components

- Making sure all defects are fixed, retested, and closed

- Verifying that all requirements have been implemented (correctly)

- Identifying defects

- Making sure defects are addressed

- Making sure defects are addressed before deployment

RUP states that testing should be an integrated part of the whole development project, and I cannot agree more. The purpose is to find defects as early as possible, when they can be fixed by using minimal effort. We find four quality dimensions along which tests are carried out (www.tcu.gov.br/tcuup/manuals/intro/im_bp5.htm):

- *Reliability*: The application/system resists failure (crashing, hanging, memory leaks, and so on) during execution.

- *Functionality*: The application/system implements and executes the required use cases as intended.

- *Application performance*: The application executes and responds in a timely and acceptable manner, and continues to perform acceptably when subjected to real-world operational characteristics such as load, stress, and lengthy periods of operation.

- *System performance*: The system executes and responds in a timely and acceptable manner, and continues to perform acceptably when subjected to real-world operational characteristics such as load, stress, and lengthy periods of operation.

Deployment Discipline

The activity in the deployment discipline needs to be planned for early in the project. The deployment is mostly focused at the end of the Construction phase and the Transition phase, but to successfully deploy an application or system, we need to plan for this even earlier. This discipline focuses on producing product releases in a successful way. It also focuses on delivering the software to the end users. Included in this work are the tasks of packaging, distributing, and installing the software as well. Furthermore, the people in this discipline provide help to users, so that deployment runs smoothly.

Configuration and Change Management Discipline

The next discipline we are looking at is the configuration and change management discipline. RUP specifies three areas when it comes to change and configuration management:

- *Configuration management*: This, of course, is the structuring of products. We also need a way to keep control of our releases and the artifacts belonging to them, and these are tasks belonging to this area.

- *Change request management*: In this second area, we keep track of all change proposals we receive for the different versions of the software.

- *Status and measurement management*: When a change request is created, it goes through different states in its workflow. It transforms from new, to logged, to approved, to assigned, to completed. This area describes how we can get reports on status of the software and its change requests and different releases. These reports are important for the project team as well as for stakeholders, so that they can feel that they have a good understanding of the project's status at the moment.

Project Management Discipline

As you have seen, we have two dimensions of a project in RUP: the four phases and the iterations within them. Project management focuses on planning the phases, which is done in the phase plan: planning how many iterations (in the iteration plan) might be needed and also how to handle risks through the project. This discipline also monitors the progress of the project. There are some things RUP does not include in the project management discipline, however. It does not cover managing people, which is usually a project management responsibility. Budget management and contract management also are not included.

Environment Discipline

The environment discipline is the last discipline in RUP. Contrary to what one might think, we do not include the software environment here. Instead we find the environment for the project—that is, the processes and tools we should use when running the project, what work products we should deliver (more about these in a moment), and so on.

Work Products, Roles, and Tasks

All through the project, various deliverables should be produced. RUP originally called these deliverables *artifacts*, and that is the term that has stuck in most people's minds. However, after IBM took over RUP responsibilities, the term *work products* was used, and I will use this new term from now on in this book.

A *work product* could be an architecture model, the risk list, the iteration plan, and so on. It is a representation of the results of a task. This term encompasses all documents and models that we produce in the project.

A *task* is a unit of work, which provides a meaningful result. A task is assigned to a role. A *role*, in turn, defines a set of related skills, competencies, and responsibilities.

Let's consider an example. The work product *iteration plan* is the result of a task, *produce iteration plan*, which is performed by the role *project manager*. Another example could be the task *defining the architecture*, which produces the result, or work product, *architecture model*. This is performed by the role called *architect*.

There are several benefits of using RUP. Many projects have completed successfully using an adaptation of this framework. I would say that project quality is significantly improved by using RUP. The problem, however, is that RUP has grown to be an almost impenetrable framework. There is too much to consider and choose from, which makes it very hard to adopt correctly. One of my colleagues said that he did not like a model that needed adaptation to that extent. And I can understand that. I also think the process is too strict and not truly iterative compared to Scrum or any other truly agile methodology. Even Ivar Jacobson, one of RUP's founders, seems to have realized that the framework has grown too immense. He has during the recent years improved upon RUP and created a new, more agile framework.

Manifesto for Agile Software Development

In 2001, a group of people met at a Utah ski resort to try to find some common ground for how the development process could be improved to better meet customer requirements and hence deliver better business value. This is part of their story:[5]

---

5. "Manifesto for Agile Software Development" (http://agilemanifesto.org).

We are uncovering better ways of developing software by doing it and helping others do it. Through this work we have come to value

- *Individuals and interactions over processes and tools*

- *Working software over comprehensive documentation*

- *Customer collaboration over contract negotiation*

- *Responding to change over following a plan*

That is, while there is value in the items on the right, we value the items on the left more.

This manifesto was signed by Kent Beck, Mike Beedle, Arie van Bennekum, Alistair Cockburn, Ward Cunningham, Martin Fowler, James Grenning, Jim Highsmith, Andrew Hunt, Ron Jeffries, Jon Kern, Brian Marick, Robert C. Martin, Steve Mellor, Ken Schwaber, Jeff Sutherland, and Dave Thomas.

The manifesto's values represented a start to a new movement in the software development community, and this movement has gained a great number of followers since. In addition to the previous list of values, the manifesto also includes the following principles:[6]

- *Our highest priority is to satisfy the customer through early and continuous delivery of valuable software.*

- *Welcome changing requirements, even late in development. Agile processes harness change for the customer's competitive advantage.*

- *Deliver working software frequently, from a couple of weeks to a couple of months, with a preference to the shorter timescale.*

- *Business people and developers must work together daily throughout the project.*

- *Build projects around motivated individuals. Give them the environment and support they need, and trust them to get the job done.*

- *The most efficient and effective method of conveying information to and within a development team is face-to-face conversation.*

- *Working software is the primary measure of progress.*

- *Agile processes promote sustainable development. The sponsors, developers, and users should be able to maintain a constant pace indefinitely.*

- *Continuous attention to technical excellence and good design enhances agility.*

- *Simplicity—the art of maximizing the amount of work not done—is essential.*

- *The best architectures, requirements, and designs emerge from self-organizing teams.*

- *At regular intervals, the team reflects on how to become more effective, then tunes and adjusts its behavior accordingly.*

---

6. "Manifesto for Agile Software Development."

I believe that most of these values and principles should be present in all software development, but sadly that is not always the truth. Many times projects I have participated in have delivered a large chunk of software after several months of development. Only then has the customer been brought in to evaluate the work, so both collaboration and incremental delivery have been neglected. Many times the customer has had a lot to say about the result, which has required writing many change requests to fix the issues or explain why the software works as it does, and not in the way the customer expected. So to me these values and principles are important and have been a key concern in my previous projects.

As you saw, many representatives from various development methods signed the manifesto. Of those, perhaps most well known are Extreme Programming (XP) and Scrum, but many of the others are well known as well.

I have chosen to cover Extreme Programming briefly and Scrum a little more extensively in this chapter. Many of the XP methods are widely used in Scrum projects (and other projects as well). I think about test-driven development, for example, which we will come back to in Chapter 6. Let's start with a short introduction to XP.

Extreme Programming (XP)

Extreme Programming (XP) is a deliberate and disciplined approach to software development. XP stresses customer satisfaction, an important part of the Agile Manifesto. The methodology is designed to deliver the software the customer needs and do this when it is needed. XP focuses on responding to changing customer requirements, even late in the lifecycle, so that customer satisfaction (business value) is met.

XP also emphasizes teamwork. Managers, customers, and developers are all part of a team dedicated to delivering high-quality software. XP implements a simple and effective way to handle teamwork.

There are four ways XP improves software teamwork; communication, simplicity, feedback, and courage. Courage, by the way is an interesting subject. It means don't be afraid to kill your darlings—in other words, be prepared to redo what you have coded, be prepared to change what you have done after a review. It also means be prepared to be persistent and not give up. It is essential that XP programmers communicate with their customers and fellow programmers. The design should be simple and clean. Feedback is supplied by testing the software from the first day of development. Testing is done by writing the unit tests before even writing the code. This is called test-driven development and has started to become a very well-used practice in many projects, not only agile ones. We will come back to this in Chapter 6. In that chapter, you will see how VSTS implements test-driven development.

The software should be delivered to the customers as early as possible, and a goal is to implement changes as suggested. XP stresses that the developers should be able to courageously respond to changing requirements and technology based on this foundation.

In RUP we have use cases and in XP we have *user stories*. These serve the same purpose as use cases but are not the same. They are used to create time estimates for the project and are also used instead of large requirements documentation. The customer is responsible for writing the user stories, which should be about things that the system needs to do for users. Each story is about three sentences of text written by the customer in the customer's terminology, without any technical wordings a developer might have used if describing the same thing.

Another important issue is that XP stresses the importance of delivering working software in increments so that the customer can give feedback as early as possible. By having a mindset that this will happen, developers are ready for implementing changes.

The last topic I want to highlight with XP is the use of pair programming. All code to be included in a production release is created by two people working together at a single computer. This should increase software quality without impacting time to delivery. Although I have never had the benefit of trying this myself, the coworkers I have spoken to who have used pair programming are confident that it will add as much functionality as two developers working separately—while providing much higher quality. I can make a reference to my old job as an assistant air traffic controller here. Many times that we sat in the tower, air traffic was so heavy that the controllers soon needed help keeping track of every airplane. I am aware that this is not the same thing, but my point is that two pairs of eyes see more than one pair, and this is what makes pair programming so tempting to me.

To learn more about Extreme Programming, I encourage you to visit `www.extremeprogramming.org`.

Scrum

Over to one of my favorite development models: *Scrum*. With all the attention Scrum has been getting in recent years, you might mistakenly believe that it is a fairly new model. The truth is that the Scrum approach, although not called Scrum at the time, was first presented as the rugby approach in 1986. Hirotaka Takeuchi and Ikujiro Nonacha described this approach, arguing that small cross-functional teams from a historical view produced the best results.[7]

It wasn't until 1990, however, that the rugby approach was referred to as Scrum. Peter DeGrace and Leslie Stahl highlighted this term from the Takeuchi and Nonacha original article.[8] The term comes from rugby originally (see Figure 3-8), where it means the quick, safe, and fair restart of a rugby game after a minor infringement or stoppage:

> *A scrum is formed in the field when eight players from each team, bound together in three rows for each team, close up with their opponents so that the heads of the front rows are interlocked. This creates a tunnel into which a scrum-halt throws in the ball so that front-row players can compete for possession by hooking the ball with either of their feet.*

> —Planet Rugby (`www.planetrugby.com`)

Have this definition in mind when you go through the description of the rest of the development version of Scrum.

---

7. Hirotaka Takeuchi and Ikujiro Nonacha, "The New New Product Development Game," January–February 1986, *Harvard Business Review*.

8. Peter DeGrace and Leslie Stahl, *Wicked Problems, Righteous Solutions: A Catalog of Modern Engineering Paradigms* (Prentice Hall, 1990).

Figure 3-8. *A real scrum!*

Ken Schwaber started using Scrum at his company in the early 1990s. But to be fair, it was Jeff Sutherland who was the first to call it Scrum.[9] Schwaber and Sutherland then teamed up and presented this approach publicly in 1996 at the Conference on Object-Oriented Programming, Systems, Languages, and Applications (OOPSLA) in Austin, Texas. They then collaborated to use their experience and industry best practices to refine the model so that it got its present look. Sutherland and Mike Beedle described the model in *Agile Software Development with Scrum* (Prentice Hall, 2001).

Empirical Process Control

So what is this model or framework called Scrum all about? First let's define two concepts to solve different problems. We touched on the problems with projects in Chapter 1. When we have a problem that is similar time after time (road construction, for instance, or implementing a standard system), we pretty much know what to expect of the various tasks at hand. We can then easily use a process that produces acceptable quality output over and over again—like the Waterfall model, perhaps. This approach is called *defined process control*.[10]

When it comes to a more complex problem, however, such as building a software system, you have seen that the traditional models do not work. We then must use something called *empirical process control*, according to Schwaber.

Empirical process control has three legs to stand on:

- Transparency

- Inspection

- Adaptation

"Transparency means that the aspects of the process that affect the outcome must be visible to those controlling the process," Schwaber writes.[11] This means that to be able to approve the outcome, we must agree on what the criteria for the outcome are. Two persons cannot say they are *finished* with a task unless they both agree on the criteria for *finished*.

---

9. Jeff Sutherland, "Agile Development: Lessons Learned from the First Scrum," 2004, http://jeffsutherland.com/scrum/FirstScrum2004.pdf.

10. Ken Schwaber, *The Enterprise and Scrum* (Microsoft Press, 2007).

11. Ken Schwaber, *The Enterprise and Scrum*.

The next leg is inspection. The process must be inspected as frequently as necessary in order to find unacceptable variances in the process. Because all inspections might lead to a need for making changes to the process itself, we also need to revise the inspections to fit the new process. To accomplish this, we need a skilled inspector who knows what he or she is inspecting.

The last leg is adaptation. You saw that an inspection might lead to a change of the process. This is one example of an adaptation. Another can be that we need to adapt the material being processed as a result of an inspection. All adaptations must be made as quickly as possible to minimize deviation further on.

Schwaber ruses the example of code review when he discusses empirical process control: "The code is reviewed against coding standards and industry best practices. Everyone involved in the review fully and mutually understands these standards and best practices. The code review occurs whenever someone feels that a section of code is complete. The most experienced developers review the code, and their comments and suggestions lead to the developer adjusting his or her code."[12]

Simple, isn't it? I could not have said it better myself.

Complexity in Projects

What makes a software development process so complex anyway? We discussed it a little previously but let's dive a little bit deeper into it here. In theory, it might seem pretty straightforward to build software systems. We write code that logically instructs the CPU to control the computer. I mean, how hard can it be? Alas, it is not that simple, I'm afraid. The people writing the code are complex machines in themselves. They have different backgrounds, IQs, EQs, views, attitudes, and so on.

The requirements might also be complex, and they have a tendency to change over time. According to Schwaber, 35 percent of the requirements gathered at the beginning of a project change during the project. And 60 percent of the features we build are rarely or never used in the end. Many times in my projects, several people are responsible for defining the requirements at the customer. Quite often the persons responsible have diverging agendas as to why and what to build. Often the stakeholders have a hard time expressing what they really want. It is when they see a first prototype of the system that they fully start to see the possibilities with the software, and only then can they begin to understand what they want.

Rarely is just one computer involved in a system either. Interaction between several machines is usually the case. We might have a web farm for our GUI, a cluster for our application tier, a back-end SQL Server, some external web services, and often a legacy system, all needing to integrate to solve the needs of the new system.

When complex things interact—as people, requirements, and technology do in a software project—the level of complexity increases greatly. So I would say it is safe to say that we don't have any simple software problems anymore. They are all complex. Schwaber realizes this as well, and in Figure 3-9 we can see his complexity assessment graph.

---

12. Ken Schwaber, *The Enterprise and Scrum.*

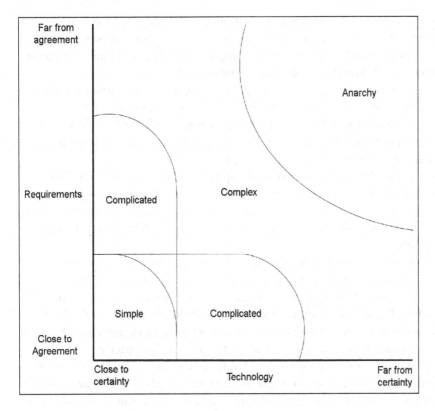

Figure 3-9. *Schwaber's complexity graph*

The projects in the Anarchy area are chaotic and unworkable. To get them to reach their finish lines, we probably need to resolve serious issues before even starting the project.

What Scrum tries to do is address this inherent complexity by implementing inspection, adaptation, and visibility as you saw in empirical process control earlier. Scrum does so by having simple practices and rules, as you will now see.

What Scrum Is

Scrum is an iterative, incremental, and powerful process. Many get fooled by its perceived simplicity, but keep in mind that Scrum can handle CMMI at level 5, which not many other processes do. Figure 3-10 shows the skeleton of the Scrum model on which we attach the rules and practices. Each iteration consists of several daily inspections.

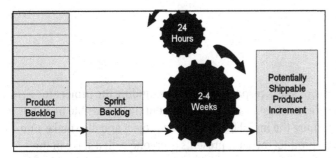

Figure 3-10. *The Scrum skeleton*

During these inspections, team members evaluate each other's work and the activities performed since the last inspection. If necessary adjustments (adaptation) are found, they are implemented as quickly as possible. The iterations also conclude with inspections when more adaptations can be made. This cycle repeats until it is no longer funded.

All the requirements that are known at the beginning of the project are gathered in the product backlog, which is one of the artifacts of Scrum. (I will soon come back to this.) The project team reviews the backlog and selects which requirements should be included in the first iteration, or *sprint* as it is called in Scrum. These selected requirements are added to the sprint backlog, where they are broken down into more-detailed items.

The team then makes their best effort to turn the sprint backlog into a shippable increment of the final product. The team is self-managing, which means they collectively decide who does what, and what is the best way to solve the problems. The increment is presented to the stakeholder(s) at the end of the sprint so they can inspect it and make the adaptations necessary to the project.

The sprint is most often 30 days, although I have seen sprints of two to four weeks in many projects. It depends a bit on the sprint backlog items. When I took my Scrum Master certification, Ken Schwaber described that he once had to have a one-week sprint in a project. The team had malfunctioned, and the shorter sprint time enabled him to more easily catch the reason for the problem and adjust the process so that the project ran more smoothly.

The stakeholders' adaptations and feedback are put into the product backlog and prioritized again. Then the team starts the process all over again and selects the backlog items they think they can finish during the next sprint. These are put into the sprint backlog for the next sprint and broken down into more-manageable items. And so it continues until the stakeholders think they have received the business value they wanted and funding stops.

If we look at the three legs of empirical process control again, we can see that Scrum covers them nicely. Transparency is implemented by letting the team and stakeholders agree on what is the expected outcome of the project and of each iteration. Inspection occurs daily and also at the end of each sprint. Adaptations are the direct result of these inspections and are necessary in Scrum.

The Roles in Scrum

There are roles in Scrum as there are in all previously mentioned models. But the difference is that Scrum has fewer roles, which are not defined in the same strict way as in the others. Scrum has the following three roles:

- The product owner

- The team

- The scrum master

Owner

Let's start with the *product owner*. He or she is responsible to those funding the project to deliver a product or a system that gives the best return on investment (ROI) possible from the project. The product owner must acquire the initial funding of the project and also make sure it is funded through its lifespan. The product owner represents everyone with a stake in the project and its result. In the beginning of a project, the product owner gathers the initial requirements and puts these into the project backlog. It is the product owner who ultimately decides which requirements have the highest priority based on ROI or business value (for example) and decides into which sprint they should go. During the project, the product owner inspects the project and prioritizes the product backlog and sprint backlogs so that the stakeholders' needs are met.

Team

The *team* is the one responsible for the development. There are no specific roles in the team. Because the team is cross-functional and self-organizing, it is their responsibility to make sure they have the competencies and staff needed for solving the problems. So it is not the scrum master who decides who does what and when, as a project manager would do in a traditional approach. These are some of the reasons behind this thought, as provided by Ken Schwaber through his scrum master course material:

- People are most productive when they manage themselves.

- People take their commitment more seriously than other people's commitment for them (for example, when a project manager commits that the person should accomplish something).

- People have many creative moments during down time.

- People always do the best they can.

- Under pressure to work harder, developers automatically and increasingly reduce quality.

The team should be seven persons, plus or minus two for optimal results. A logical team consists of one programmer, one tester, a half-time analyst/designer, and a half-time technical writer. The optimal physical team has 2.5 logical teams.

The team decides which items in the backlog they can manage for each sprint based on the prioritized backlog. This whole thinking is a giant leap from traditional project management and takes some getting used to. Some people do not accept this and find it impossible to work this way.

Scrum Master

The *scrum master* is responsible for the Scrum process and has to make sure everybody in the team, the product owner, and anyone else involved in the project knows and understands the process. The scrum master makes sure that everyone follows the rules and practices of the Scrum process. So the scrum master does not manage the team; the team is self-managing. If a conflict occurs in the team, the scrum master should be the oil that makes the team smoothly work out their problems. It is also the scrum master's responsibility to protect the team from the outside world so they can work in peace and quiet during the sprint, focused on delivering business value.

The following lists the scrum master responsibilities, again according to Ken Schwaber's course material:

- Removing the barriers between development and the customer so the customer directly drives development

- Teaching the customer how to maximize ROI and meet their objectives through Scrum

- Improving the lives of the development team by facilitating creativity and empowerment

- Improving the productivity of the development team in any way possible

- Improving the engineering practices and tools so each increment of functionality is potentially shippable

The Scrum Process

Now that you know the basics of Scrum, it is time to take a look at what happens during a Scrum project.

The product owner, after arranging initial funding for the project, puts together the product backlog by gathering functional as well as nonfunctional requirements. The focus is to turn the product backlog into functionality, and it is prioritized so that the requirements giving the greatest business value or having the highest risk come first. Remember that this approach is a value-up paradigm, where we set business value first.

Then the product backlog is divided into suggested releases (if necessary), which should be possible to implement immediately. This means that when a release is finished, we should be able to put it into production at once so that we can start getting the business value as quickly as possible. We do not have to wait until the whole project is done until we can start getting return on our stakeholders' investments.

Because the Scrum process is an adaptive process, this is just the starting point. The product backlog and the priorities will change during the project as business requirements change and also depending on how well the team succeeds in producing functionality. The constant inspections will also affect the process.

When a sprint is starting, it initiates with a *sprint planning meeting*. At this meeting, the product owner and the team decide, based on the product owner's prioritization, what will be done during this sprint. The items selected from the product backlog are put into the sprint backlog. The sprint planning meeting is time-boxed and cannot last more than eight hours. This strict time-box enables the participants to avoid too much paperwork related to what should be done. The meeting has two parts. The first four hours are spent with the team and the product owner; the latter presents the highest-priority product backlog issues, and the team questions him/her about it so that they know what the requirements mean. The next four hours are used by the team so that they can plan the sprint and break down the selected product backlog items into the sprint backlog.

When the project is rolling, each day starts with a 15-minute daily scrum, or stand-up, meeting (see Figure 3-11). This is the 24-four hour inspection.

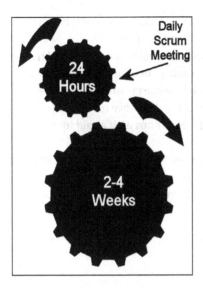

Figure 3-11. *The sprint in Scrum*

During this meeting, each team member answers three questions:

- What have you done since the last daily scrum meeting?

- What do you plan to do on this project until the next daily scrum (your commitments)?

- What impediments are in the way of you meeting your commitments toward this sprint and this project?

The purpose of this meeting is to catch problems and hence be able to make timely adjustments to the process. It is the scrum master's responsibility to help the team members get rid of any impediments they may have.

When a sprint comes to an end, a *sprint review* is held. This meeting is also time-boxed, but at four hours instead of eight. The product owner and the stakeholders get a chance to see what the team has produced during the sprint and reflect on this. But it is important to remember that this meeting is not a demonstration; it is a collaborative meeting of the people involved.

Now there is only one meeting left: the *sprint retrospective*. The sprint retrospective takes place between the sprint review and the next sprint planning meeting. It is time-boxed at three hours. The scrum master encourages the team to adjust the development process, still within the boundaries of the Scrum process and practices framework, so that the process can be more effective for the next sprint.

What happens if we have a larger project than one with only a team of approximately seven people? Can Scrum scale to handle this? According to Mike Cohnin, we can use a process called *scrum of scrums:* "The scrum of scrums meeting is an important technique in scaling Scrum to large project teams. These meetings allow clusters of teams to discuss their work, focusing especially on areas of overlap and integration. Imagine a perfectly balanced project comprising seven teams, each with seven team members. Each of the seven teams would conduct (simultaneously or sequentially) its own daily scrum meeting. Each team would then designate one person to also attend a scrum of scrums meeting. The decision of who to send should belong to the team. Usually the person chosen should be a technical contributor on the team—a programmer, tester, database administrator, designer, and so on—rather than a product owner or scrum master."[13] By using this technique, we can scale Scrum infinitely, at least in theory.

That's basically it. Scrum is a lean process and appeals a great deal to me. I have had the privilege to achieve my Scrum Master certification through a course held by Ken Schwaber himself, and this was a very uplifting experience. Unfortunately, some customers or stakeholders can find Scrum a bit vague, so they won't try it. They think they have more control by continuing to follow their previously adopted methods and are perhaps a bit afraid to embrace this modern way of doing projects.

Some even think that documentation and planning are not necessary in Scrum. Developers salute this because they don't want to write documents, and stakeholders tremble at the thought. But nothing could be further from the truth. Scrum does not say we do not document or plan. The contrary is true. Planning, for instance, is done everyday during the daily scrum (see Figure 3-12).

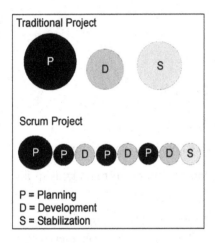

Figure 3-12. *Planning in Scrum*

Documents should also be written, but we scale away documents that are not necessary—documents that are produced only for the sake of documentation and almost never are read after they are produced. We document what is needed for the system and the project. We document our code; we document traceability, and so on.

I have found that some companies think they are using Scrum just because they develop iteratively. In many cases, they have changed the Scrum process so that it will not help them solve their development problems, problems that are clearly visible in a true Scrum project. Instead they have used Scrum as make-up covering the bad spots, and when the project still ends up failing, they argue that Scrum doesn't work either, that they still do not deliver value or still have overruns, and so on. So when implementing Scrum, follow the process and framework, and adjust the organization to Scrum, not the Scrum process to the organization.

How about architecture, the IT architect shouts. Don't we need to set the architecture before we start coding? Well, no! Scrum uses the concept of emerging architecture, which means we create a base architecture during the first sprint. This is evolved and built upon as the sprints continue. So the architecture is emerging as we go along, giving us agility in this concept as well.

13. Mike Cohnin, "Advice on Conducting the Scrum of Scrums Meeting," May 2007, www.scrumalliance.org/articles/46-advice-on-conducting-the-scrum-of-scrums-meeting.

When a customer is hesitating, we must use our most persuasive skills to get them to at least do a pilot on a project and see how it goes. It is my firm belief that most customers will be pleasantly surprised afterward. When the customers see that they get a product better meeting their requirements and giving better ROI in a shorter time than traditional projects, they usually melt.

Essential Unified Process (EssUP)

The *Essential Unified Process*, or *EssUP*, is a new software development process that builds on established and modern best practices (www.ivarjacobson.com). The founders claim that it is a practice-centric process integrating best practices from three leading processes or frameworks:

- The unified process

- The process maturity process

- The agile processes

From these three we get different things. The unified process makes sure we get structure, which is something we could see in the preceding description of RUP that it definitely provides. The process maturity process contributes with process improvement, and the agile methods give us agility.

Furthermore, this model claims to give us core processes that are very different from other models and frameworks. EssUP relies on the idea of separation of concerns (SOC). This is also called aspect-oriented thinking, meaning that we identify and address specific concerns in order of priority.

Wikipedia describes separation of concerns as follows: "In software engineering, the programming paradigms of aspect-oriented programming (AOP), and aspect-oriented software development (AOSD) attempt to aid programmers in the separation of concerns, specifically cross-cutting concerns, as an advance in modularization. AOP does so using primarily language changes, while AOSD uses a combination of language, environment, and method."[14]

This is said to make it easier to tailor-make our software development process so that it better suits our concerns.

The Practices of EssUP

EssUp relies heavily on the concept of practices. Ivar Jacobson defines a practice like this:[15]

A practice provides a way to systematically and verifiably address a particular aspect of a problem.

It is important to note that:

- *A practice does not attempt to address the entire problem. Rather, a practice attacks a particular aspect of the problem.*

- *A practice is systematic in that someone can articulate it—it is not a black art. A practice has a clear beginning and end, and tells a complete story in usable chunks.*

---

14. http://en.wikipedia.org/wiki/Aspect-oriented_programming

15. Ivar Jacobson, Pan Wei Ng, and Ian Spence, "Enough of Processes—Let's Do Practices," http://www.jot.fm/issues/issue_2007_07/column5/.

- *A practice includes its own verification, providing it with a clear goal and a way of measuring its success in achieving that goal. Without verification, the practice is not complete.*

- *Because of these qualities, practices can be developed, learned, and adopted separately, and that can be used in conjunction with other practices to create easily understood and coherent ways of working.*

In short, a practice is a proven way of approaching or addressing a problem. It is something that has been done before, can be successfully communicated to others, and can be applied repeatedly producing consistent result.

So which practices do EssUP give us? We have five foundation practices and three supporting practices (see Figure 3-13).

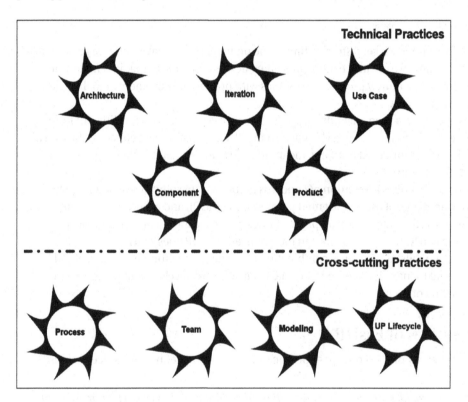

Figure 3-13. *The practices of EssUP*

The development and technical practices are as follows:

- Iterative Essentials

- Architecture Essentials

- Use-Case Essentials

- Component Essentials

- Model Essentials

These are the social engineering processes and other practices:

- Product Essentials

- Process Essentials

- Team Essentials

Iterative Essentials

In the Iterative Essentials, we find practices to "break the project up into a series of smaller, self-contained, time-boxed, mini-projects."[16] These practices will give us better possibilities to manage risks, money, quality, cost, and change requests. They will give us the agility and flexibility that we seek to successfully run the project with quality in mind.

Figure 3-14 shows the artifacts that we are supposed to produce and how they relate. You can see that some of the ideas from Scrum are reflected in EssUP, such as the product backlog, for instance.

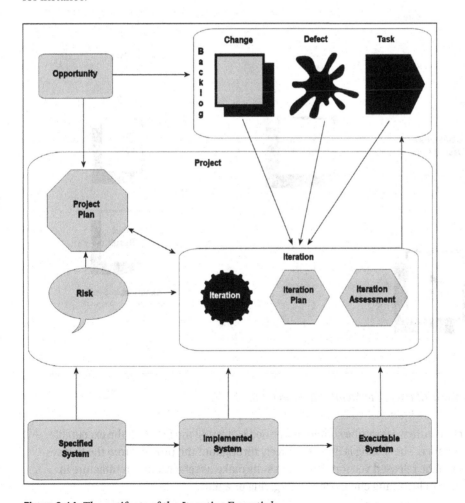

Figure 3-14. *The artifacts of the Iterative Essentials*

---

16. Ivar Jacobson International, "Iterative Essentials," www.ivarjacobson.com.

Architecture Essentials

The Architecture Essentials create a firm foundation for the development of a robust, high-quality system. We should use these practices to address the technical risks we see in the project. We should also use them to establish an appropriate architecture. Figure 3-15 shows the artifacts we are expected to deliver.

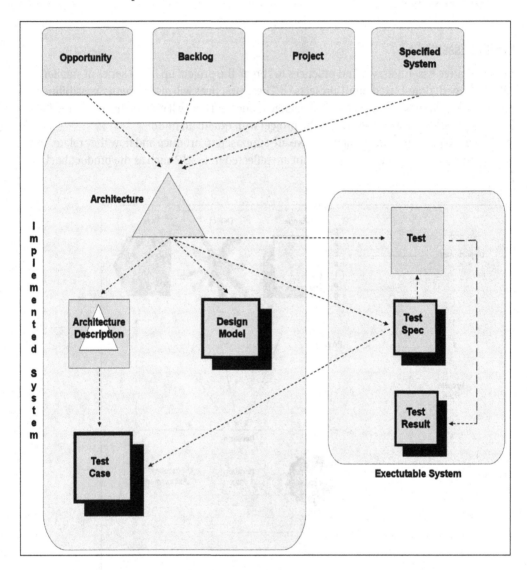

Figure 3-15. *The artifacts of the Architecture Essentials*

The architecture we describe should be verified by testing the builds of the executable system we produce. The testing is done iteratively throughout the project, from the first system skeleton to the released version. The test results make us refactor the architecture in coordination with incoming change requests, giving us agility.

Use-Case Essentials

Use-Case Essentials are the practices that give us an agile approach to requirements management, development, and system testing. Together with the customer, the team captures the essential requirements for the system and identifies the value expected from it.

In Figure 3-16, you see which artifacts are produced here. Use cases are still pretty much what they are in RUP: they describe a sequence of actions that happens when an actor wants something from the system (the actor is a role played in the use case, which can be a human, a computer, or another software system). For instance, we can have the use case customer purchase a book from our new web site. The use case would describe what happens during this process, in the form of sequential actions.

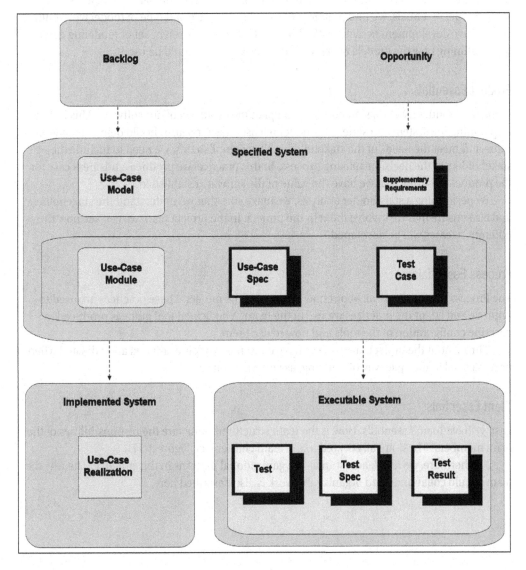

Figure 3-16. *The artifacts of the Use-Case Essentials*

You can see in Figure 3-16 that we have use-case-based requirements specifications, scenarios, and test cases. These are derived from the requirements we have produced.

Component Essentials

EssUP focuses hard on component-based development. The designers produce a design model showing the components and how they work together to implement our system(s). We also create source code and unit tests for each component.

Model Essentials

Models are created to communicate the requirements structure and behavior of a system. In the Model Essentials, we find practices to establish the style and type of model we should use to drive development activities. We should establish a lightweight set of modeling guidelines outlining how the models are related and the way they should be used.

Product Essentials

Using the Product Essentials practice, we can plan the evolution of our software. This is done by planning the system as a series of product releases. Each release should deliver business value and meet the needs of the stakeholders. To accomplish this, we need to include the stakeholders in the decision-making process. In this practice, we produce a business case for the product, ensuring that we have the value of the software established.

By performing a stakeholder analysis, we make sure that we understand the stakeholders and also ensure that we involve them in the project. In the project plan, we can see how the different releases will be developed.

Process Essentials

The Process Essentials are all about how we work in the project. These practices are used to improve and adapt the practices we use in the team. A dedicated tool guide is produced to describe configuration of the tools and how to use them.

Throughout the project, the way we have chosen to work is evaluated and adjusted when necessary, all in the agile way of thinking, as you will soon see.

Team Essentials

Last we have Team Essentials. How is the team structured? What are the responsibilities of the team members? These are all covered in the team charter (see Figure 3-17).

Furthermore, we find leadership and organizational patterns in this practice. The way the team should collaborate and organize the work is also described here.

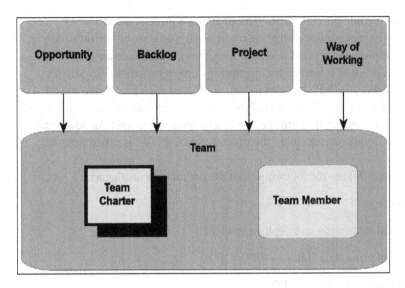

Figure 3-17. *The team charter*

Implementing EssUP

How do we implement this process? According to EssUP, we should use what we have and improve on that, one practice at a time. We are supposed to use what we need and what we think the organization can use without any severe risks. The process itself is supplied with a base set of practices, including guidelines. These will help us adapt our own practices.

This all might seem fine and not so rigid as RUP. Still, I am not sure what I think because I have not tried this in real projects. Speaking with Tomas Jacobson, son of Ivar Jacobson, I understand that EssUP is offered free when one purchases consulting from the Ivar Jacobson International company. So it is not a framework we can just start practicing without any help. Some aspects of it seem nice, but my concern is that we still have a great deal of overhead just for getting the model to work. The reason I mention it in this chapter is that it is an evolution of RUP. Another is that Ivar Jacobson has collaborated with Microsoft (and IBM) in developing the process. This has resulted in a process template (not free of charge because it is custom-made for each customer) for VSTS. This gives us access to EssUP directly from inside of VSTS.

Capability Maturity Model Integration for Development (CMMI-DEV)

Before moving on to the Microsoft Solutions Framework (MSF), I want to say a few words about the *Capability Maturity Model Integration for Development,* or *CMMI-DEV* (referred to simply as *CMMI* from now on in this book). One of the implementations of MSF uses CMMI as a basis, and we need to know more about CMMI before we cover MSF for CMMI. CMMI provides a way for an organization to implement process improvement and show the level of maturity of a process (www.sei.cmu.edu/cmmi/).

CMMI can be used to guide process improvement across a project, a division, or an entire organization. The model helps integrate traditionally separate organizational functions, set process-improvement goals and priorities, provide guidance for quality processes, and provide a point of reference for appraising current processes. CMMI contains four process areas (PAs), Each PA has one to four goals, and each goal is composed of practices. There are 22 practices in all. These goals and practices are called *specific goals and practices*, as they describe activities that are specific to a single process area. An additional set of goals and practices applies across all of the process areas; this set is called *generic goals and practices*.

The process areas in CMMI are the following, with the practices beneath each:

- Process Management

  - Organizational innovation and deployment (OID)

  - Organizational process definition + IPPD (OPD)

  - Organizational process focus (OPF)

  - Organizational process performance (OPP)

  - Organizational training (OT)

- Project Management

  - Project planning (PP)

  - Project monitoring and control (PMC)

  - Supplier agreement management (SAM)

  - Integrated project management + IPPD (IPM)

  - Risk management (RSKM)

  - Quantitative project management (QPM)

- Engineering

  - Requirements management (REQM)

  - Requirements development (RD)

  - Technical solution (TS)

  - Product integration (PI)

  - Verification (VER)

  - Validation (VAL)

- Support

  - Configuration management (CM)

  - Process and product quality assurance (PPQA)

- Measurement and analysis (MA)

- Decision analysis and resolution (DAR)

- Causal analysis and resolution (CAR)

The CMMI levels of maturity are based on Philip Crosby's manufacturing model.[17] The following levels exist:

- 0: Incomplete process.

- 1: Performed process. Little or no control of processes. The project outcome is unpredictable and reactive. All the process areas for performed processes have been implemented and work gets done. However, the planning and implementation of processes have not yet been implemented.

- 2: Managed process. The organization has satisfied all requirements for implementing managed processes. Work is implemented by skilled employees according to policies.

- 3: Defined process. At this level, a set of standard processes within the organization can be adapted according to specific needs.

- 4: Qualitatively managed process. All aspects of a process are qualitatively measured and controlled. Both the operational as well as the project processes are within normal control limits.

- 5: Optimizing process. At this level, there is a continuous process improvement. CMMI level 5 focuses on constant process improvement and also on reducing common cause variation.

CMMI isn't a prescriptive model with regard to how we satisfy practices; instead it demonstrates that we can perform the practices effectively, based on evidence. The model is as much focused on the meta-issues of managing and improving processes, risk profiles, and organizational effectiveness as it is on good development practices. CMMI also offers implementation choices, including continuous and staged models. As you can see, CMMI is a complex model covering many areas in the ALM process.

Microsoft Solutions Framework (MSF)

The *Microsoft Solutions Framework (MSF)* came out in its first edition in 1991. Microsoft started the MSF project because customers and partners were querying Microsoft Consulting Services about how Microsoft handled its projects. MSF's goal has been to provide a framework that enables us to use the parts we want, as we see fit—just as with RUP. Microsoft used industry best practices as well as the best practices of the Microsoft Internals Operations and Technology Group, Microsoft Consulting Services, and others (see Figure 3-18).

---

17. Philip Crosby, *Quality is Free: The Art of Making Quality Certain* (McGraw-Hill, 1979).

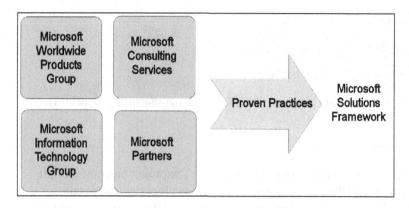

Figure 3-18. *The origin of MSF—Microsoft Solutions Framework*

Since 1991, MSF has constantly evolved and has now reached version 4. With the latest edition of MSF, Microsoft provides us with two prescriptive instances of the framework, taking a step away from providing only a framework and now moving closer to giving clear examples of how we can use it. The two instances are shipped with Visual Studio Team System and are called MSF for Agile and MSF for CMMI. I will come back to these in a while with little more detail.

Figure 3-19 shows an overview of how MSF is designed.

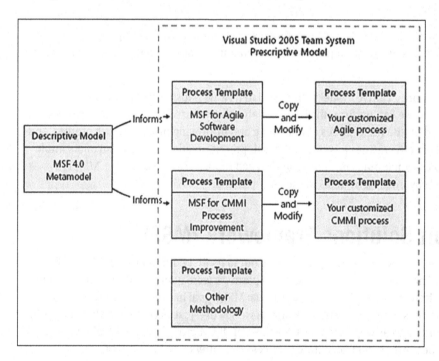

Figure 3-19. *The design of MSF*

The core is the descriptive model on the left, the metamodel of MSF. This has been used as a basis for MSF for Agile and MSF for CMMI, the two prescriptive models. And as you also can see, the model can be used as a base for other methodologies based on MSF as well. Microsoft has intended for the MSF for Agile and MSF for CMMI models to be examples of how to implement MSF, and actively urges us to use these VSTS templates as an inspiration for our own development models, not to use them as they are. This is something I think many customers have overlooked.

Key Elements in MSF

MSF version 4 consists of a number of key elements. We are free to use them all or individually. They are as follows:

- Foundational principles

- Mindsets

- Models

- Discipline

- Proven practices

- Recommendations

We are now going to take a little closer look at these.

Foundational Principles

The *foundational principles* are the core principles on which MSF is based. They are the guiding concepts of how the project team should work together. Most of the nine principles are very much soft values, but some are not:

- *Foster open communications*: Team members and the organization in which the project works need information of various degrees. MSF urges us to be as open and inclusive with our communications as possible—both internally in the project as well as externally with stakeholders.

- *Work toward a shared vision*: Compare this to the idea in Scrum where it is said that everybody involved in the project must know the goals of the sprint and the project so that they all can agree when the criteria for being finished are met. It is the same thing in MSF. We need to know and agree on what we are working on and what we are supposed to accomplish.

- *Empower team members*: This next principle simply means that we should trust that our team members will deliver what they have committed to deliver. If we, as team members, feel that we are trusted, empowered by our mates, we often feel more accountable for our decisions and hence more responsible for the outcome of the project.

- *Establish clear accountability and shared responsibility*: This principle relates to empowerment.

- *Deliver incremental value*: This is the agile speaking in MSF. There are no other reasons for having iterations in MSF than there are in Scrum or RUP. The thought is that the team should work iteratively to deliver (business) value to the stakeholders.

- *Stay agile, expect and adapt to change*: This principle also comes from the agile world. There really is nothing else to say about this principle; *stay agile, expect and adapt to change* says it all.

- *Invest in quality*: The definition of quality in MSF is the following: "meeting or exceeding customer expectations . . . at a cost that represents value to them."[18] When everybody feels accountable for the project outcome, they all are responsible for the quality. So if we invest in empowerment (as an example), we can get better quality in the end.

- *Learn from all experiences*: "Those who do not remember the past are condemned to repeat it," said author George Santayana in his book *The Life of Reason*. This is very true, and many organizations have tried to do something to avoid this pitfall. MSF speaks about the possibility to learn from all experiences. We need to foster an environment where we can capture and share both technical and nontechnical experiences so that we can adapt and adjust to lessons learned. This must be done within the project from iteration to iteration, but also from earlier projects.

- *Partner with customers*: Success is a joint effort; think nothing else. We need to involve stakeholders in the project process to succeed—the same idea as in Scrum, basically. This is the only way to make sure their expectations are met.

Mindsets

The next key element is *mindsets*. This whole concept is focused on how to get the individuals in the team to focus on maximizing success. There are several mindsets MSF speaks about:

- *Foster a team of peers*: Everyone shares responsibility for project success or failure.

- *Focus on business value*: Here as in Scrum, we try to provide business value as the primary target.

- *Keep a solution perspective*: This mindset aims for team members to see where their project fits into a broader picture.

- *Take pride in workmanship*: If we take pride in our work, we will deliver better quality.

- *Learn continuously*: Learn from successes and failures and adjust as needed.

- *Internalize qualities of service*: Not only stakeholders need to understand quality of service. This way, we design quality of service (QOS) into the solution from the beginning.

- *Practice good citizenship*: We as persons should be trustworthy, honorable, responsible, and respectful in all aspects.

- *Deliver on your commitments*: Trust and empowerment are earned by us delivering on our commitments.

---

18. H.J. Harrington and J.S. Harrington, *Total Improvement Management: The Next Generation in Performance Improvement* (McGraw-Hill, 1994).

Proven Practices

Proven practices, or best practices, is the next key element. Some of the proven practices in MSF are as follows:

- *Use small, multidisciplinary teams*: Small teams are more agile than larger. When the project is large, try breaking the whole into several smaller teams.

- *Enable teams to work together at a single site*: If we work closely together, we can be more effective.

- *Motivate*: Motivated teams are more effective.

- *Get specific early*: Move from the abstract to the specific early. This helps the team align its thinking and reach consensus on how to implement a shared vision.

Models, Disciplines, and Recommendations

There are three other key elements left. I will not go into these in deeper detail here, because the ones I've already mentioned are the most important ones. But to give you an overview of what they mean, I will say a few words:

- *Models*: With models we mean schematic descriptions, or perhaps I should say mental maps, of how we can structure our team and processes. Among these is the governance model.

- *Disciplines*: These are areas of practice using a specific set of methods, terms, and approaches—for instance, project management or risk management.

- *Recommendations*: These are optional, but MSF suggests these practices and guidelines in the application of the models and disciplines.

Roles in MSF

MSF has more roles defined than Scrum. This doesn't mean that these roles are not present in a Scrum project, however. It simply means that the framework itself doesn't speak about them or define them. If we want to land a Scrum project, I'd say the different roles have to participate as members of the team, but because a Scrum team is self-organizing, it is up to the team to decide which competencies are needed. When you see them, you will agree that these are roles present in almost all development.

Figure 3-20 shows the seven roles, or, as MSF puts it, *advocacy groups*.

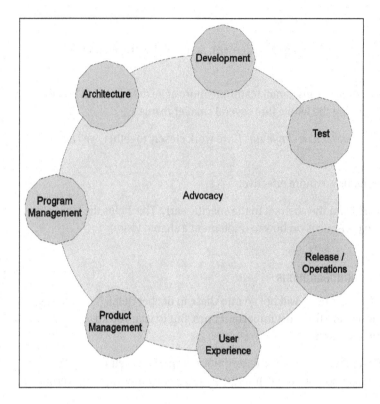

Figure 3-20. *The advocacy groups of MSF*

The key here is that they are all equally important and there really is no group hierarchy. If one fails, the project fails. It is as simple as that. Table 3-1 summarizes the advocacy groups and what each advocates for.

Table 3-1. *What the Advocacy Groups in MSF Advocate For*

MSF Advocacy Group	Advocates For
Product Management	Solution definition. To satisfy stakeholder needs and expectations.
Program Management	Solution delivery. To satisfy sponsor(s) needs and expectations.
Architecture	Solution design. To satisfy all needs and expectations.
Development	Solution construction. To satisfy design.
Solution Verification	To make sure solution works as specified.
Test	Solution validation. To make sure solution works as specified.
User Experience	Solution usability. To make sure solution has an effective, productive, and efficient UI.
Release/Operations	Solution deployment. To make sure solution is deployed smoothly and integrated into the infrastructure.

These groups are responsible for the key quality goals that must be achieved for a project to be considered successful. This fact stresses that all groups are equally important, because if one group does not reach its quality goal, the project might be unsuccessful. Table 3-2 shows us the goals that each group is responsible for.

Table 3-2. *The Goals of the Advocacy Groups*

MSF Advocacy Group	Key Quality Goals
Product Management	Satisfy stakeholder. Define solution within constraints.
Program Management	Identify and coordinate project constraints and deliver solution within these constraints.
Architecture	Design solution within the project constraints.
Development	Build solution according to spec.
Test	Make sure solution meets, or preferably exceeds, the defined quality levels.
User Experience	Maximize usability.
Release/Operations	Make sure deployment and transition to operations is smooth.

The MSF Lifecycle

When we look at the different phases of MSF, we can see many similarities with RUP or perhaps, dare I say it, the Waterfall model. The project goes through six major phases (see Figure 3-21):

- Envision

- Plan

- Build

- Stabilize

- Deploy

- Governance (where the customer has accepted the solution)

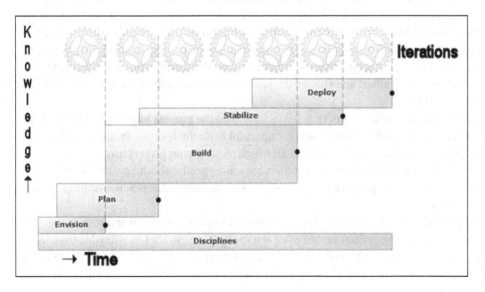

Figure 3-21. *The phases in MSF*

The major difference between the phases in MSF and the phases in the Waterfall model are that MSF advocates iterations within the phases. This could look acceptable from the beginning, but consider this: even though envisioning and planning could be performed iteratively, doesn't that still mean that the specs and architecture are fixed after they are done and these phases completed? In that case, the iterations do not add much value or flexibility. To be fully agile, we need to be able to change the architecture, for example, as the project is under way and new or clearer issues emerge. To me, it is more attractive to have an emerging architecture as in Scrum instead of having our architecture decisions controlled by plans made at the beginning of the project, when we did not know all difficulties.

MSF for Agile and MSF for CMMI

As I said earlier, Microsoft has included two process templates for VSTS based on MSF. You will have a closer look at these in Chapter 6, when you start diving into VSTS itself. The templates are as follows:

- *MSF for Agile* is the Microsoft way of building software in an agile way. Although a lot of the thoughts from the agile community have been adopted, I still think it is just something in between. It is not truly agile because it does not let go of the more rigid RUP-inspired way of running projects. I don't think it handles requirements changes enough throughout the process. There are iterations, sure, but we still have phases that need to be approved before moving on to the next. When one phase is finished, we don't seem to go back and change it if needs arise. It doesn't really matter whether the phases themselves are iterative, if we have the rigidity to not go back a phase if necessary. You will see more examples of the agile process later in this book, so I will not go into greater detail here.

- *MSF for CMMI* has a slightly different approach. MSF for CMMI can help an organization to CMMI level 3. This process differs from MSF for Agile in that it has very specific process steps in its guidance. MSF for CMMI also has more documentation and checkpoints.

You might think that an agile development framework such as Scrum could not apply a CMMI level, but that isn't true. According to Ken Schwaber, Scrum reaches CMMI level 5 at this time. CMMI level 5 focuses on constant process improvement as noted earlier, which is the core of the Scrum process. Scrum focuses on adapting the process continuously. We have the daily Scrum meetings, sprint reviews, sprint retrospectives, and so on, all encouraging (or even demanding) us to adapt and change the process to deliver better business value with the software we develop.

What Scrum doesn't do, however, is tell us how to do the process improvement or how to do the process itself. It tells us only that it is important to do the reviews; for the specifics we need other models or frameworks, such as XP, which many Scrum project use, or MSF for Agile. CMMI, RUP, MSF, and many of the others are more specific about how things are to be carried out. CMMI has its practices, such as the process management practice or project management practice.

I think Scrum's demand that we focus on process improvement continuously is the strong side of Scrum. We are not forced to do it a specific way, so it's more flexible than the others. On the other hand, not saying how to carry out process improvement can be Scrum's weakness as well. If we use a method or model that is unsuitable for this, we will fail in our improvement efforts.

At the MSDN web site (http://msdn.microsoft.com), you will find more information about these two processes. I encourage you to visit this site if you want to learn more about them or about MSF in general. When writing this, I am in the middle of a discussion with the Microsoft process team in Redmond about the future of the VSTS process templates. I cannot reveal any details yet because it is far from decided which way Microsoft will go, but interesting things are happening.

Summary

This chapter has focused on describing some development frameworks we can use for our development processes. Even though I suggest you consider using Scrum, I have included the others here as well, so that you compare them and make a decision for yourself.

For me, working in an agile project such as a Scrum project is very satisfying. I like the fact that everybody is involved in the project, and that we focus on customer participation and, more important, on delivering business value. It is so easy to forget this when the process becomes too elaborate. RUP, for instance, has a tendency to almost drown the project with documentation for the sake of documentation itself, not because it adds business value, and I don't like that.

For some projects, one model is more suitable than another. I have seen many companies use several development models, and they select the one that best addresses the requirements of the project. If it is a medical company that has to comply with FDA regulations, perhaps a more regulatory model such as MSF for CMMI is best, and for other projects Scrum is better. This is a decision that has to be made within the organization, because it depends on many combined and organization-specific factors.

At Know IT in Gothenburg where I work, we have selected the Scrum process with many of the XP practices for our in-house development projects. In those cases, we make sure that the customer has a product owner who closely collaborates with the team, just as he or she would if we were sitting on the customer premises. We can offer this project setup at the customer location as well. However, if the customer so wishes, we use RUP or any other process. We can always make suggestions based on what we think will benefit the customer most, but in the end it is the customer's decision.

Remember that choosing the process model is important because it affects the outcome of a project. So before implementing VSTS, please consider this topic and do not rush into MSF just because it is included out of the box. MSF out of the box can be used as a start, but Microsoft encourages us to change these templates to fit our organizations. Keep in mind that in a truly agile manner, we must always be prepared to change and adjust our process template, no matter which process we choose. Start with a pilot project and go from there.

CHAPTER 4

■ ■ ■

The Agile Enterprise—Or How We Could Bridge the Gap

A few days ago, I interviewed a woman for a job at Know IT here in Gothenburg. She was working as a consultant for a large shipping company based in Sweden, mainly on the company business side. During the interview, we talked about the gap between companies' business and IT sides. We agreed that we had seen this gap in most companies we had worked for over the years. And we were amazed that so little has been done to bridge the gap, despite the fact that everybody seems aware of it.

At the shipping company, this gap was even physical. The business people resided in a building on one side of a heavily trafficked road, while the IT people had their nest on the other. The only thing connecting the two (physically) was a rickety bridge high over the traffic. She told me that not many ventured to the other side, cementing the two organizations within the company. Unfortunately, the gap was having an impact on the organization as well, making it hard for IT to support the business processes and goals. Changes to processes were hard for the company to implement in their IT systems, and the cost was pretty high even for smaller changes. We both agreed that this was a schoolbook example of how the gap interferes with the organization and its goals.

ALM, in my opinion, is all about improving our processes so that we deliver better business value to our organizations. As you saw in Chapter 2, Figure 2-1, the ALM process starts with business need(s) in some way and should result in business value somewhere down the line. We cannot deliver the best business value unless we bridge the gap between the business and IT. If we focus our efforts only on improving the development process, we will not come all the way in our ALM efforts. We need some way to bridge the gap.

The *Harvard Business Review* recently published an interesting article on this topic.[1] The authors, Andrew McAfee and Erik Brynjolfsson, suggest that after we have improved our processes, we cannot stay content with the results. Our competitors are trying to improve their processes in the meantime as well. To win in such a competitive market, the authors suggest we take an approach that focuses on three areas:

- Deploy a consistent technology platform, rather than stitching together a jumble of legacy systems.

- Innovate better ways of working—meaning we should improve our processes continuously.

- Propagate those process innovations widely throughout your company by using IT.

---

1. Andrew McAfee and Erik Brynjolfsson, "Investing in IT That Makes a Competitive Difference," July–August 2008, *Harvard Business Review*.

These views are interesting and thoughtful and connect very well to the topics in this chapter. This chapter covers two topics that help to bridge the gap:

- Service-oriented architecture (SOA)

- A redefined view of the architect role(s)

SOA can help us reach a consistent technology platform while at the same time achieving the agility we need to more easily adjust our IT systems to changes in the business processes, hence delivering better business value. SOA provides a way to implement and automate business processes in our IT infrastructure in a flexible way. To fulfill the SOA vision, we need to make sure that the business processes we have in our organizations are implemented in the technological platform. This also means that we need to have both business and IT sides on board to make SOA really useful, and hence a great way to bridge the gap. The traditional way of architecting software has not entirely made us attain this agility. To deliver business value, we need to incorporate a different architecture that can help us close the gap.

Because all business systems or applications should map into some (or many) business processes, it is essential that SOA is a part of the ALM process as well. This process cannot disregard SOA because business value will suffer.

Traditionally, an IT architect is a person who is very knowledgeable in the technical side of IT development and who is doing architecture focused on solving purely technical problems. By redefining our architect roles, we can make the definitions and contents of these roles broader and incorporate both business and IT in the architect process. In the end, this too will help us bridge the gap. By doing this and starting to consider other architect roles in our organization, we can gain a lot. At the same time we will improve the ALM process, because architecture and development are important parts of this process. You will see two models outlining architect roles later in this chapter.

Architects have a big influence on how our business processes are implemented and automated in the IT infrastructure. Business architects are responsible for the way we work in our companies and how the business processes are defined. IT architects are responsible for how these business processes will be realized in IT. To implement SOA, we need to make sure the architects from both the business and IT sides focus on this architecture. If these architect roles do not communicate well, the mapping between business processes and their IT representation will suffer. This makes it even clearer that SOA and architect roles are big parts of a successful ALM strategy.

This chapter focuses on two ways to bridge this gap. In Chapter 6, you will see how Visual Studio Team System can help us implement these ways as well. To really have a useful and cost-effective ALM process, we need to address this issue; otherwise, we will not get the best result out of our ALM investments. Keep in mind, however, that a tool such as VSTS won't do all the work for us, but can help in achieving the final goal: an agile company ready to adapt to new business challenges. The ALM process plays an important part in reaching these goals.

However, first let's take a look at an example of a success story from the Japanese retail-banking world. I find this story exciting because it proves that by changing the way we do our work and the processes by which we work, we can achieve great things.

Radically Simple IT

In a recent issue of the *Harvard Business Review*, David Upton and Bradley Staats presented an example of how the Shinsei Bank in Japan "turned IT from a constraint into a launchpad for growth."[2]

When Masamoto Yashiro took over the helm of the bank in 2000, he wanted not only to make it more profitable, but also to revolutionize retail banking in Japan. At that time, services that (at least here in Sweden) were standard for a bank to offer its customers, such as 24/7 ATMs free of charge and Internet banking, were not included in the portfolio of the Shinsei Bank (or in most other Japanese banks either, for that matter). Yashiro wanted to offer high-quality products and services to customers so his company would gain a tremendous advantage in the retail-banking sector.

The problem in the Shinsei Bank was that the IT infrastructure was antique and had problems supporting even the existing business in a good way, never mind being able to support the new solution. Yashiro got more or less carte blanche in transforming the business into a bank that "could scale with growth and adapt to new opportunities." Even so, that did not mean that he had unlimited resources in terms of time or money, so he had to find effective ways to transform the bank. He started by gathering a group of people whom he knew had the skills necessary to help him succeed in his mission. Many of these were people Yashiro had previously worked with and knew well.

The team decided to abandon the idea of implementing the new system(s) in a big bang approach, that is, they did not find it attractive to develop everything and deploy it all at once. Even if the solution might work, the impact on users would be too great to risk such an approach. Even developing it all in an iterative way was discarded because the team members believed they would need three to five years for that. What they did was choose to implement the solution in parallel with the existing systems and build it in a modular way. This would let the team little by little introduce new applications to the users and not scare them by making a big switch at one time. Yashiro realized that he needed to have the employees on board for the system to be fully successful. He wanted it to sell itself to the users, instead of forcing them into a new way of working. Pretty smart approach, if you ask me.

Yashiro and the team were well aware of the gap between IT and business. First of all, Yashiro and his closest coworkers invested time into understanding IT. They wanted to be able to explain to customers how and why they used IT. They studied IT theoretically and also talked to and visited the IT organization within the organization. Regular meetings were set up between the two sides so that communication could run freely. By doing so, the sides slowly but safely came to speak the same language. Business users educated IT people about the business needs, and in return IT people showed prototypes of ways to implement these needs in the IT infrastructure. The goal was not only to bridge the gap but to forge the two sides together.

The Shinsei team also decided to aim for cutting down the number of standards used in the company. This means that things such as networking protocols, operating systems, and platforms were reviewed and decimated. The purpose was to strive for extreme simplicity and in return get a lower cost for maintenance and operations. By simplifying the IT infrastructure, they reduced complexity, deepened the expertise knowledge into only a few areas, and increased the possibility of reusing elements of the system. This reduced maintenance costs and increased the amount of money available for development.

---

2. David M. Upton and Bradley R. Staats, "Radically Simple IT," March 2008, *Harvard Business Review*.

A radical approach the Shinsei Bank took was to discard all mainframe systems and switch to a pure Microsoft environment instead. This was extremely rare at the time. Most banks shuddered at the thought of having Windows as a platform for their mission-critical banking systems. However, the bank succeeded, and the amount of money saved in lower maintenance and operations costs immediately saved the bank $40 million in expenses annually (a mainframe system costs roughly 15–20 percent of the initial investment in annual maintenance).

Note Windows was not yet seen as the stable platform it actually is at the time the Shinsei Bank started its change process, and most organizations still kept their mainframe systems because of their reliability over the years. The more Windows 2000 was used, the more its stability and reliability was accepted. These days, almost nobody questions the use of Windows for mission-critical systems.

Another thing the team members did was to look for simple solutions to business problems, solutions that could be reused down the line. They took a business problem, broke it down into smaller parts, and then decided how to technically solve it. If they had no in-house solution, they looked for an off-the-shelf solution. If that turned out negatively, they turned to one of their Indian software service partners and had the solution custom made. No matter which solution was chosen, it had to be reusable and communicate with the outside world in a standards-based way.

Building systems or applications in modules is nothing new. The Shinsei Bank went one step further, however, and aimed for a truly modular environment. By focusing hard on specifying the interfaces between modules, the bank made sure that a module could be developed and redeveloped internally without breaking compatibility with other modules using it. This is a nice feature you will soon recognize in service-oriented architecture. The Shinsei architecture allows the team to build solutions to local problems without breaking the whole system architecture.

Users were also involved, as mentioned earlier. They were involved not only in the development process, but also beyond the rollout. The users' ideas for improving the system were greatly appreciated by the team, and many suggestions were used in the new systems, making the users feel like they really could affect the outcome and the continuous improvement process.

All in all, this approach helped the bank tremendously. By June 2007, the bank had more than 2 million retail customers, which should be compared to the mere 50,000 they had in 2001 when the project was started. They have also been proclaimed as the number one bank in terms of customer satisfaction in Japan in 2004, 2005, and 2006.

The Shinsei Bank with Yashiro at the helm did some amazing things. In addition to deciding to revamp existing commercial-banking operations, Yashiro formulated a plan for revolutionizing retail banking in Japan by offering a value proposition that was unique in the country at that time: high-quality products and services provided on a convenient, easy-to-use, low-cost basis. He then set off to implement these things in his organization, delivering real business value sprung from the business needs of the bank.

So why am I telling you all this? Well the ideas in this success story map very well to what I will cover next. The solutions might not be the same, but the efforts aim to solve the same things. Hopefully, this will give you inspiration to new approaches in your own company.

The next topic in this chapter is enterprise architecture. The Shinsei Bank really focused on how to improve this by looking at how they could simplify and automate their business problems and processes. In the end, they were very successful in their mission.

Enterprise Architecture

Enterprise architecture (EA) in an organization is often defined as the organizing logic for business processes and IT infrastructure. The primary purpose of creating enterprise architecture is to ensure that business strategy and IT investments are aligned. Enterprise architecture should make it possible for an organization to achieve traceability from the business strategy down to the technology used to implement that strategy.

The practice of enterprise architecture has come to include activities that help decision makers understand, optimize, justify, and communicate the structure, including relationships between business entities and elements. This practice also looks at the situation today (*as-is architecture*), where the company or organization wants to be (to-be architecture), and how to reach this wanted state. This task is very important for improving the business. We find the following broad range of activities here:

- Organizational structure

- Process architecture

- Business architecture

- Performance management

These activities are important issues for an organization's ALM process as well. The ALM process includes roles involved in decisions concerning these areas, so architecture is not separate from the ALM process in any way. This means that we can use architecture to better fulfill our ALM goal, which ultimately is to deliver better business value.

Within the US federal government, the practice of modeling enterprise architecture has become more and more common over the years—especially in the context of the Capital Planning and Investment Control (CPIC) process. A reference model called the Federal Enterprise Architecture (FEA) serves as a framework for guiding federal agencies in the development of their architectures. Many other companies have also started to apply enterprise architecture in order to improve business performance and productivity. Among them we find companies such as BP (formerly known as British Petroleum), Independence Blue Cross, Intel, and Volkswagen AG.

To organize enterprise architectures into different views, we often use enterprise architecture frameworks. The purpose is to use views that are meaningful to the stakeholders of the systems. Such an architectural framework defines how to organize the structure and views associated with enterprise architecture. Because the whole discipline of enterprise architecture is so large and broad, these models have a tendency to become large and broad as well. Taking into account that large companies are the most common users of these frameworks, we can see that their complexity drives the size of the frameworks as well. These models need to be comprehensive in order to be able to describe the architecture.

To handle this scale and complexity, an architecture framework defines complementary projections of the enterprise model called *views*, where each view is meaningful to different system stakeholders. The frameworks are often standardized for both defense and commercial systems. Frameworks may specify a process, method, or format of architecture activities and products. Not all frameworks specify the same set of things, and some are highly specialized.

Table 4-1 shows some common frameworks and their applicability to the architecture levels defined in the 2006 FEA practice guidelines from the US Office of Management and Budget.[3]

Table 4-1. *Applicability of Common Enterprise Architecture Frameworks*

Applicability of Common Frameworks	FEAP	EAP (Spewak)	Zachman ZIFA	IEM	IDEF	DODAF (C4ISR)	TOGAF	UML
	Federal Enterprise Architecture	Steven Spewak's Enterprise Architecture Planning	Zachman Enterprise Architecture Framework	Information Engineering Methodology	ICAM Definition Languages	Department of Defense Architecture	The Open Group Architecture Framework	Unified Modeling Language Framework
Enterprise architecture	Yes	Yes	Yes	No	No	No	Unknown	No
Segment architecture	No	Unknown	Yes	Yes	Yes	Yes	Unknown	No
Solutions architecture	No	No	Yes	Yes	Yes	Yes	Yes	Yes

Service-Oriented Architecture

Over the years, new architectures and technologies have popped up in the world of IT. Some have been endorsed by only a few user industry groups, while others have become widely accepted. Quite a few of them have been hyped by developers and, to some extent, decision makers alike, but these solutions perhaps have not managed to create a real breakthrough and become used in the way they were intended. Some argue that this has happened to component-based development (CBD) and that this has paved the way for service-oriented architecture (SOA).

SOA is an exciting way of architecting our business software and systems and has been much talked about in recent years, because it offers some really nice benefits for an organization.

Background to SOA

We have seen an evolution: from procedural programming to functional development to object orientation to component-based development. These techniques have all had their benefits, and object orientation, for example, is probably something that won't ever be unnecessary, no matter which architecture you design your applications with.

---

3. Wikipedia, "Enterprise Architecture," http://en.wikipedia.org/wiki/
   Enterprise_Architecture#cite_note-1.

It's been a long, winding road to reach the latest, but probably not last, stop on the architecture tour—service-oriented architecture. However, SOA seems to have been one of the architectures that has been widely accepted. How can this have happened so soon? Well, CBD promised all kinds of benefits, such as reuse and an open market in components. These benefits would (purportedly) drastically reduce the time it takes to develop new applications and systems, according to Lawrence Wilkes and Richard Veryard in a recent article.[4] Many companies used, and still use, techniques such as the Common Object Request Broker Architecture (CORBA) or the Component Object Model (COM), but they never achieved the breakthrough and the results that were promised to them. You may wonder why this has happened, and I wouldn't be surprised. But if we look back, we really can't say that the component market blossomed as it was promised or that companies reuse components to a great extent.

According to Wilkes and Veryard, many companies saw other benefits instead. Some of these were improved scalability and the capability to replace components as needed, for instance.

But, I think that the reason that companies have failed to reuse components lies more with us: the developers and architects. How much effort did we really put into reusing components? Think about it for a while; how many times have you reused components compared to the number of times you have reused code snippets? I can honestly say that for me, code reuse has been greater than components reuse. It's been easier to build a new component by reusing code snippets than it has been to adapt old components to new requirements. In my projects, we do make sure that we build systems by using components and object orientation, but we don't build them based on the principles of CBD.

Research has also been done by the Software Engineering Institute (SEI) and other organizations that ties much of the blame for the lack of reuse on immature processes and practices. For example, if we can't communicate effectively and we don't follow the same process (including documentation, test standards, and so on) from team to team or even from project to project (when on the same team), we're not going to trust those other components to reuse them. CMMI by SEI, just to mention one model, focuses on process improvements and is a result of these problems. This could definitely also be one of the reasons why SOA has emerged as a means to standardize these issues.

In 2003, Microsoft architect Don Box, speaking at the XML Web Services One conference, likened objects to software-based integrated circuits and said that programmers would do better to focus on services instead.[5] I agree with Box, and I and Rickard Redler tried to push for this in the first edition of our book, *Designing Scalable .NET Applications* (Apress, 2003).

In 2000, something happened in the IT business. Web services initiatives were announced throughout the industry: IBM introduced web services, Hewlett-Packard introduced E-Speak, Sun Microsystems introduced ONE, and Microsoft introduced .NET. When web services emerged a few years ago, new ideas for architecture came to the surface. Web services provided us with benefits in several areas:

4. Lawrence Wilkes and Richard Veryard, "Service-Oriented Architecture: Considerations for Agile Systems," April 2004, *The Architecture Journal*, http://msdn.microsoft.com/en-us/library/aa480028.aspx.

5. Vincent Shek, "Microsoft Architect Touts SOAs," August 2003, *eWeek*, www.eweek.com/article2/ 0,1759,1655790,00.asp.

- *Platform independence*: We can use web services built on any platform, as long as they use standard protocols for communication—that is, SOAP, Extensible Markup Language (XML), and Web Services Description Language (WSDL). We really don't care how they've been implemented, so long as we know how to contact them and what their interface is.

- *Loose coupling*: Components hold a connection; clients using web services simply make a call. Loose coupling describes a resilient relationship between two or more systems or organizations with some kind of exchange relationship. Each end of the transaction makes its requirements explicit and makes few assumptions about the other end.

- *Wrapping existing systems*: SOA can also be used to wrap existing systems when these have no way of exposing their functionality in a standardized way. Many legacy systems, for instance, communicate in only proprietary ways. This would be hard to have in a flexible architecture, where we need to share business functionality between different platforms.

- *Discovery*: We can look up a specific service by using a directory service such as Universal Description, Discovery, and Integration (UDDI), a less formal catalog maintained in a wiki, or perhaps an entry in an Lightweight Directory Access Protocol (LDAP) directory.

These features of web services fit nicely into the more and more connected world of today. But if we're going to build systems in large enterprises in the future, we need to change the way we look at architecture. This is where *service orientation (SO)* comes in to service-oriented architecture. Remember, though, that many of the problems of large organizations are present in smaller ones as well, so we are not forced to use SOA for large organizations only. It can be very handy in small or medium-sized organizations as well.

What Is a Service?

Before SOA started to emerge, component-based software development was used extensively. This architecture has by no means disappeared, but its shortcomings make it more scarcely used for new development. Component-based software development can be compared to gluing prefabricated components together, much as in the field of electronics or mechanics. We take one component for customers, for instance, and connect this to the order component to implement part of the sales process. What really is the glue here is that these components must share the same programming language for this to be successful. This also means that we cannot share components across platforms, and because most organizations have several platforms and legacy systems, this can (and has) become a problem.

To understand what SOA is, we first must answer the following question: what is a service? Many people have a hard time understanding services. At one of my .NET courses, the students and I were involved in a long discussion until a revelation occurred among the participants. At first they couldn't stop thinking in a traditional, component-based way, but after several discussions, the coin finally dropped down. After that first barrier, when they got rid of their views on the traditional way of building software and started to look beyond that, all our architecture discussions went very smoothly, and suddenly there wasn't any problem at all. The students now had lots of ideas about how to implement services in their own projects.

Let's start with a real-life example to illustrate what a service really is. I recently applied for a renewal of my driver's license from the Swedish Road Administration (SRA). The SRA's whole procedure for handling this can be said to be a service. The service, in this case, is to process my application and then, based on various (and for me, hidden) facts and procedures, they either issue me a new license or reject my application. I don't need to bother about how the SRA processed my information or which routines they followed internally to process my application. In this case, my application is a request to a service, which SRA exposes, and their answer (whether a new license or a rejection) is the response to my request.

So, a service doesn't have to be a mystery or something hard to understand. Think of it as something that encapsulates a business process or an information area in your business. A common scenario could be the management of order information, something that many companies have to deal with. A service called OrderManagement, for example, could expose extensive functionality, based on the input parameters. For instance, we can find functions that let us add new orders, update order information, delete orders, return order information, and lots of other things concerning order management. One of the keys is that the user of the service, the consumer, does not have to know what goes on under the hood. All the processing is hidden from the consumer, who needs to know only how to call the service.

One common problem is deciding how much business logic a service is going to cover. We need to make sure that the service we are about to develop is valid and does not cover too much or too little. For instance, the OrderManagement service could, if we wanted, be designed as a service handling all aspects of order management. Would this be okay? Possibly, but we could almost certainly break the logic of such an extensive service down into smaller parts and implement these as separate services instead. This would probably be better if we need to reuse some of this logic later in other systems and applications. We will discuss this depth of services later in this chapter.

What Is This Thing Called SOA?

If we built a cool web service that our company uses, does this mean we have implemented an SOA? Definitely not, I say. Web services are only parts of a service-oriented architecture. What a web service really is, to be honest, is just a set of protocols by which services can be published, according to David Sprott and Lawrence Wilkes of CBDI Forum (www.cbdiforum.com). Web services are programmatic interfaces to capabilities that conform to the WS-* specifications. (WS-* is just an acronym for all the parts of web services available to us, such as WS-Security, WS-Federation, and so on.)

■ **Note** Web service specifications are occasionally referred to collectively as *WS-**, though there is no single managed set of specifications that this consistently refers to, nor a recognized owning body across them all. The reference term *WS-** is more of a general nod to the fact that many specifications are named with a WS- prefix. Read more about them at http://en.wikipedia.org/wiki/List_of_Web_service_specifications.

But who are Sprott and Wilkes? Why should you listen to them? These two guys are perhaps not as well known as Don Box, but they have been in this business a long time and are considered experts. They both work for CBDI Forum, which is an independent analyst firm and think-tank, and Sprott is one of its founders. They both give plenty of lectures and write numerous articles on various aspects of business software creation, including, to a large extent, web services and SOA.

But web services aren't a must in SOA either. We can expose our services by other means as well (using message queues, among other things), although web services will probably be the way we implement SOA in the foreseeable future.

If you look around on the Internet, you can find different definitions for SOA. The World Wide Web Consortium (W3C) defines SOA as "a set of components which can be invoked, and whose interface descriptions can be published and discovered." This sounds like web services, doesn't it? This view might perhaps be a tad too technical and probably not entirely correct either.

Sprott and Wilkes define SOA as "the policies, practices, and frameworks that enable application functionality to be provided and consumed as sets of services published at a granularity relevant to the service consumer. Services can be invoked, published and discovered, and are abstracted away from the implementation using a simple, standards-based form of interface." This definition is both wider and more correct, if you ask me.

Another way, and probably the best way, to define SOA would be to say that SOA is an architectural design pattern that concerns itself with defining loosely coupled relationships between consumers and producers.[6] SOA has in itself no direct relationship with software, programming, programming languages, or technology in any way. I think this is an important distinction to make. SOA can be implemented with any technology and on any platform as long as its interfaces are implemented by using a standards-based protocol, usually SOAP, Hypertext Transfer Protocol (HTTP), or XML. When I discuss SOA here, I am discussing the use of web services, SOAP, HTTP, and XML if nothing else is noted.

Why Use SOA?

There are several implications to consider when implementing SOA in an organization. SOA is much more than simply developing a few web services and thinking you're finished. If you're going to successfully make the move to service orientation, you'll need to have the whole company management on the bandwagon as well. So how do you do that?

Let's start with considering *enterprise application integration (EAI)*. EAI can be defined as the use of software and systems and their architectural principles in order to integrate a set of enterprise applications. One major problem that many large organizations struggle with is the integration of their existing applications into their new infrastructure. The problem is that many times they succeed in exposing functionality in only a proprietary way, shutting out everybody who doesn't speak this language.

The solution, in many cases, has been developing interfaces sitting on top of these systems. This way, a lot of legacy applications have had their functionality exposed to new applications in a convenient and standards-based way. The problem with this is that we have to develop the interfaces that enable this integration, and this obviously costs a lot of money. Imagine if the architects implementing the legacy applications had a way of making sure that the applications could easily be accessible by the new systems without new development being necessary!

---

6.   Pat Helland, TechEd EMEA, 2007.

With SOA, this isn't just a dream anymore. Because the whole idea is to expose services through a standards-based interface, not proprietary to anyone, we can make sure that their functionality can be easily accessed by new systems. This way, we don't have to build special interfaces to give access to their functionality.

By using Transmission Control Protocol (TCP), XML, SOAP, web services, and any other standards-based technology, we can build systems today that will still be accessible to all new applications fulfilling these standards in the future. And because they are industry standards, we have a whole lot more certainty that they will be around in 10 or 20 years.

This will save companies a lot of future development costs. This is evident when we look at the costs many companies have had with integration issues over the last decade or so. And let's face it. It won't have to be 10 or 20 years before we can start calculating savings from this approach. Enterprises have new systems coming out all the time, and by using SOA we make sure that we can reuse functionality in a far better way than we could with component-based development. This, however, will not happen unless we carefully consider which services we want to use to solve our business problems and the level of granularity for these. SOA in itself cannot take us all the way; we have some considerations to make when implementing it that will be necessary as well.

One of the greatest benefits I can see is that SOA enables us to implement the same things as the Shinsei Bank team did, as discussed at the beginning of this chapter. As you will see as you read more about the characteristics of a service later in this chapter, SOA gives us the flexibility to work on the internals of a service while not breaking its contract with existing consumers. This gives us the flexibility we need to be able to quickly adjust to new business opportunities and changes in business processes. By using services, we can also reuse our business logic in many places without writing as much custom code as we would have to do in a component-based environment. The aim in the Shinsei example was to have an IT infrastructure that allowed for reuse and for including flexibility in the development of the system, which is what SOA gives us.

Another important benefit is that we can use SOA to map our business processes to our IT systems. If we do that, we have come a long way in improving our ALM process. Let's face it: if we don't deliver business value in our IT projects and with our IT systems, the organization will be in trouble sooner or later. The new systems we develop must map well into the structure of our existing infrastructure. SOA helps us with this mapping in a way that I don't think component-based programming ever could. Organizations are so complex these days, with even more complex infrastructures, that we need to make better architectural decisions. So in order for the ALM process to deliver the greatest business value possible, it is essential to include architecture decisions in it as well. You will see later that Visual Studio Team Editions have tools that will help us architect and develop services, while at the same time providing possibilities for improving collaboration between many of the ALM roles discussed in Chapter 2.

SOA is not something that we implement in an organization without careful consideration. It's no walk in the park to implement SOA. It will take a whole lot of consideration before it can be rolled out properly. It requires so much more than to merely start using web services. SOA is not intended for single applications either, but for organizations as a whole. This means that if we're going to be successful, we need to incorporate SOA in the enterprise IT plan and have that in mind for all architectural decisions we make from day one. If SOA isn't considered for all new development or all the future enhancements for the existing systems, we will fail in implementing service orientation.

In my experience, many of the companies that have started to use SOA have seen improvements in their ROI. But so far none of these companies have implemented SOA for all their business activities. They often do new development with an SOA mindset and implement business logic and processes as services, but they still have many applications and systems that are not implemented as services. They have not converted all their processes to services either, so maybe it is too early to tell. We might need to wait a few years before we really see ROI improvement. But once we start letting SOA influence all IT issues in our organization, we make certain that the ROI will be great.

Characteristics of Services: The Four Tenets of Don Box

To better understand what a service is and why we must think of architecture in a slightly different way than we did with object-oriented programming and components, we'll now look at the four important tenets that Don Box, of Microsoft's Windows Communication Foundation team, identifies as crucial.

Note For complete coverage of this topic, please see "A Guide to Developing and Running Connected Systems with Windows Communication Foundation" by Don Box. This document is available on the Microsoft web site and is well worth its time.

Boundaries Are Explicit

Box's first tenet is that *boundaries are explicit*. When services that build up an application or system are spread across large geographical areas, things get more complex. We might run into large geographical distances, multiple trust authorities, and perhaps different execution environments. Communication in such an environment, whether between applications or even between developers, gets potentially costly, as complexity is great and performance may suffer. An SO solution to this is to keep the surface area as small as possible, by reducing the number and complexity of abstractions that must be shared across service boundaries. This can be accomplished by using an XML document as the input and output parameter and not using multiple parameters in the call of the service, for instance. Service orientation, according to Box, is based on a model of explicit message-passing, rather than implicit method invocation, as it is in component-based development.

Services Are Autonomous

Box then states that *services are autonomous*. Services must always assume that nobody is in control of the entire system. Having total control of a system would be impossible in a service-oriented architecture. Component- or object-oriented programs are often deployed as a unit, even though many efforts have been made to change this over the last decade. In SO this isn't always the case, if it ever can be. Service-oriented systems are often deployed across a large area instead. The individual services are often deployed as a unit, but the whole system is dispersed. An SO system never actually stands still, because new services may be added all the time and old services given new interfaces. This increased ubiquity of service interaction makes it necessary for us to reduce the complexity of this interaction.

When a service calls another service, it can't expect a return value because messages are passed only one way. We can get a return message of course, but this can disappear on the way and we can never be certain it arrives in the end. This means that the service and the consumer are independent of each other. They are autonomous, or sovereign as web services expert Bruce Johnson puts it.[7] So in a scenario where a service calls another service and gets no expected return message, the service must be self-healing so that there isn't a noticeable impact. The caller must not have to depend on anybody else to complete the invoked method.

In a connected world, many things can go wrong with communication, and our services must take this into account. When a service accepts an incoming message that is malformed, or even sent for a malicious purpose, the service must be able to deal with it. The way to do this is to require the caller to prove that he has all the rights and privileges necessary to get the job done. This burden is never placed on the service itself. One way to solve this is to set up trust relationships instead of per-service authentication mechanisms.

We can compare this tenet with what is referred to as the Fallacies of Distributed Computing.[8] These are a set of common but flawed assumptions made by programmers when first developing distributed applications. In 1994, Peter Deutsch, working at Sun at that time, drafted eight assumptions that architects and designers of distributed systems are likely to make, which prove wrong in the long run. This resulted in all sorts of troubles and pains for the solutions and architects who made the assumptions. I will give a short list of them here so that you can compare them with what Box is really saying. You will notice that Box is basically restating some of them:

- The network is reliable.

- Latency is zero.

- Bandwidth is infinite.

- The network is secure.

- Topology doesn't change.

- There is one administrator.

- Transport cost is zero.

- The network is homogeneous.

Services Share Schema and Contracts

The third tenet is one of the most important ones: *services share schema and contracts, not class*. In object-oriented (OO) programming, abstractions are developed in the form of classes. They are very convenient, as they share both structure and behavior in a single named unit. This is not the case in SO, as services interact based only on schemas (for structure) and contracts (for behavior). Every service we build must advertise a contract that describes the messages it can send or receive. Even though this simplifies things, we must still be aware that these schemas and contracts remain stable over time. We can't change these after they are implemented, because if we do, we break the contracts with all existing service consumers.

---

7. Bruce Johnson, Bruce Johnson's SOA(P) Box, www.objectsharp.com/Blogs/bruce/.

8. Arnon Rotem-Gal-Oz, "Fallacies of Distributed Computing Explained," http://www.rgoarchitects.com/Files/fallacies.pdf.

To increase future flexibility, we can use XML element wildcards and/or optional SOAP header blocks, so that we don't break already deployed code. We might even have to build a new service function instead and make that available.

Service Compatibility Is Based on Policy

The last tenet that Box mentions is that *service compatibility is determined based on policy*. Every service must advertise its capabilities and requirements in the form of machine-readable policies, or operational requirements, in other words. One example is a service that requires the caller to have a valid account with the service provider. Another could be a situation where all communications with the service should be encrypted.

These four tenets seem very attractive and pretty straightforward to me, and I strongly agree with them. I like the idea that services give us the ability to be platform independent. Many times I have seen customers struggling with their systems. They want to share information between systems built on different platforms but have large problems doing this when one platform cannot call functions on the other without a lot of rewrites and hard work. The thought of having black boxes communicating in standardized ways appeals to me as well, because a lot of the problems I have seen over the years are caused by updates to logic in one component resulting in problems for the users of that logic. I want a solution where I can continue developing my logic, still knowing that my existing users will have a working interface.

These are the four tenets that Box came up with early on. These have been well accepted in the IT business since then and are now standard for developing services. I will now discuss these in a little more depth just so we can see how we can implement these in our SOA. I will do so by taking an example from Sundblad and Sundblad.

More on Characteristics: Sundblad and Sundblad

Let's now take a look at what Sten and Per Sundblad, Microsoft regional directors in Sweden and suppliers of .NET architect training to Microsoft, say about SOA.

I like the Sundblads' approach to SOA, and the possibilities it gives an organization to automate business processes. If we are to be successful in this task, we need a way to make automation flexible so that we can follow the changes on the market and in business requirements. We do not want to be stuck with an implementation that is hard-coded; we want a flexible, agile way of handling process automation. And this model can help us reach this goal.

Let's first take a look at the SOA basics that Sten Sundblad describes.[9] These lay the foundation for the way we should use services to automate our business processes.

Sundblad starts by pointing out that the idea of SOA is to organize IT systems as a set of services that can be reached through a message-based interface. It builds on the same foundation as SOAP and XML, but is not dependent on either. The idea itself is nothing new—it's been around for more than ten years and was started in the CORBA community in the 1990s. But now, thanks to XML, SOAP, and web services, the idea has been getting the attention it deserves. Sundblad continues that the reason for this is obviously that these building blocks have made it possible for a service to be both language- and platform-independent.

Sundblad also states five characteristics that are usually mentioned when talking about services. We'll now take a closer look at each one of these. Note that we can recognize Box's tenets in here as well:

---

9. Sten Sundblad, "Service Oriented Architecture—An Overview," 2004, www.2xsundblad.com. (Or, as it's called in Swedish, "Serviceorienterad arkitektur—En översikt.")

- A service should be autonomous.

- A service should have a message-based interface.

- A service should have its own logic that encapsulates and protects its own data.

- A service should be clearly separated from and loosely coupled to the surrounding world.

- A service should share schema—not class.

Autonomy

You'll recognize this characteristic from Box's four tenets. *Autonomy* means that the service should be possible to develop, maintain, and evolve independently of its consumers. The service must take full responsibility for its own security and be suspicious of anything and anybody who tries to use it. If I use a service, I do not need to know anything about it except the way I should communicate with it. The service is a black box, and what's going on inside is none of my business. It doesn't matter which programming language has been used to implement the service either, as long as the interface is based on open standards. Box also stresses that these features are important for a service to possess.

Message-Based Interface

When we talk about services, we have two roles: the service and the service consumer. The *consumer* is any system using the functions of a service. It could be another service, a Windows application, or anything else capable of communication with the service. No consumer should ever be in contact with the inner logic of a service. You must develop the services so that they are accessible only when you send a message to them with a wish to get the service performed (see Figure 4-1). It's the logic of the service that handles the message and determines whether to process the request.

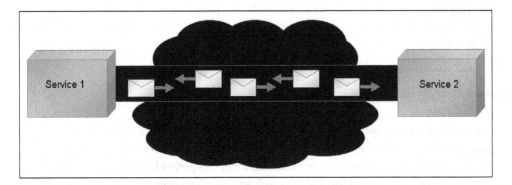

Figure 4-1. *Services communicate through messages and nothing else.*

There is no other way to interact with a service but to send a message to it and get a return message in response (see Figure 4-2). The *schema* of the service defines the format of the individual messages that the service handles—that is, which messages and formats it accepts, and which response messages and formats it returns. The service *contract* defines the allowable sequences of messages that the service accepts.

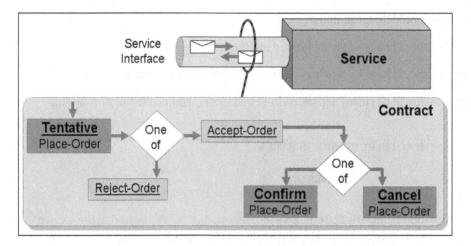

Figure 4-2. *Contracts define how we can communicate with a service.*

Services also do only a limited number of things for their consumers (see Figure 4-3). These things are defined in the schema and contract and are the ways a service binds its trust. It is the business logic within the service that makes sure only the externally published operations are allowed to happen. We must write the service so that it carefully evaluates the incoming message and makes sure it conforms to the schema and contract before executing any logic.

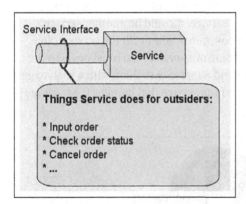

Figure 4-3. *Defining the trust of a service*

Let's take a little example from real life by continuing to look at the driver's license renewal process I described earlier. When I recently applied for a renewal of my driver's license, I got a form sent to me via snail mail. This form was preprinted with text, leaving spaces for me to insert information about myself and attach a photo showing my best side. I also had to sign it, so that my signature could be printed on the license. The form's instructions explained how I should fill it out and how to return it to the authorities. After a few weeks, I would either get a new license or an answer as to why my application was not approved. (And yes, I was approved.) Nowhere in this process did I have to know how the authorities handled my application or how they would process my information. The only thing I needed to care about was filling my form out correctly and making sure I sent it back to the correct address.

If we translate this experience into our examination of services, we can say that the form I filled out was a message that was being sent to the service. I also got a message in return, in this case either a new license or a rejection. But these messages are totally asynchronous. They don't depend on each other in any way, except for the fact that my application must come in before the agency's reply. But otherwise, there is no connection between the authorities and me during the waiting period. So, this example shows not only a message-based interface, but also the autonomy of this service.

Even though we often talk about web services when SOA is discussed, I must firmly point out that this does not have to be the case. There are other ways to display a message-based service, including by using a message queue. But, to be realistic, we could probably assume that most service-oriented solutions will use web services.

One thing worth noticing here is that using a message-based interface means that we should send all parameters encapsulated in the message. This goes for both the consumer and the service. We don't build a service, for instance, that takes integers as parameters—instead we embed the integers in an XML document and send this to the service. In return, we'll get an XML document with the result of our request. A benefit of this procedure is that it's easy to add new parameters for future needs without changing the signature. The only thing that has changed is that the content of the message and both old and new messages will now work.

Encapsulation of Data

One of the important aspects of a service is that it should be autonomous, as we have learned from all of the previously mentioned authors. According to Sundblad, this also means that a service should encapsulate its data. No other service or application should be allowed to touch the data (see Figure 4-4).

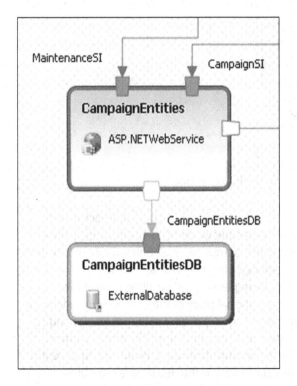

Figure 4-4. *A service should encapsulate its own data.*

The only way that your service's data should be reached is when a user sends a message requesting that some modification of the data is to be performed. If the consumer is validated and has the correct credentials, and has sent a well-formed message according to the service specifications, the consumer's request will be performed. It's the logic of the service that touches the data, never the message itself.

■**Note** A service's data can be both persistent and nonpersistent. The objects in a service often have non-persistent data in their RAM, just like any other object, but instead of relying on another component to save persistent data, in this case the service itself saves this to the database.

To further elaborate on this, we can say that data is different from the inside than it is from the outside. The data transferred to and from the service is passed in messages, and both the sender and the receiver must understand these messages and the format of the data. The schema helps them achieve this understanding (see Figure 4-5). This means that the schema must use an independent definition so that the schema does not change over time. A consumer using a schema will have problems if we update it. A schema change can break the consumer's implementation of the service if we don't handle changes in a good way. The schema describes what data should be sent with the request and what data we will get in the response of the service.

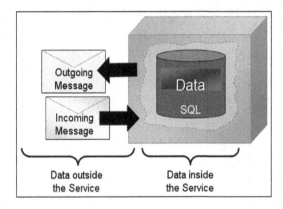

Figure 4-5. *Data is different from the inside and outside of a service.*

If we update the schema, we must make sure to version-control it, so that each service consumer knows which version of the schema it uses and we do not break anything after such an update. We need to have all versions of the schema available at all times; if we don't, we will cause problems for consumers of a specific version if that version disappears.

The service itself must then be able to handle requests based on all versions of the schema. All versions must be accessible from an external place so they can be truly independent. The data inside the service can be stored in any way we choose as long as service and consumer agree on the external format. The data that is sent out from the service is often refined in some way from the format it has in the internal database. It could be that the data sent is a consolidation of many table rows or data sources within the service but exposed as one data set (see Figure 4-6).

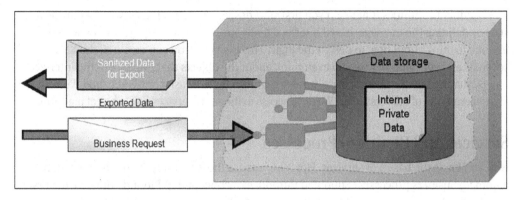

Figure 4-6. *Encapsulating change and reads of data*

Only the service can modify its data in any way. The service provider is responsible for writing the business logic that handles this. By encapsulating changes and reads in this way, we can make sure that the integrity of data and work of the service are protected. We can also ensure that the privacy of the service is protected by controlling what is exported from it.

Clearly Separated from and Loosely Coupled to the World

As you may already understand, a service must be clearly separated from its surrounding world—just like the driver's license renewal process, where the service (renewal) was separated from the message sender. The service has its clear borders, and the only way we communicate with it is through the published interface; it does not share anything about its implementation to anyone outside the service. The driver's license example also showed that the process of determining whether the application for a new license was approved (or not) was loosely coupled to the renewer—that is, none of the parties involved knew anything about the other except for the way they could communicate. The renewal service is not dependent on the license renewer to work either; the service will still exist even if the renewer (in this case, me) disappeared. If the whole process had been over the telephone, for instance, we would have been forced to keep the line open all through the process, and thus have a stronger relationship by not being separated for the time the process took place.

The same goes for services in service orientation. The renewer, in the case of the driver's license, sent a message to the authorities, waited, and finally got the reply. No persistent connection between the two existed at any time. When a consumer sends a message to a service, no persistent connection should exist either. If a new message needs to be sent, a new nonpersistent connection has to be made. The only thing that the consumer and the service share is the structure of the message and the contract that controls the communication between the two.

Share Schema—Not Class

For SOA to work, the consumer and the service have to agree on the schema that determines the structure of the message.

Because the object model of consumer and service might be completely different, the service doesn't need to (and shouldn't) share its object model. It should share only the schema of the message structure. In our driver's license example, the schema would be the form and its instructions. When we are talking about web services, the schema would be the WSDL file.

Sundblad continues that when you first start designing your services, you should always start by defining the message-based interface that your service will expose. After you do this, it's time to think about how to design the logic. This is so that you can create all the XML schemas and contracts before you even think about the objects that implement the interfaces.

By sharing schema and not class, we also get the benefit of easier reuse (the modularity in the Shinsei example) of business logic. We have access to the same services, irrelevant of platform.

Services and Business Processes

Now you know the basics of services. How can you use these features in your organization to automate business processes? Sundblad introduces a concept that I found attractive the first time I read about it. I have tried to analyze some of the organizations where I have worked over the past ten years, just to see whether this model could be applied to these. Much to my joy, I found that the model would do very well and would greatly improve the way these companies work.

What most people agree on is that the concept of services encapsulates a whole business process or business information area. All businesses have somewhere between 10 and 20 higher-level services, according to Sten Sundblad.[10] Higher-level services could include the purchasing process or the sales process, for example.

Sundblad pushes for doing a process-oriented analysis of the business in question when you're implementing your SOA. As you do this, you'll find that there are at least four kinds of services that should implement the functional requirements:

- Entity services

- Activity services

- Process services

- Presentation services

Entity services are rather persistent or stable over time. A business is not likely to change these processes, because they supply and protect the information that the business is depending on. An example of an entity service could be a customer service exposing stable functions such as retrieving customer information or updating, adding, or deleting customers. If you think of these different kinds of services as four layers, entity services would be the foundation at the bottom level, as shown in Figure 4-7.

Activity services are slightly less stable than entity services. In other words, they may be changed over time. Activity services are placed one layer up from entity services, and are the services that perform the actual work in one or more processes. They can be said to orchestrate a number of entity services in order to perform the work of the service. Let's say that we want to retrieve all orders for a specific customer. A call from a higher-level service requests a list of orders for customer X. The customer activity service calls the order entity service, retrieves the information, and packages this into a result set that it sends back to the higher-level service. It is the activity service that decides how many and which entity services it needs to access to get all the information it needs.

---

10. Sten Sundblad, "Service Oriented Architecture and Processes," 2004, www.2xsundblad.com (unfortunately available only in Swedish).

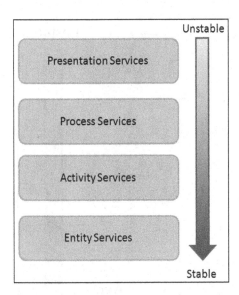

Figure 4-7. *Four kinds of services in a business*

High-level *process services* are in the next layer. These can be seen as the conductor orchestrating the workflow in a process. The workflow can consist of calls to one or more lower-level services or perhaps to external services. It's probable that process services will change over time, because they often reflect the changes in a company's way of doing business and are often enhanced to give competitive benefits when the company needs them. When we change these, no lower-level services should have to change. Many vendors use a language such as the Web Services Business Process Execution Language (WS-BPEL) for this workflow.

Wikipedia provides this definition: "WS-BPEL provides a language for the specification of executable and abstract business processes. By doing so, it extends the web services interaction model and enables it to support business transactions. WS-BPEL defines an interoperable integration model that should facilitate the expansion of automated process integration in both the intra-corporate and the business-to-business spaces."

Presentation services compose the top layer. These are the user interface services that provide users with a way of accessing other services. As you probably recognize from your own company, these kinds of services are very likely to be changed as time goes by. When changes occur in the way a company does its business, the user applications usually change as well. By having easy-to-change UIs, we can adjust swiftly, giving us the capability to gain competitive advantages.

By using these types of services, we can build our IT representation of the business processes in our organization (see Figure 4-8). This representation is done by using the architect designers of Visual Studio Team Edition for Architects. A user interface (presentation service) can access different business processes implemented as services. The UI (in this case a web page) connects to a process service that handles the workflow in a process. Figure 4-8 shows an example of a UI that calls the order process. This process service coordinates all efforts needed to process an order from our web site. For instance, it first calls the warehouse service to check whether the product(s) is in store for shipping and probably also reserves the product(s). It then calls the customer service (activity service) to either fetch, update, or add customer information.

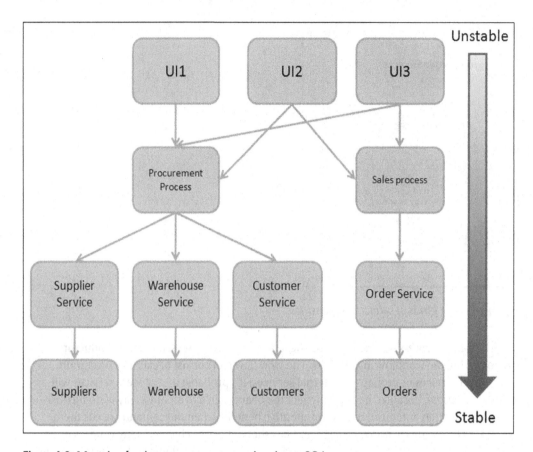

Figure 4-8. *Mapping business processes to services in an SOA*

It also calls an external credit card service for credit card verification. When all information is gathered and the credit card has been debited, it persists the reservation of the product(s) and sends a message to the shipping system so that the customer's order will be sent.

When changes need to be made in any of the services, we can do that as long as we support the contracts we have already set up. If the UI needs to be changed, we can change it. If a process service needs to have its workflow adjusted due to changes in a UI or to an additional UI being added, for example, we can do that as well without breaking compatibility with the other presentation services. We can also add new service interfaces to any service and still have the existing ones supported. This gives us the flexibility and reusability the Shinsei Bank was aiming for (and actually implemented, in their own way).

It might also be easier for business people to look at a map of the IT services and get an understanding of them when they are described in this way instead of in a nerdy technical way. We can then discuss whether the processes are implemented in an optimal way or should be changed to better reflect the business, bridging the gap even more. If your business stakeholders don't care about the service, you haven't captured it at the right level of granularity, and you might want to consider reworking it.

Other Benefits of Automating Business Processes

What other benefits of implementing our business processes in an SOA can we find? I have found some topics I think greatly enhance the result of a successful implementation of processes in the IT infrastructure apart from the ones already mentioned. These are factors that are important no matter whether we implement an SOA or some other architecture.

First of all, I think that the result of an automated process implementation should be visible directly. We must make sure that we can see that the process has been automated, so that the people involved in the process can see the change and start using the process quickly, even if the process involves many people. Having the process built into the IT infrastructure can help us with this.

We can also eliminate the human factor in following a process. Even though written guidelines may exist for a process, we tend to invent our own way of complying with these. Automating the process makes it easier to know that the way of working is the same for everybody.

We must also see that the process is executed the same way every time. It will be confusing if the process behaves differently from time to time, and from location to location (if we have a large organization). Automating the process makes this easier to enforce.

There must be a way to monitor the execution of the process. Automating the process makes it possible to include monitoring not dependent on manual monitoring. This way, we can track events, activities, and status information in a whole new way.

A Redefined View of the Architect Role(s)

I've been working in the IT business since 1998 or so. Over these years, I have done a lot of different things: system development, project management (the traditional way), Scrum mastering, and also IT architecture. When I am in contact with customers and coworkers, I sometimes have referred to myself as an IT architect. More and more I have started to feel that the tasks I've filled that role with maybe aren't architecture at all. My role has been as a person deeply involved and competent in technical matters. I have done software architecture—deciding how a system should be a layered, where the components should reside (on which server), how scaling should be considered, what the interfaces should be like, which systems should cooperate, and so on. I have also done those Big Up Front Designs that the agile world (not only them, of course) detests so much. I have focused very little on how best to map business processes with IT systems or how to best fulfill the business needs and goals.

As you saw in Chapters 1 and 2, this lack of focus on business value among IT people is one of the things ALM tries to solve. Many surveys have shown that managers in different organizational positions want this improved. We need a way to make sure that we include collaboration between IT architects and business architects somehow. If we don't include this perspective when defining our ALM process, we will never deliver the most business value.

I think that many of you would agree that the technical stuff that I've mentioned springs to mind when you think about IT architecture, right? When I speak to customers and coworkers, I find that they also agree with this. But I have started to ask myself lately whether this approach is correct. Let's start by looking at what architecture really is all about before answering this question.

When we think of constructing buildings, roads, or any other physical object, I think we can more clearly define what architecture is. We often think about architecture in terms of the blueprint, with all its measures and figures. The blueprint is the document telling engineers and construction workers what to build and what it should look like. It doesn't necessarily tell us the specifics of how to build it—how to mix the concrete, where to hammer nails, or how to attach boards to walls. It instead shows the big picture. It shows what object should be built and what it should look like from an external point of view. The how, or the internals of the object, are left to the engineers and construction team to figure out. This clear separation has sprung from thousands of years of experience of constructing buildings and roads, where we have found that the architect has no way of knowing all the details of the process, especially because complexity has increased over time in construction work.

Another thing that differentiates construction architects from software architects is that construction architects are more concerned with the goals for what they are building. A house, for instance, is designed for the people who are going to live in it; they have their needs and requirements, and the architect is focused on fulfilling these. This has not been the case in IT until recent years.

With this as a background, we might wonder why the IT industry has believed for so long that an IT architect should focus so heavily on technology implementation. In the companies I have worked for, the architects have focused way too much on IT and technical matters and not so much on business aspects. Many of my coworkers who claim to be architects talk technology, and not so much business value. This might have changed lately but is still true in many cases.

Over the years since computers were introduced in the 1940s, software development has increased in complexity enormously. There is a huge difference in software between 1940 and today as well, which adds to the complexity we see today. From the beginning, there was no need for a conscious development process for designing software. Or perhaps we should say that the need was there but nobody really saw it because the applications were pretty simple and not interacting with each other—software was seen as individual programs. This does not mean that their logic was simple, just that they were not very complex. As a result, we did not see the need for architecture; many of these programs were designed as they were programmed. But much has happened since then. Over time at least, people realized the need for designed software (that is, designed before it was programmed) to improve the results. Sometimes during the 1960s or 1970s, software engineering was increasingly talked about, but architecture still wasn't a focus area, if it was talked about at all.

I think it was Frederick Brooks who was the first, or at least one of the first, to talk about the importance of architecture for complex software systems (in this case the IBM System/360 operating system): "By the architecture of a system, I mean the complete and detailed specification of the user interface. For a computer, this is the programming manual. For a compiler, it is the language manual. For a control program, it is the manuals for the language or languages used to invoke its functions. For the entire system, it is the union of the manuals the user must consult to do his entire job."[11]

The observant reader notices that he doesn't say anything about the technical inside of a system, but speaks only about what can be observed from an external point. Software engineering, on the other hand, is all about what is going on, on the inside.

---

11. Frederick Brooks, *The Mythical Man-Month* (Addison-Wesley Professional, 1975).

Sten Sundblad wrote the following:

"With a sharp line between architecture and the implementation of architecture, it becomes possible to create an architecture and then discuss different ways to implement it. It also becomes possible to change the implementation, while keeping the architecture unchanged, if the implementation turns out to be less effective than the engineers thought when they originally designed it. The implementation could also be changed when new options for the implementation become available."[12]

With this view, we can see how we could achieve what the Shinsei team succeeded in doing. That is, we could change the inside of our system and not break the whole picture. The viewpoint also elevates architecture higher than most often do today. Sundblad continues saying that "architecture should tell us about what we must build to respond to business and usage requirements, but not about how we should build it. Keeping the how away from all communication between the architect and the business people or users makes such communication so much easier." I think this is a very healthy way of looking at architecture and the connection to business requirements.

So if we draw a line between architecture and engineering, where what does and what doesn't affect usage behavior, we could more easily see architecture in an SOA perspective. Architecture, according to Sundblad, is about the details of the contract, while engineering is about which language we write a service with, which design pattern we use, or which database it should store its data in. Even though there might be a gray area here, I tend to agree on this point for drawing the line. This way, we make sure that we can change the inside of a service without breaking the big picture—as long as we do not change architecture, or in this case the contract. Because when we change the inside, we do not change the usage behavior.

So in my definition of architecture, architecture is all about mapping owner and usage needs and requirements (business requirements) to a technical solution. Or perhaps mapping a technical solution to business requirements. We architect the outside and usage behavior, not the inside. Architects provide the frame for the people working with the inside; they don't provide the blueprint for the details. We leave that very important job to the software engineer. It is the software engineer's skills that are needed to accomplish that. When we implement an SOA, we should not forget how a new system maps to our existing enterprise architecture either, because this is extremely important for the architecture of the system.

Enough about architecture in itself. You might not agree on what I have just written, but let it sink in for a while and consider it some more before continuing reading.

Let's now continue with the architect role(s).

Architect Roles According to IASA Sweden

The International Association of Software Architects (IASA) is an international (the name itself should have given me a clue to this fact) and independent organization focused on IT architecture and the IT architect role(s). IASA was founded in 2002 and has approximately 6,000 members worldwide. This makes it the biggest organization for professional architects today, and is actually *the* organization for architects. Most others are too small to have the influence that IASA has.

IASA members saw a lot of problems on the Swedish architecture scene that they wanted to address. There seemed to be great confusion over the architect roles and their definitions.

---

12. Sten Sundblad, "Software Architecture vs. Software Engineering," 2007, www.2xsundblad.com.

They suspected that there was a great need, at least in Sweden, for guidance regarding which architect roles should exist in an enterprise and how these roles should cooperate. IASA identified four major problems:

- The same architect role could have different tasks in different organizations.

- Different companies have different role names for the role responsible for the same tasks.

- There is a lack of an independent recommendation about which competences were required within the different roles.

- There is no independent certification to verify such competence.

To address these issues, the Swedish IASA Reference Group (SIRG) set off to work in 2006/2007 to produce recommendations for companies. SIRG had three primary goals:

- Specify the deliverables that architects work with

- Position these deliverables on a map, covering areas from business and strategies to technical architecture

- Cluster these deliverables to roles and get consensus around naming conventions

SIRG positioned the deliverables within three levels, as you can see in Figure 4-9.

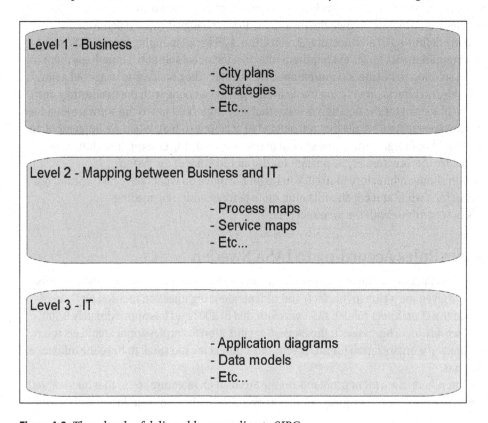

Figure 4-9. *Three levels of deliverables according to SIRG*

Within the first level, there is a strategic dialogue between IT and the business side. On this level, strategic architectural principles are produced and strategic decisions are made about policies connected to these principles. These will be valid for the entire organization. Decisions are also made here regarding the kind of IT that the enterprise should invest in.

At the second level, we are somewhere in the twilight zone between IT and business. Here reference models are created, helping in getting the business clearly understood by the different sides and also in setting the frames for technology. This is the level where architects try to understand the business processes and figure out ways to improve these by using IT.

The third level addresses the technical architecture and how this should be realized, while still adhering to the policies set at level 1. At the third level, suggestions for standards (open or internal) are produced based on solution patterns.

The preceding levels do not necessarily map to a specific architect role because roles can sometimes work with deliverables on different levels.

SIRG came up with the idea of four architect roles, as you can see in Figure 4-10, based on an IT perspective. I think this assumption is worth noticing, especially when we compare these roles to the Sundblads' recommendations in the following section of this chapter. IASA has a pure IT perspective on their architect roles.

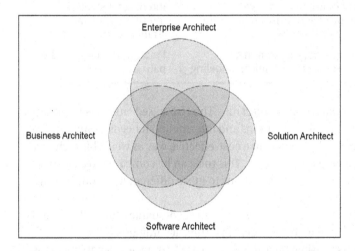

Figure 4-10. *The architect roles IASA found for Sweden*

Besides not focusing on business architecture, SIRG also chose not to consider some other architect roles in an enterprise. For instance, they do not mention infrastructure architects, an area I think is extremely important to include in all development projects early on, to avoid deployment problems later. In a Scrum team, for instance, I think it is essential to include this competence because we develop and deploy new stuff with every iteration. SIRG also does not talk about security architects or data architects.

The results were finally that IASA recognized four architect roles in Sweden. These are the IASA recommendations as of November 1, 2007:

- Enterprise architect

- Business architect (most often referred to as business analyst)

- Solution architect

- Software architect

As you saw in Figure 4-10, these roles overlap in some areas. There is no reporting hierarchy between them either. Table 4-2 shows the competences that the people in the four architect role should possess as well as the artifacts produced.

Table 4-2. *Competences and Artifacts of the Four IASA Architect Roles*

Architect Role	Competences	Artifacts
Enterprise architect	Deep business and IT knowledge, leadership and negotiation skills, governance experience, project management, economy, enterprise architecture, and business modeling	IT strategies, capability maps, city plans, integration strategies, as-is/to-be analysis, architectural principles, gap analysis, lifecycle analysis, application portfolio strategies
Business architect	Deep business knowledge, process modeling, requirements analysis, workshop leadership kills	Process maps, use cases, information models
Solution architect	Broad and general knowledge, deep knowledge about infrastructure, data models, service orientation, good understanding of enterprise architecture	Application diagrams, system maps, service interfaces, technical interfaces, integration strategies
Software architect	Deep knowledge in programming, frameworks, standards, technical modeling	Frameworks, class models, patterns, aspects

Let's start with exploring the *enterprise architect* role. The IT-focused enterprise architect should make sure the enterprise has the IT solutions and information it needs to support the business strategy. This should naturally be done in a cost-effective way as well. This architect role reports to the CIO or maybe to a chief architect. This role can be compared to a city planner who uses strategies, planning, rules, and regulations to make different functions in a city work together effectively.

The enterprise architect role is probably immature in most companies, but will grow as IT and business are more closely aligned in the foreseeable future, according to IASA.

The enterprise architect is responsible for artifacts such as IT strategies, capability maps, city plans, integration strategies, as-is/to-be analysis, architectural principles, gap analysis, life-cycle analysis, and application portfolio strategies.

The *business architect* works very close to the business and should have a deep understanding of how the company works. These people model the business processes for IT use. Because they also have good knowledge of how the IT systems support the business processes, their responsibilities include suggesting improvements to the IT system as well. This work is often done in collaboration with the enterprise architect. The business architect also supports the solution architect with analysis and requirements to new or existing solutions. This role is responsible for making sure projects deliver business value. The artifacts produced include process maps, use cases, and information models.

A *solution architect* could be seen as an evolution of the traditional system architect role. This person is responsible for taking the business requirements and transforming them into an IT solution design, while at the same time making sure existing IT capabilities and services are used in an effective way. Reuse is natural for this role.

With the help of prioritizations and compromises, the solution architect balances the functional and nonfunctional requirements into a realistic design. The aim, is of course, to make the projects as successful as possible. It is also this role that is responsible for aligning new solutions to the existing architectural principles so that standards are followed and new systems integrate well with the organization.

This architect role produces the following artifacts: application diagrams, system maps, service interfaces, technical interfaces, and integration strategies.

The last IASA recommended role is the *software architect*. The role works with the structure and design of software systems. System attributes such as flexibility, performance, reusability, testability, and usability are topics important for this role. The work is probably executed in cooperation with the solution architect for best prioritization and optimization of these attributes, so that cost and other constraints are considered.

A software architect focuses on the project at hand, while the solution architect has a wider focus on policies, regulations, and reuse of existing assets. Frameworks, class models, patterns, and aspects are artifacts produced by the software architect.

IASA has produced a matrix so that we can more easily get an overview of the focus areas of their recommended architect roles (see Table 4-3). The boundaries between them are not waterproof, and in many organizations the architect roles share responsibilities, which I think is essential if we want to reach the goal of a project. In a large project, we need much more cooperation between the roles and the teams to be truly successful.

Table 4-3. *Focus Areas for the IASA Roles*

Goal	Make Organization More Effective		
	IT	Processes	Humans
Enterprise architect	X	X	X
Business architect	X	X	
Solution architect	X		
Software architect	X		

There are some primary goals of the architect roles IASA stresses. They should work to make the company more effective, support the business, and, if possible, innovate it with the help of IT. We can see three primary means of control for helping a company implement change:

- With the help of innovative and efficient processes

- By organizing, empowering, and training the staff to possess the best competence available

- By using technological innovations through the help of IT, for instance

These were the thoughts of the Swedish IASA organization. I am glad that they have realized that we need to extend and redefine the architect roles. But I am not sure that I agree with everything they present. I still think they focus too heavily on technological issues in their roles. That is, I think they focus too much on the internals of a system in some roles, and this just isn't architecture in my view. The software architect, for instance, is a role I would rather name software engineer. IASA states that this role produces frameworks, class models, patterns, and so on for a specific project. These are implementation and hence engineering skills, not architecture.

I also think they miss the clear business side in these roles. Or rather, they probably lack another architect role. I do not think we can solve the whole gap problem by just looking at the IT side of the architect roles. Instead we need to integrate the business more. This doesn't mean that I discard IASA's work. It is a good start that will help enterprises and other organizations get a long way toward bridging the gap. I can also see a pedagogic point in just focusing on the IT side. That way, we do not have to start the whole discussion with the business side at one time, but could perhaps ease the business people into this thinking piece by piece. By showing greater results on the IT side, giving direct better results to the business, the business side will be curious about how the IT side did it and the discussion could evolve from there.

For an organization to reach even further, I would like to have a more elaborate model to start with. Even though it might not be implemented all at once, I would like the model to have a clear plan on how to bridge the gap. Fortunately, there is one more to my taste, which we will cover next.

The Sundblads' Architect Roles

This section describes a view on architect roles that really appeals to me. I like its mix of business and IT architect roles. In my eyes, architecture is such a big area that I don't think we can have a single architect role accomplish everything. IT architecture cannot be seen as separate from business architecture either. The two go hand in hand, and we need to provide a framework for their integration. One person, or role, cannot fulfill this.

The Sundblads have a take on architect roles that will help us get the collaboration we need in our projects between the business side and the IT side. Using this approach, we can make sure the ALM process will run more smoothly and help us deliver better-quality business software.

The Sundblads believe that "one of a software architect's most important qualifications must be an ability to understand business problems and to define IT solutions which are actively meant to help solve these business problems, and also an ability to understand business goals and define IT solutions meant to help reach these goals."[13] The two writers continue that they think that a skilled architect also should have the guts to suggest ways to improve business performance. As a basis for these suggestions, the architect should use knowledge of the IT opportunities, both those within the company or organization as well as those available on the market. Because we don't expect business people to have detailed knowledge of IT, it is the architect who has to input his or her IT knowledge to the business people in order to bridge the gap. And the other way around of course, because IT people probably lack the deep business knowledge necessary.

The Sundblads continue that they don't think it is enough that software architects learn the business thinking, or for that matter that business people learn the deep technical stuff. They suggest that we need a whole new set of architect roles to produce business software that really supports the business processes—and also at the same time provides software with the agile ability to transform when changes occur in the business, increasing business performance and competitiveness. I agree with their assumption on redefining the architect roles. We cannot expect every business or IT person to be as driven and motivated as was the case in the Shinsei Bank.

---

13. Sten Sundblad and Per Sundblad, "Business Improvements Through Better Software Architecture," January 2007, http://msdn.microsoft.com/en-us/library/bb266336.aspx.

The Sundblads suggest five architect roles that are needed to develop good business software (see Figure 4-11). We will now take a deeper look at these and see what they can accomplish.

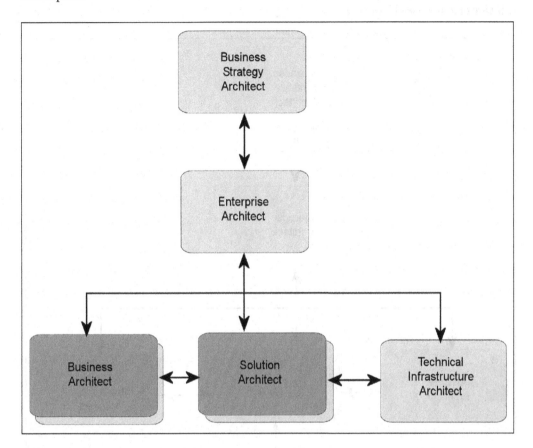

Figure 4-11. *The Sundblads' five architect roles*

In Figure 4-11, you can see that information and communication flow between the five architect roles. This should not be seen as a reporting hierarchy, but more as an information flowchart.

The Sundblads also stress that they are talking about roles and not about people in their article. So a business-oriented solution architect could probably play the role of business architect as well as the role of solution architect. This person could perhaps also be acting as a software developer or engineer. When somebody plays multiple roles, it is essential that the person manages to keep the roles apart. This is often a tough task.

There are some constraints in this figure as well. It doesn't cover every possible IT or business architect role available. For instance, no organizational architect role is included, because that role is most often not necessary for software development. The figure only concerns architect roles important for specification and development of business software. The Sundblads also reason from an SOA perspective, which is the second constraint. SOA is an important architecture if we want to build the agile electronic company the Sundblads aim for.

If you look carefully at Figure 4-11, you can also see that it has no application architect role. This is because the tasks concerning this role are not architecture, according to the reasoning earlier in the chapter. Those tasks are internal to the system and are performed by the software engineer (see Figure 4-12).

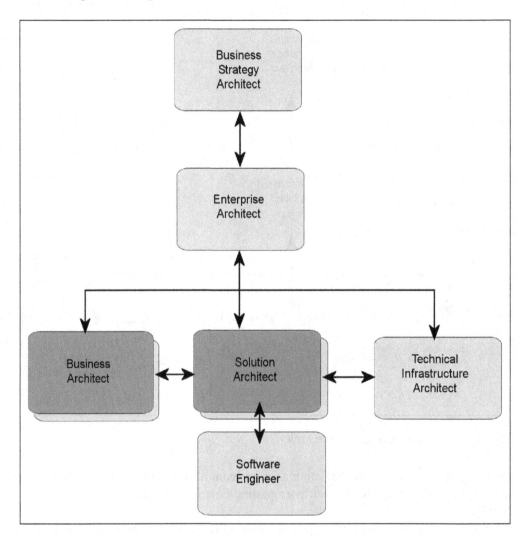

Figure 4-12. *The software engineer role is placed below the solution architect role.*

What is the primary difference between business architects and IT architects? According to the Sundblads, "the big difference . . . is that the business architect's primary focus is set on improving the functionality of the business, while the software architect's primary interest is—or should be—to design software that supports the business and helps improve the functionality of the business." To me, this makes good sense. Let's now see how the Sundblads suggest that we realize this.

Business Strategy Architect

The *business strategy architect* is a role that the Sundblads never thought of as an architect role before. But as you can see, the idea is pretty good, because we always consider the tasks and results of this role in our development process (or at least we should consider it). The business strategy architect focuses only on business strategy. In order to have any influence over this area, this role is probably a member of, or closely associated with, top management in the organization.

For those of you who are familiar with the works of Peter Drucker, we know that every organization (commercial as well as noncommercial) has a purpose and a mission.[14] Drucker's book on management was something that I had heard of before reading the Sundblads' article, but had never read. After reading the article, I ordered it from Amazon.com (one of my favorite sites) and found it very interesting indeed. I highly recommend it if you have the slightest interest in this area.

Drucker states that the purpose describes why the organization was started and also why it still exists. If we have a commercial company, for example, the purpose is probably to make money for its owner(s). The mission, Drucker continues, tells us what the organization should do and for whom it should do it. To determine the mission of an organization, Drucker suggests we ask three specific questions; the answers should be stated in terms of customer value:

- What is our business?

- What will our business be?

- What should our business be?

The answers to these questions should drive strategic planning and work, which brings us back to the business strategy architect role. This is something this role should work with. The strategic plan will tell the business what markets it should go for and also what kind of products the organization should offer. The business processes and activities all should have the purpose of producing business value so that they contribute to the value streams of the organization. The strategic plan should guide this work with its goals and objectives. The business strategy architect is the role responsible for defining, negotiating, and documenting the strategic plan, including the goals and objects in it.

The Sundblads define a set of competencies based on Microsoft competencies and add their view on which level of competency is needed (see Table 4-4). This matrix is great for evaluating the role of business strategy architect.

Table 4-4. *Level of Competency for the Business Strategy Architect*

Competency	Level of Competency Needed
Leadership	Very High
Strategy	Very High
Technological breadth	Low
Technological depth	Very low
Organization dynamics	Very high
Tactical/Process	High
Communications	Very high

14. Peter Drucker, *Management: Tasks, Responsibilities, Practices* (Collins Business, 1993).

Business Architect

The *business architect* is the next role we'll discuss. Do not for a moment confuse this role with the business strategy architect; there is a lot that differs between them. "The business architect's job is not to architect software," according to the Sundblads.[15]

Instead this role focuses on finding out how we can best organize the work in the organization so that the strategies and objectives that the business strategy architect has defined can be fulfilled. So the business architect should look at how the business and the way it is run should be architected. Software architects should then use this work as a basis for how they design the software solutions.

The business architect should break down and map the activities in the organization's business processes. This person must evaluate in which way these activities are important to the results of the organization. Furthermore, the business architect must consider how well an activity performs and how well it needs to perform. This work could provide advantages over competitors, so it's important to perform these tasks well.

Note The business architect does not have to consider how the activities are performed. Instead, he focuses only on which level of activity is needed—for example, what input does an activity need, what output does it provide, what are the responsibilities of the activity, and so on.

We can understand that it is hard and detailed work to evaluate and define the business processes and their activities at such a level that we could make decisions on them. These decisions in turn must always be evaluated against the business strategy so that we know how much effort we should put into improvements in relation to the payoff we can get from them.

The problem in deciding how to take advantage of IT so that we can support the business is that probably no single role can have the required knowledge of both IT and business issues. Therefore, the Sundblads suggest that the best way to "improve an organization's ability to function well and to gain competitive advantage in the marketplace" comes when the business architect closely collaborates with the solution architect. If you look back at Figure 4-11, you can see information running between these two roles. You can also see that an organization could have several business architects depending on its size.

The Sundblads have put together the level of competency needed for the business architect in Table 4-5.

Table 4-5. *Level of Competency for the Business Architect*

Competency	Level of Competency Needed
Leadership	Medium
Strategy	High
Technological breadth	Medium to high
Technological depth	Very low
Organization dynamics	High
Tactical/Process	Very High
Communications	High

---

15. Sten Sundblad and Per Sundblad, "Business Improvements Through Better Software Architecture."

Solution Architect

Now we have come to the *solution architect*. Remember that one of the cornerstones of the Sundblads' theory was that we are talking SOA. So we are always thinking with a service-oriented mindset when we discuss the architect roles that the Sundblads suggest. Figure 4-8 earlier showed how we could use SOA to map the IT systems (services) to our business processes. Furthermore, we could also let several services use a specific service by letting them all have their own service interface for accessing the functionality the services expose (see Figure 4-13).

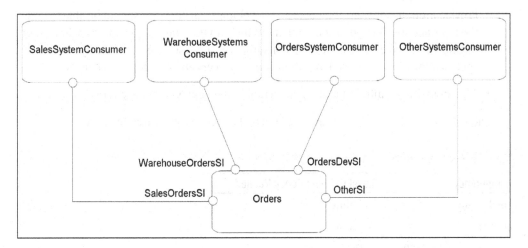

Figure 4-13. *A service can expose multiple service interfaces.*

The way services should be implemented lets us add new service interfaces when we need them. We also have the capability to add new features to a service by exposing a new service interface, still allowing the existing interfaces to be untouched. The architecture of a service, based on the discussion earlier in this chapter, is all about specifying the service interfaces—by that, I mean the complete and detailed specification of the service interface(s).

The solution architect should be responsible for architecting technical solutions to our business problems—in the agile, service-oriented organization, this means the design of the service interfaces. Still, the solution architect does not have to bother with implementation. That is instead the job of the software engineer. The job of the solution architect isn't very technical at all. The role needs technical understanding of course, but it also requires an understanding of business issues and needs. Compare this to the skills we usually see in an application architect today (for example, IASA's software architect role), and we find a totally different focus. However, many of IASA's competences for a solution architect map very well with the Sundblads' if we compare them, so maybe that is the role we should really compare with.

If we let the solution architect and the enterprise architect work together and they perform their jobs well, they can definitely make sure that the technical solutions fit into the enterprise architect's vision of the future system's portfolio. (The role of the enterprise architect is discussed later in this section.) This is an important brick in realizing the agile, service-oriented enterprise.

The Sundblads describe three main tasks for the solution architect. I have added a fourth task as well:

- Help the enterprise architect implement the agile, service-oriented enterprise. This can be done only by elevating the perspective from the specific object and seeing the present and future environment.

- Help the business architect solve business problems and improve functionality. The solution architect should understand the business and how it is performed, and also suggest changes and improvements in the business behavior by making better use of IT. The solution that the solution architect designs must satisfy the goals and requirements of the business as well.

- Provide input to software engineers and developers. An engineer should be able to take the interface specifications and implement these in the solution as services, while other engineers should be able to develop consumers of these services, based only on the specifications. So a close collaboration with engineers and developers is needed.

- Together with the infrastructure architect, plan the deployment of systems.

Table 4-6 shows the level of competency needed for the solution architect.

Table 4-6. *Level of Competency for the Solution Architect*

Competency	Level of Competency Needed
Leadership	Medium
Strategy	Medium
Technological breadth	Very high
Technological depth	Medium to high
Organization dynamics	Medium
Tactical/Process	Medium
Communications	High

Technical Infrastructure Architect

I am glad that the Sundblads include the *technical infrastructure architect* in their theory. All too often projects run into problems during deployment for the sole reason of forgetting to include infrastructure professionals in the design phase. In my eyes, this role is as important to have in any IT project as a developer or engineer. The infrastructure architect deals with high-level issues of hardware, network, operating systems, security, and system software.

Note We do not include data or information infrastructure in this role.

In order for a project to successfully deliver business value, it is essential to include infrastructure in design and architecture planning. We need this skill so that we fully take advantage of the technical infrastructure in our organizations.

Enterprise Architect

The final architect role has been saved for last for a good reason: "The enterprise architect role collects all the other architect roles within it"[16]—except of course for the business strategy architect role. The Sundblads argue that the enterprise architect role consists of business, solution, and technical infrastructure architecture. Of course, other architect roles such as security or organization architects could be included as well; it all depends on the definition of the term *enterprise architecture*. The Sundblads, however, state that talking about enterprise architecture only in terms of the fundamental technology structure for IT strategy might be misleading and therefore go with a definition found on Wikipedia:

"Enterprise architecture is the practice of applying a comprehensive and rigorous method for describing a current and/or future structure and behavior for an organization's processes, information systems, personnel and organizational subunits, so that they align with the organization's goals and strategic direction. Although often associated strictly with information technology, it relates more broadly to the practice of business optimization in that it addresses business architecture, performance management and process architecture as well."

The Sundblads believe that enterprise architecture is about all aspects of importance for business performance, which fits this definition well.

So what does an enterprise architect do according to the Sundblads? Well, this role focuses on the big picture. The enterprise architect should know about which business processes exist in the company. He doesn't have to know the details that, for example, the business architect has to know, but he should know the high-level details and have access to the specifics when needed. It is essential for the enterprise architect to know what the processes do, how they relate to business value streams, and how they help achieve the overall business goals.

If we speak SOA, which we do here, this role also needs to know which services exist in the organization. If there is a sales process, the enterprise architect should know about it. He should also know which entity services are available. He doesn't, however, need to know about the details of each service, the same way he doesn't need to know about the details of the processes. The enterprise architect is controlled and led by business strategy and should in turn control and lead business, solution, and technical infrastructure efforts, as you saw in Figure 4-11 earlier.

One of the biggest artifacts that the enterprise cares for and produces is the city plan. This is, for those unfamiliar with this concept, a large-scale map of the business architecture and the IT resources used to support the business. Table 4-7 compares enterprise architecture to real city planning (I mean planning a city with buildings and stuff).

Table 4-7. *Comparison Between City Planning and Enterprise Architecture*

City Plan Is to . . .	As Enterprise Architecture Is to . . .
Zones	Organizational structure
Buildings	Applications and systems
Building materials, interface specifications	Infrastructure hardware, design specifications, and development languages

16. Sten Sundblad and Per Sundblad, "Business Improvements Through Better Software Architecture."

Some of the topics in a city plan are listings of business processes, strategic information areas, interactions between these two, cross-references of applications and services to business processes and information areas, and much, much more. It is also essential to include information about who owns what, and who pays for changes to services and applications—very important in budget discussions when starting projects.

"All development of business software should be based on the enterprise architect's strategic road map towards the future state"[17] of the organization. The enterprise architect should know where we can gain the highest payoff with development efforts in any area. If fruits are hanging low, the enterprise architect should naturally pick them, so to speak.

Table 4-8 shows the competencies the Sundblads have specified for the enterprise architect.

Table 4-8. *Level of Competency for the Enterprise Architect*

Competency	Level of Competency Needed
Leadership	Very high
Strategy	High to very high
Technological breadth	High to very high
Technological depth	Low to medium
Organization dynamics	Very high
Tactical/Process	High
Communications	Very high

Comparisons of All Roles

To make comparisons among all of the architect roles described by the Sundblads, you can use Table 4-9.

Table 4-9. *Comparisons Among the Competencies for the Architect Roles*

Competency	Level of Competency Needed					
	Business Strategy Architect	Enterprise Architect	Business Architect	Solution Architect	Technical Infrastructure Architect	Software Engineer
Leadership	Very high	Very high	Medium	Medium	Medium to high	Low to medium
Strategy	Very high	High to very high	High	Medium	Medium to high	Low
Technological breadth	Low	High to very high	Medium to high	Very high	Very high	High
Technological depth	Very low	Low to medium	Very low	Medium to high	Medium to high	High to very high

Continued

---

17. Sten Sundblad and Per Sundblad, "Business Improvements Through Better Software Architecture."

Competency	Level of Competency Needed					
	Business Strategy Architect	**Enterprise Architect**	**Business Architect**	**Solution Architect**	**Technical Infrastructure Architect**	**Software Engineer**
Organization dynamics	Very high	Very high	High	Medium	High	Medium
Tactical/Process	High	High	Very high	Medium	High	Medium
Communications	Very high	Very high	High	High	High	Medium

Conclusions on Roles So Far

Now you have seen two approaches to defining the architect roles in an organization. As you already know, I lean toward the Sundblads' version because I find that more attractive as it includes the business side more than IASA does.

I think that if we truly want to have a well-running ALM process, we need to include the business side in our IT projects. And to me, the Sundblads' theories could help us achieve this. I'm not saying we could just go out and change our organizations overnight. Things like this take time to implement and understand. But if we start the discussion, we can open some eyes and make it happen more quickly.

When I have given speeches about the need for redefining architect roles at various conferences and customer seminars, the Sundblads' approach has been well received indeed. Both business people and IT people find the ideas attractive and worth investigating further. I like its combination of business and IT architects roles. In my eyes, architecture is such a big area that I don't think we can have a single architect role and believe that this role can accomplish everything. IT architecture cannot be seen as separate from business architecture either. The two go hand in hand, and we need to provide a framework for the integration of them both. One person, or role, cannot fulfill this.

In Visual Studio Team Editions, covered in Chapter 6, you will find tools to at least partly help you support these architect roles found in both of these architect theories.

Summary

This chapter covers two of my favorite topics: SOA and architect roles. I have tried to provide a good overview of how I think we can bridge the gap between the business side and the IT side in an organization. The aim of bridging this gap is to reach the level of success we saw in the Shinsei Bank example.

SOA is an architecture framework that can help us implement and automate our business processes in the IT infrastructure. This is what makes it such a great part of an ALM process. SOA is built up of separated services, each encapsulating part(s) of our business logic. These services communicate with each other by sending messages.

The architects have a big influence on how our business processes are implemented and automated in the IT infrastructure. Business architects are responsible for the way we work in our companies and how the business processes are defined, and IT architects are responsible for how these business processes will be realized in IT. To implement SOA, we need to make sure that architects from both the business and IT sides focus on this architecture.

If we are to fulfill the goal of a good ALM process that really gives business value to our organizations, we need to consider more than just the process itself. We need to tie the strings together from the business needs to the delivered business value. If we do not include both business processes and their implementations and architecture as IT systems in our ALM process, we will never deliver enough business value.

It is my belief that SOA is a great thing, the best right now for architecting our business systems. It gives the flexibility we need to quickly adapt to new business challenges. I do realize that this cannot be achieved too quickly. You just don't change an organization's IT infrastructure all at once. But if we start to investigate the business processes in our company, we could see where we can get the best ROI in changing to a service orientation. Do it the Shinsei way, little by little at a relatively fast pace and with an incremental approach. Be alert for the business needs and always have business value in the back of your head. And stay agile.

The same obviously goes for redefining the architect roles. We need to have architect roles that cover business issues as well as IT issues. I don't think that this can be achieved with only one architect role; instead we need to think about architecture on the business side as well. These architect roles then need to collaborate, to make sure the business processes are implemented and automated in IT. I have shown two great examples of how we can define our architect roles, even though I favor one of them over the other. Start a discussion in your organization, and see if you can figure out which roles are needed for you, or which approach is best suited for your organization.

CHAPTER 5

■ ■ ■

ALM Assessments

Often in my work I need to perform an assessment of a given situation. I could be describing a system's present architecture and then coming up with a plan for improving it, or I could be assessing how a system scales. The more I've started working with people instead of technology, my focus when doing the assessments has been on a different level: suddenly I need to consider human factors and not only technological topics. Before VSTS entered my life, I conducted surveys of how a department functioned, for instance. I have done such assessments by interviewing people from the organizations and thereby getting a picture of the situation.

For these interviews, I have used my previous experiences from my studies for a bachelor's degree in psychology. Interviews are complex and result in a lot of information that you need to process afterward. Mostly I have prepared by writing questions on a form that I use for the interviews. Any follow-up questions that came up have been carefully documented and included in later assessments. So this form started to become my tool, even though I did not have it in an application. I used a Word document that I updated and printed out for each interview.

However, I have been a bit reluctant to use only tools. I thought about digitalizing the questions into a web application or the like and letting the subjects answer the questions themselves, but I didn't want to abandon the interview part. Tools can help, but they can also hinder because you can become too dependent on them. Another aspect of using tools for this purpose is that if I let a single person answer my questions in, let's say a web form, I wouldn't be around to ask the follow-up questions. These questions enable me to learn so much more than I would if I only looked at the answers to the original bunch of questions.

When I started working with Visual Studio Team System a few years back when the product was new, I felt that it was a good foundation for taking control of an ALM process. It lacked (and still does in some cases) some of the support I wanted, but it was a good start, and nothing else was offered on the Microsoft platform to compete with it. The more I dived into it, the more I started thinking of how I best could evaluate an organization to implement VSTS at their site. I wanted to take the assessment concept I had and make an ALM assessment out of it, because ALM started to get my attention. I realized very quickly that ALM was an important part of an organization's ability to improve their software development cycle, and if I could find a way to help them with this, the market potential (for me as a consultant) was great.

Fortunately, Microsoft released their ALM assessments on the web (www.microsoft.com/almassessment), including the Application Platform Optimization (APO) assessment. Microsoft has provided its APO model to help IT organizations understand and adopt a more flexible and agile application platform. These felt like a good start, so I set off to figure out how to best use these tools to help my customers implement VSTS. Previously, I had found that many of my customers used only a fragment of the true potential of VSTS (most often the version-control system only). If I could show them why they should use more features, they would get so much more out of it and at the same time be more successful in running their projects.

The thing that concerned me was that Microsoft's assessments were tools much like a web questionnaire of my previous assessment would have been. That is why I, together with a coworker, set off to work on creating a business based on Microsoft's Application Platform Capability Assessments, but mixed with an interview part as well. The reason for this is that a tool cannot read between the lines. It cannot hear what a person says apart from what is actually answered. We wanted to have the capability to ask follow-up questions, enabling us to clarify and discuss where needed. The value of follow-up questions was one of the things that I had learned from my psychology classes.

I also realized that the assessments from Microsoft gave me a great advantage. After everything was entered into the tool, the tool could handle much of the data processing. This would decrease the labor attached to the manual processing of the large amount of data an interview gives you. I "only" needed to make sure that I entered the most realistic values into the system, and that's where the interview part could help me out. My coworker and I knew that if we used the questions as a form for our interviews (similar to my Word document in the previous scenario), we had a good foundation for the interviews. Then we would use the results of the interviews, including our follow-up questions and our own observations, to enter data into the assessments form, giving us the capability to reflect on each question and choose the best answer for the organization we were working with.

In this chapter, I will describe the Microsoft Application Platform Optimization model. I'll walk you through the two Application Platform Capability Assessments I use as well as the Microsoft Assessment Builder (a.k.a. Roadmap Builder). Finally, I'll show you one way of carrying out an assessment of an organization's IT department.

Microsoft Application Platform Optimization (APO) Model

APO is one part of Microsoft's Dynamic IT initiative that also includes the Infrastructure Optimization model and the Business Productivity Infrastructure model (see Figure 5-1). There are four primary goals of the Dynamic IT initiative:

- Manage complexity and achieve agility

- Protect information and control access

- Advance the business via IT solutions

- Amplify the impact of your people

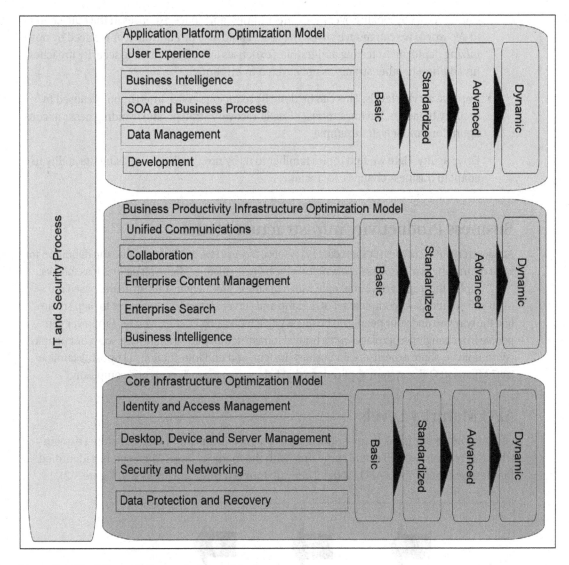

Figure 5-1. *The Microsoft Dynamic IT model*

The preceding models are aimed at helping customers better understand the current IT capabilities in their organizations, and based on these results take the capabilities to a higher level of maturity.

In this section, I'll give you a brief overview of the Infrastructure Optimization model and the Business Productivity Infrastructure model before focusing on APO.

Infrastructure Optimization Model

With the Infrastructure Optimization model, Microsoft focuses on four areas: the desktop infrastructure, the server infrastructure, the remote infrastructure (which covers how to handle remote offices or locations), and virtualization. Based on best practices internal to Microsoft as well as on feedback from customers, Microsoft has provided an approach they say will do three things:

- Control costs by looking over hardware, utilities, and space expenses in the data center to see where we can reduce costs. The costs could also be controlled or reduced by optimizing deployment testing and training expenses as well as reducing security breaches (in addition to other strategies not covered in this book).

- Improve service levels. This can be done by reducing service interruptions caused by security breaches, having a robust disaster recovery strategy, and avoiding desktop configuration conflicts, for example.

- Drive agility. Here we find topics familiar to us by now, such as increasing the ability to adapt to business changes, for instance.

Business Productivity Infrastructure Model

At `www.microsoft.com/businessproductivity/about/overview.mspx`, we can find the definition for what optimizing our *Business Productivity Infrastructure* means. Microsoft defines it as follows:

"Amplify the impact of your people with a business productivity infrastructure based on Microsoft solutions—a complete set of desktop and server software and services to help streamline the way you and your people do business while increasing IT effectiveness. Empower your people in a changing workplace with a unified infrastructure that simplifies the way your people communicate, share expertise, gain business insight, and find information, all by using familiar 2007 Microsoft Office system applications that help you manage IT costs and complexity."

APO Maturity Levels

Let's now move our focus to the Application Platform Optimization model. Before I explain what this really is, we will spend some time with the maturity levels Microsoft has identified for the assessment of the APO model. There are four optimization levels (see Figure 5-2).

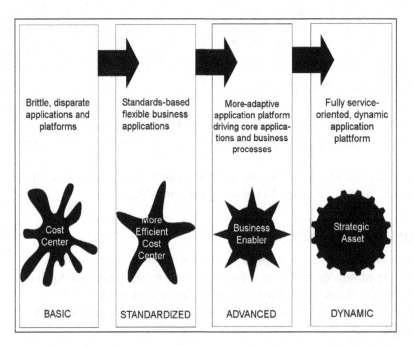

Figure 5-2. *The four optimization levels for categorizing an IT organization*

Basic

When a company is classified as a *basic* organization, it is characterized by brittle, disconnected applications and platforms. This fact hinders rapid adjustments to business changes and also hinders the rapid development and interoperability of business-critical applications. The organization makes no real use of business processes, or these processes (if they exist) are often ill-defined. The processes are definitely not automated in any way. Such an organization probably has no tool for collaboration between teams and team members, and definitely lacks the clear connection between IT and business that is crucial for a company to have.

The development process is probably quite rigid, which makes development hard to control. All in all, this leads to higher costs, application backlogs, and lower IT productivity. The IT department is probably seen as just a cost to management and its true potential as a strategic asset is clouded by all problems.

According to a 2007 study by Forrester Consulting and commissioned by Microsoft,[1] 22 percent of the organizations included in this study considered themselves at this basic level (see Figure 5-3). Even though this figure had dropped from 47 percent since the first examination two years earlier, the number remains quite big.

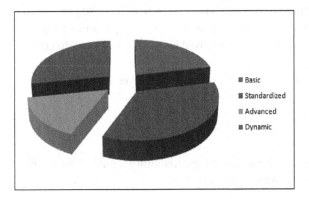

Figure 5-3. *Findings of the Forrester study from 2007 concerning maturity level in organizations*

Standardized

The *standardized* organization has begun to use industry standards broadly across departments as well as with business partners. These standards could be as simple as starting to use XML, for instance. Furthermore, such an organization has also started to take control of their development and data infrastructure, enabling the use of business intelligence reports and analytics. They have also started to automate some of their business processes. The IT department has slowly begun to be seen as a business enabler that could provide help in building more-adaptive systems quickly.

According to the Forrester report mentioned previously, 35 percent of the organizations considered themselves at this standardized maturity level (up from 28 percent two years earlier).

1. Forrester Consulting, "Many Organizations Embrace Converged Application Platforms, but Adoption Barriers Remain," October 2007, http://download.microsoft.com/download/b/3/5/b3561c68-e641-4137-abdd-df09ac51742c/Forrester%20Consulting%20-%20Application%20Platform%20Optimization%20Study%2010-2007%20-%202.pdf.

Advanced

At an *advanced* level, IT is truly seen as a business enabler and partner. Now infrastructure and systems are more easily managed throughout their lifecycles. The business processes are well-defined and well-known. The business side has begun to truly take advantage of IT and can rely on the IT department to quickly make adjustments when changes in the business occur. Such a company has standardized a robust and flexible application platform for the most critical systems and processes.

The Forrester report showed that 16 percent of the companies considered themselves to be at this advanced level, an increase as compared to the 5 percent in the previous measurement.

Dynamic

A *dynamic* organization is fully aware of the strategic value of their infrastructure. They know it can help them run the business efficiently and stay ahead of market competitors. Costs are controlled to the company's maximum ability. All processes are automated and integrated into the technology, enabling IT to adjust to business changes and needs. The collaboration between the business and the IT department is working smoothly as well. It is also possible to measure the effects of business benefits of IT investments, which is a strong argument when showing the value of IT. This kind of organization has also used SOA to the fullest so that cost-effective systems can be developed.

Forrester showed that 28 percent of the organizations were at this level (according to themselves), which was an increase from 14 percent previously.

APO Capabilities

With this as a background, you are ready to have a look at the capabilities included in the APO model. Microsoft defines five capabilities, as shown in Figure 5-4.

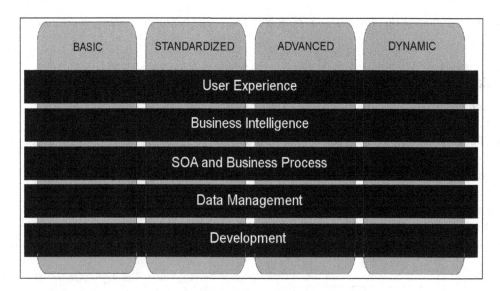

Figure 5-4. *Microsoft has defined five capabilities for their APO model.*

User Experience

The next capability is another unappreciated area. *User experience (UX)* is important, but most often this capability is not included in projects as a special field. We far too often rely on developers solving UX problems without thinking of the effects this could have. Not many developers are skilled in this area, and the importance and value of this field is included in this capability. Usability should be a higher priority in most cases. I have seen projects that were considered failures because the user experience was too technical. The developers had a technical view on how to work in the application (or system) and had designed it with this as the primary viewpoint. The design was not in line with how the end user really worked, so the user interface needed a lot of rework, resulting in higher costs and a delayed project.

Business Intelligence

Microsoft identifies *business intelligence (BI)* as a capability as well. Microsoft and many others have a vision that business insight should be provided to all employees. This is certainly the keyword to success in my own company, Know IT. This leads to faster, more-reliable, and more-relevant decisions in the organization, because all members of the organization have access to the right information to support good decision making. We find areas such as data mining, reporting, data warehousing, data integration, analysis, and more here.

SOA and Business Process

SOA and business process is the second capability. SOA is a great way to implement our organizations, as you saw in Chapter 4. This capability focuses on the integration between Business Process Management (BPM) and SOA. This integration is something Forrester believes must be intimately linked.[2]

This is an immature market according to Forrester, as only 33 percent of their respondents in the survey said they had a combined strategy for SOA and BPM (see Figure 5-5). A significant two-thirds of the organizations had no such strategy, in other words. This might be good for me as a consultant because the market exists for helping out, but could be disastrous for some companies if they don't change this fact.

Having effective business processes that we are able to quickly adjust to new or changed business needs is essential for an organization these days. We need ways to manage our processes and then automate them in our IT infrastructure. BPM will help with managing the processes, and SOA will help with implementing them in our IT environment.

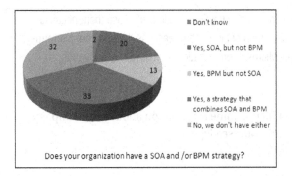

Figure 5-5. *Only 33 percent of Forrester respondents had a combined strategy for BPM and SOA.*

2. Forrester Consulting, "Many Organizations Embrace Converged Application Platforms, but Adoption Barriers Remain."

Data Management

Data management covers what an organization should consider when integrating data management and analysis software. How is the data storage handled? Will it support the business-critical systems reliably? This capability also covers how database development is being carried out, how well the database team is integrated into the development projects, and so on. The main focus is to determine how best to build an integrated, well-managed, and always-connected data infrastructure to support our most demanding and mission-critical applications.

Development

Let's first look at the *development* capability. Here we find the things that can enable an organization to develop applications that connect business processes to meet business needs. It covers areas such as what kind of development platform the organization uses, whether a development process is in place, how the development team and projects are organized, how visibility into the process of a development project is going, and so on.

The APO Assessment

Now you're ready to take a look at the assessment program itself. In this section I'll show you the application and walk you through a couple of example questions. Finally, I'll show you how to see the results.

Starting the Assessment

The APO assessment can be found at `www.microsoft.com/business/peopleready/appplat/default.mspx`. The assessment is available free to anyone wanting to assess their IT processes. It consists of approximately 40 questions divided into the five capability areas mentioned earlier. Some areas are divided into subgroups, for instance the Development section includes questions about the development platform, Application Lifecycle Management, and custom applications. Microsoft presents the questions in a multiple-choice format; you can't type in answers.

■Note The tools I discuss in this chapter are developed and supplied by Microsoft. I use them because they are good, and they help me a lot in my work. But the most important reason is that they are platform-independent. I have used the assessment on a non-Microsoft organization as well with good results.

Before starting an assessment, you must fill out some information about your company and choose which assessment you want to carry out (see Figure 5-6).

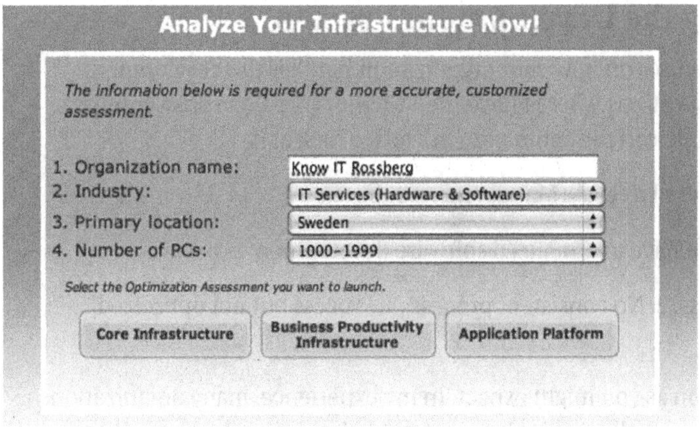

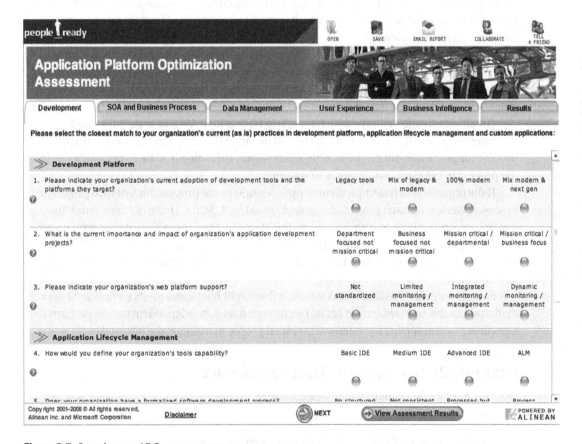

Figure 5-6. *Choosing an assessment*

Next you get right into the Application Platform assessment, as shown in Figure 5-7.

Figure 5-7. *Starting an APO assessment*

To give you an idea of how the questions are asked, I will give you a few examples and then discuss them and my experiences of them a bit.

Example 1: Assessing the Development Process

This first example question focuses on how your organization handles the development process. This is one of those questions where I have seen CIOs or managers answer more positively than the real situation is in the company. Let's take a look at it.

Development—Application Lifecycle Management subarea

Q: Does your organization have a formalized software development process?

A: 1. No structured process, 2. No consistent process, 3. Process but not optimized, 4. Process optimization

Answer 1 is not as common as you might expect. In my experience, many organizations report that they have no process at all, or at least do not think they have. However, all organizations have a way of working, a way that has evolved over the years. It's just that in many cases, that process is not documented. Because an organization has no documented process, someone answering this questionnaire themselves might answer "1" because they interpret the lack of a documented process as having no structured way of working. So this question needs some extra thought, and this is why it is good to have an independent assessment leader doing the interviewing.

At times when participants have spontaneously answered 1, we have discussed this and found the correct answer to be 2. They have a process—not documented—but they do have it. Perhaps the process isn't consistent, because consistency is hard to attain if you have not documented and structured the process.

Other organizations I have seen have started using RUP, MSF, or some other well-documented process. But to answer 3, I would like them to really have started to use the process (or processes) for all projects. In other words, there needs to be a consistent use of the process in development projects to answer 3.

If the organization has implemented optimization of the process, for instance project process reviews after each project, the answer would be 4. So far, I have not seen more than one or two companies that have fully taken this step. Most use some kind of review on paper but rarely go through with the full retrospective after a project is finished. It's a little bit like knowledge reuse: it's nice to talk about and say you have, but unfortunately not many really implement it.

So a question like this that seems simple at first might hold some pretty complicated information about the organization. So again, I recommend that an independent person perform the assessment by conducting interviews with several people to really get the best answer.

Example 2: Assessing the User Experience

The next question asks about your user experience, especially about how you see this area in your projects.

User Experience—Client and Web Development subarea

Q: Does your IT organization have awareness of the user experience you provide to customers/users, and is this a priority?

A: 1. Not considered critical, 2. Appreciation of impact, 3. Deep understanding of needs, 4. Critical element

This is also a question I think we should dive down on in our interviews. Nobody wants to say that they don't focus on the user experience, but sadly this is the case in many projects. By asking follow-up questions, I try to really get to know how UX is regarded.

The user is important to the success of the project, and if we don't consider this aspect, projects will be seen as failures even if they have great functionality. So a low-hanging fruit for many organizations is taking control of the UX. That way, the organization has more satisfied end users (be they internal or external), which can be accomplished fairly easy and at a low cost.

■**Note** To perform an assessment as an interviewer, you have to be well prepared. You need to understand the questions and probably should do some research beforehand so you can discuss the questions with the participants. The first time I did an assessment, I was not as prepared as I should have been, and I regret that still. My results on later assessments were much closer to the real situation in the companies than the first was.

Viewing the Results

After answering all the questions, you click the View Results button and are shown a screen summarizing the results (see Figure 5-8).

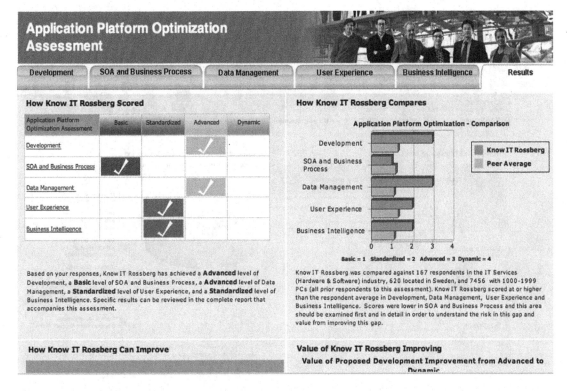

Figure 5-8. *Viewing the results of an APO assessment*

Here you can see a nice table presenting information about the organization's score for each of the five capabilities. You can also see how these scores compare to those of similar companies (based on the short information provided on the first screen). This can be useful information for a decision maker, or for an IT manager who wants to show off the department's skills.

Furthermore, you'll also find information on each capability that indicates how to improve from the level you are assessed at to the next level. This information is provided in short bullets leading the way forward. An example on this is the following excerpt from a demo assessment I did for a dummy company called Know IT Demo:

How Know IT Demo Can Optimize the Application Platform

Business process and service-oriented architecture (SOA) (advance from Basic to Standardized)

To advance from the current Basic level to Standardized, we recommend the following projects:

- *Automate key departmental processes in your organization.*

- *Talk with other company decision makers about the value of web services and service-oriented architecture.*

- *Develop a specific plan to enhance your current web services.*

- *Establish standards-based business-to-business integration.*

As seen in Figure 5-9, you also get some information about the value of advancing a level. These results are given in the local currency.

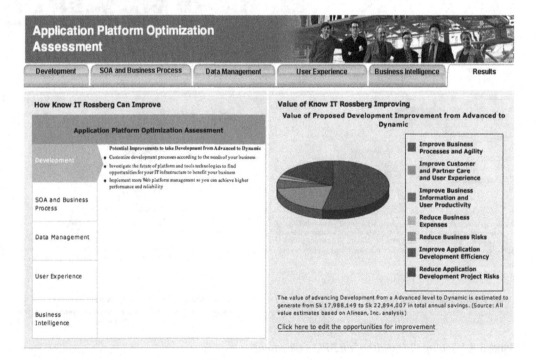

Figure 5-9. *Viewing more of the results of an APO assessment*

If you want to, you can access a more advanced screen by following the Click Here to Edit the Opportunities for Improvement link. You can then provide input for your company so that these values are based on real figures for your organization (see Figure 5-10). There are many fields that you can provide input into, and providing these additional answers requires a good understanding of the business.

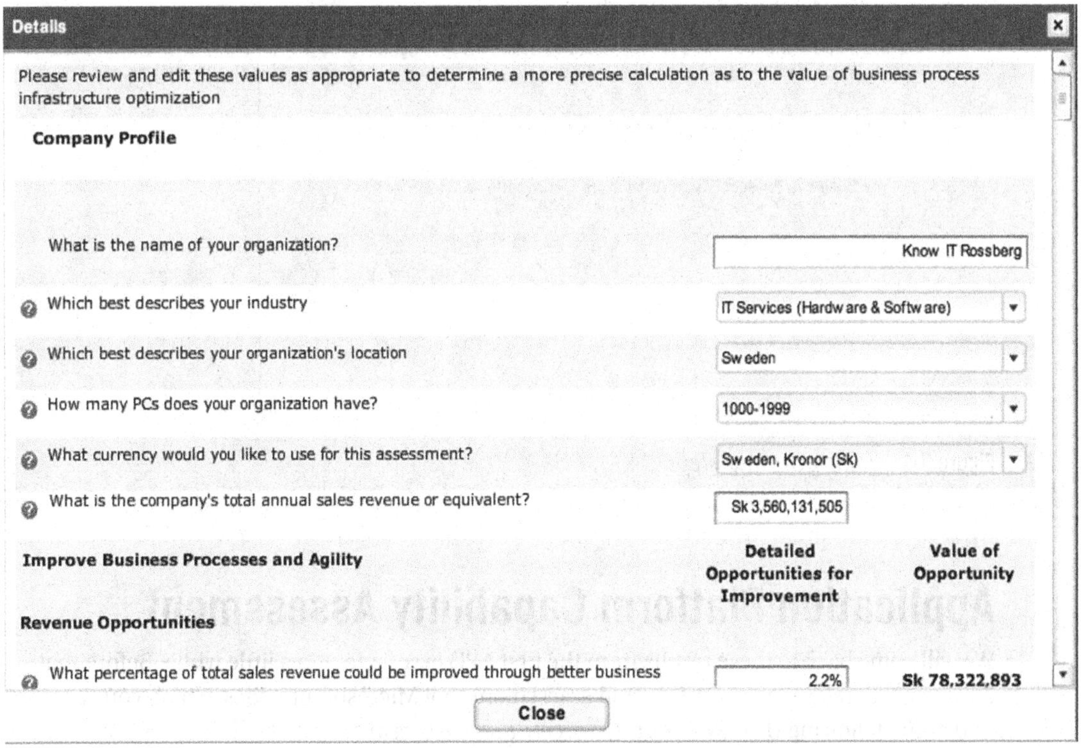

Figure 5-10. *Providing input for evaluating the value of advancing on the maturity scale*

After you are happy with the input and want to close or save the assessment, you can click Take the Next Steps and see how Microsoft encourages you to go on (see Figure 5-11). A nice feature is that you can have the assessment results e-mailed to you and hence have the opportunity to go over them in more detail. The document that is sent has more-extensive results as well, so you can dive deeper into the results.

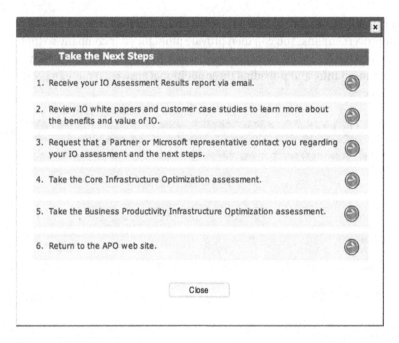

Figure 5-11. *Taking the next steps*

Application Platform Capability Assessment

We will come back to these results from the first APO assessment in a little while. Before that, however, let's take a look at the second assessment tool Microsoft provides, which you can find at the following URL: www.microsoft.com/almassessment.

This assessment is called the Application Platform Capability Assessment and exists in five versions, of which one is deprecated:

- ALM Assessment for Individuals (Lightweight)

- ALM Assessment for Teams (Comprehensive)

- ALM Baseline Assessment—deprecated, use ALM Assessment for Teams instead

- Business Intelligence Quick Assessment—provides a quick snapshot of an organization's strategic and technological capabilities

- SOA and Business Process Capability Quick Assessment

We will use the ALM Assessment for Teams (Comprehensive) for discussions in this book, because this one is most relevant for covering the development process and the ALM process. It covers all aspects of the ALM process and is very extensive. So in order to get good coverage on what parts of the ALM process you can improve, this is the assessment you should use.

One big difference with this assessment, aside from the number of questions and the detail level in them, is that it is intended to be filled out by more than one person. It is no longer a self-assessment as the APO assessment is. Microsoft also encourages the use of a partner when gathering information about your organization. The best thing about using a partner for such an assignment is that you get an independent view on the answers and the state of the organization.

The ALM Assessment for Teams (Comprehensive) includes more areas than the previous APO assessment we looked at; it has eight practice areas, all divided further into a various number of practices. The assessment has about 200 questions (this figure is subject to change), so it covers a great deal more material.

The eight practice areas and their practices are shown in Table 5-1.

Table 5-1. *Practice Areas and Practices of the ALM Assessment for Teams*

Practice Area	Practices
Architecture and Design	Architecture framework Analysis and design Database modeling
Requirements Engineering and User Experience	Elicitation Requirements analysis Requirements management Traceability UX research UI design and prototyping UI implementation End-user documentation
Development	Code writing Code analysis Code reuse Code reviews Quality metrics Database development
Software Configuration Management	Collaborative development Database change management Version-control repository Release management Build management Change management
Governance	IT governance maturity Application portfolio management Compliance management
Deployment and Operations	Designed for operations Deployment Environment management Operations Customer support Database deployment
Project Planning and Management	Project initiation Project planning Project monitoring and control Risk management Stakeholder management Project close
Testing and Quality Assurance	Test resource management Test planning Test management Test types Database testing

■**Note** Does anybody but me wonder why Microsoft put Requirements Engineering and User Experience together in the same practice area? Sure, the user experience provides input to requirements, but I don't see the direct connection. Please let me know if you have a good answer.

Starting the Assessment

When you start an assessment, you begin with filling in some information about the company. You can see in Figure 5-12 that you also set a time frame indicating the period that you'll allow people to add information into the assessment. You also can fill out the name of the partner you work with during the process.

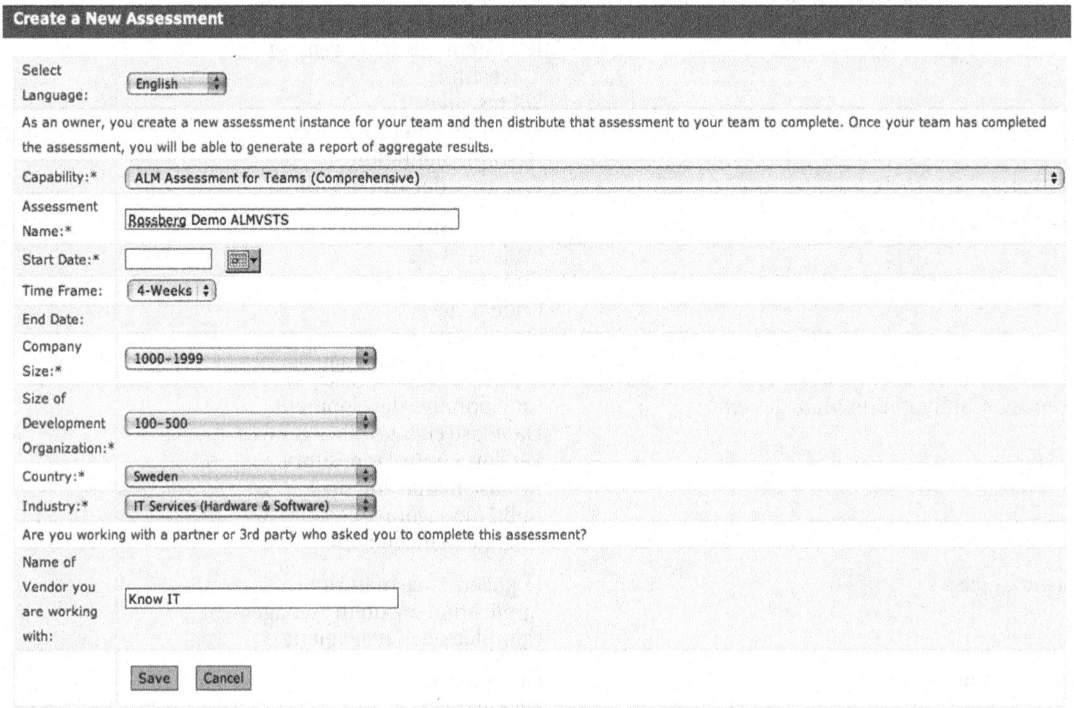

Create a New Assessment

Select Language: [English ◆]

As an owner, you create a new assessment instance for your team and then distribute that assessment to your team to complete. Once your team has completed the assessment, you will be able to generate a report of aggregate results.

Capability:* [ALM Assessment for Teams (Comprehensive) ◆]

Assessment Name:* [Rossberg Demo ALMVSTS]

Start Date:* [   ] [📅▼]

Time Frame: [4-Weeks ◆]

End Date:

Company Size:* [1000–1999 ◆]

Size of Development Organization:* [100–500 ◆]

Country:* [Sweden ◆]

Industry:* [IT Services (Hardware & Software) ◆]

Are you working with a partner or 3rd party who asked you to complete this assessment?

Name of Vendor you are working with: [Know IT]

[Save] [Cancel]

Figure 5-12. *Starting an Application Platform Capability Assessment as owner*

The creator, or *owner*, of the assessment sends an e-mail to all contributors containing a token that is entered on the assessment contributor page (see Figure 5-13).

When you enter the assessment, you'll have one page for each of the eight practice areas. As you know, these practice areas are divided into practices, and these are displayed as tabs on each practice area page. Clicking each tab displays the questions for each practice (see Figure 5-14). Some practices have only one question, and others have close to 20, so variance is great.

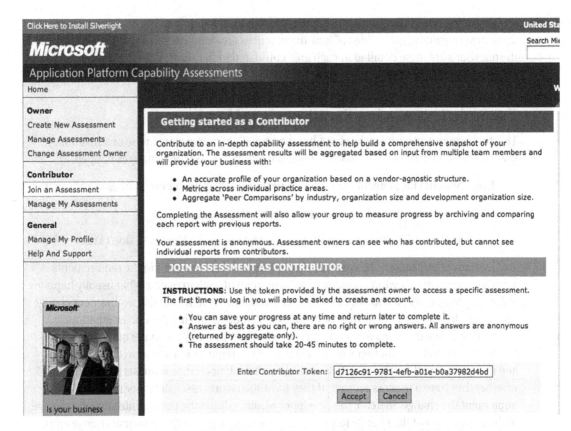

Figure 5-13. *Starting an Application Platform Capability Assessment as contributor*

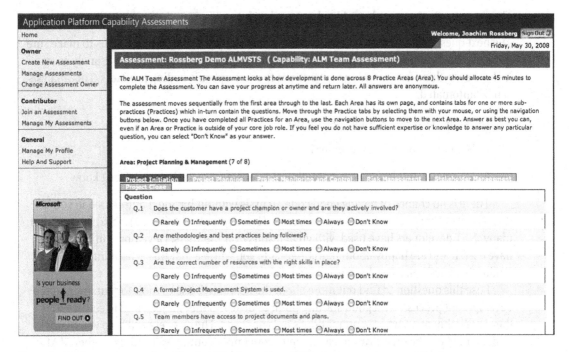

Figure 5-14. *Answering an Application Platform Capability Assessment as contributor*

So what kinds of questions can you expect from this assessment? I will show some of them next so you can get an idea of how the practices are examined. Just as you would expect, the questions are more detailed in each area compared to the shorter APO assessment. Let's take a look at two examples.

Example 1: Assessing Requirements Handling

This first example question asks about how you handle requirements in the organization. It tries to find out whether you update the original requirements when changes happen.

Requirements Engineering and User Experience—Requirements Management practice

Q: Are requirements updated as requirements change?

A: 1. Rarely, 2. Infrequently, 3. Sometimes, 4. Most times, 5. Always, 6. Don't know

In many organizations, I have seen the requirements remain fixed in the requirements specification no matter what happens to the requirement itself in reality. What usually happens is that the developers go ahead and change the functionality to reflect the requirement change (that might have come as an e-mail or by phone), without changing the documentation.

So discussing this question at the interview will tell you more than the question itself would. I try to find out whether the organization has a requirements system or application, and if they do, whether it is used. I also ask about how their change requests are handled, whether they have a process for that. If they have such a process, a developer would not implement the change. Instead, the developer would redirect the person initiating the change to the correct step of the change request process—usually by sending a formal change request to the project manager or whoever is in charge of this.

Example 2: Assessing Code Analysis

The next question I will show you covers code analysis. Code analysis enables us to make sure that developers follow a set of rules indicating how code must be written. Code analysis can include everything from naming conventions to more-specific coding practices. This analysis can be automated.

Development—Code Analysis practice

Q: Is there good static code analysis?

A: 1. Rarely, 2. Infrequently, 3. Sometimes, 4. Most times, 5. Always, 6. Don't know

There is no chance of having good code analysis without having it automated in some way. FxCop (`http://msdn.microsoft.com/en-us/library/bb429476(VS.80).aspx`) is a tool that many .NET developers have used with great results over the years. Developers in my projects have used it and are happy about it. In Chapter 6, you will see that this is built into Visual Studio Team System, so we have access to it from there.

I use this question to find out more about the company's use of tools for automating the development process. It's a good starting point to dive into this subject, and to see whether they have other areas where automation is or is not used. The answers will help you better understand how the organization can benefit from implementing VSTS (or any other ALM tool), for instance.

Viewing the Results

When all participants have answered their assessments, the assessment owner closes the assessment so that no one can enter any more information. To see the results, the owner then clicks the Generate Report button (see Figure 5-15).

Assessment Summary

Capability	Assessment Name	Status	Creation Date	Start Date	End Date	Competency Level	Action	Report
ALM Team Assessment	Rossberg Demo ALMVSTS	Finished	5/29/2008	5/29/2008	5/30/2008		Modify	Generate Report

Figure 5-15. *Generating a report for an Application Platform Capability Assessment*

The questions are rated on a five-degree scale (1, 2, 3, 4, and 5) with a sixth choice being the possibility to answer "Don't know." The best score is 5, and the lowest is 1. (This is exactly like the scoring system we had in the Swedish schools a few years ago.)

The system calculates the medium score for each capability, for each capability area, and for the whole assessment and presents it graphically to the user (see Figure 5-16).

Current report for an assessment: Rossberg Demo ALMVSTS

Capability: ALM Team Assessment

Executive Summary

Scale:

Basic	Standardized	Advanced	Dynamic
0	2	3	4	5

Contributor(s): Joachim Rossberg

The score of this assessment was a **4.26**, which places your organization at the **Dynamic** level. **8** development areas were measured during the assessment, and the final assessment score reflects the weighted average score across the **8** areas. Within each development area there are one or more practices, which contribute to the area score. The table below provides a general description of the areas covered in this assessment.

Area	Description	Score
Architecture & Design		4.31
Requirements Engineering & User Experience		3.90
Development		4.21
Software Configuration Management		4.70
Governance		4.08
Deployment & Operations		4.16
Project Planning & Management		4.47
Testing & Quality Assurance		4.24

Figure 5-16. *The report for an Application Platform Capability Assessment*

You will see a text overview of the whole assessment. Our demo here shows a pretty good score of 4.26, which puts this organization at the Dynamic level. In the table below this score, you can see the individual practice area scores. You can see the maturity level of each area as well. This information is a pretty good summary for management to look at. But if you want to see more-detailed information, you can scroll down the web page to see the score and maturity level for each practice, as seen in Figure 5-17.

Area	Practice	Score
Architecture & Design		**4.31**
	Architecture Framework	4.25
	Analysis & Design	4.17
	Database Modeling	4.50
Requirements Engineering & User Experience		**3.90**
	Elicitation	4.75
	Requirements Analysis	4.25
	Requirements Management	4.00
	Traceability	4.00
	UX Research	4.00
	UI Design and Prototyping	3.33
	UI Implementation	3.83
	End-User Documentation	3.00
Development		**4.21**
	Code Writing	4.60
	Code Analysis	4.50
	Code Reuse	4.33
	Code Reviews	3.50
	Quality Metrics	4.33
	Database Development	4.00
Software Configuration Management		**4.70**
	Collaborative Development	5.00

Figure 5-17. *A report detail from the score for each practice*

Now you can pinpoint any problem practices, which are practices with a lower score. You would look for the color red or yellow in the right column (*not* shown in Figure 5-17) to quickly identify such a practice. A manager might want to dive even deeper into the results, so farther down you will find the score for each question (see Figure 5-18). This setup gives you the capability to identify exactly where you have problems, in which practice—and then to use this information for planning corrective measures.

Area	Practice	Question	Basic	Standardized	Advanced	Dynamic
Architecture & Design						**4.31**
	Architecture Framework					**4.25**
		Architecture definition follows a formal process.				4.00
		There are tools for documenting & sharing Architecture models?				5.00
		Is the architecture well documented?				4.00
		Do major architectural decision follow a defined process?				4.00
	Analysis & Design					**4.17**
		Do all team members have access to the design diagrams?				5.00
		Are the diagrams updated throughout the project lifecycle?				5.00
		Are these diagrams stored and version controlled?				5.00
		Is forward/backward engineering performed between the code and the diagrams?				4.00
		If using UML, are Sequence Diagrams created?			3.00	
		If using UML, are State Diagrams created?			3.00	
	Database Modeling					**4.50**
		Do you use formal modeling methodologies?				5.00
		Is your Database being documented?				4.00

Figure 5-18. *You can see the score for each question in the assessment.*

You probably want to be able to download this report so you can use it internally, and Microsoft allows you to do this. You can choose to save the report in two file formats: Excel (of course) and XML (see Figure 5-19). The XML file can be used in another Microsoft tool, called the Assessment Builder, or Roadmap Builder in its earliest version. This tool helps create a roadmap showing how you can start implementing improvements on the issues the assessment has shown.

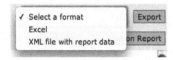

Figure 5-19. *You can export the report in two different formats.*

■**Note** You do not get any financial information in the Application Platform Capability Assessment report, only maturity scores at different levels of detail.

The Assessment Builder

The Assessment Builder, or the Roadmap Builder as it was called in its early days, is available from Microsoft (www.microsoft.com/almassessment/default.aspx) or from Incycle Software (http://preview.incyclesoftware.com/vstsroadmapbuilder.aspx). Incycle Software developed the Roadmap Builder for Microsoft.

I have always used the Assessment Builder provided by Microsoft, and as far as I can tell, both versions are exactly the same. After installation of the tool, you can access it directly from the Visual Studio IDE.

When you have finished the ALM Assessment for Teams (Comprehensive), you can export the results to an XML file as shown earlier. This file can be used as an input to the Assessment Builder (see Figure 5-20).

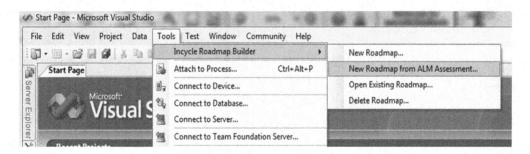

Figure 5-20. *The XML file can be used as an input to the Assessment Builder.*

After the file has been loaded, you are directed straight into the tool. If you are familiar with Visual Studio, the look and feel is the same. A toolbox is on the left, which can autohide as other toolboxes can. The canvas you have to work with has all practices and their respective areas grouped so that we can easily retrieve the ones we are looking for (see Figure 5-21). To the right is a diagram, which I will soon get back to.

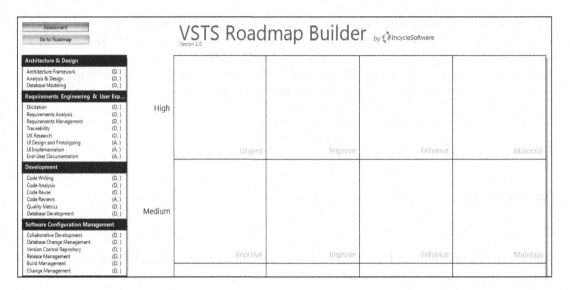

Figure 5-21. *Inside the Assessment Builder*

If you double-click on a practice, a window opens, containing information about that practice. For instance, you can see that the maturity level indicated by the assessment results is included at the bottom of the window (see Figure 5-22).

You have the option to discuss each practice in more detail with the participants if you want, and you can also change the maturity level based on new facts. There are some discussion points you can use as a starting point when deciding which level you are at. If you want, you can also add extra discussion points or information in the Observations field.

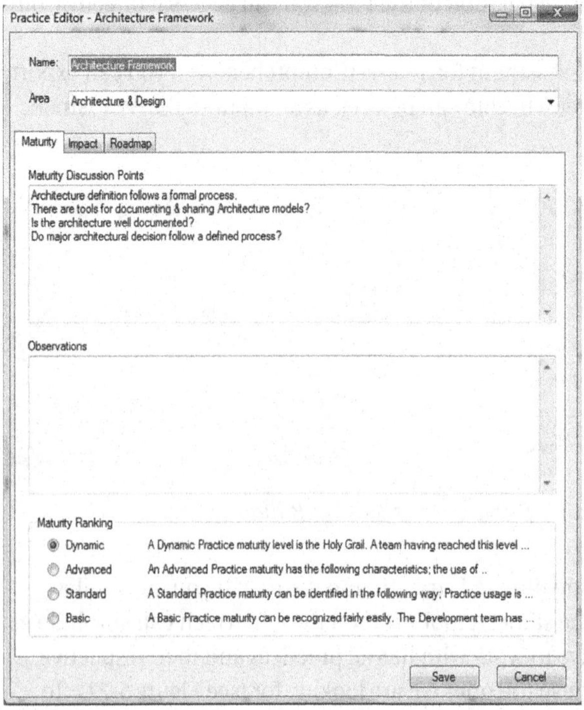

Figure 5-22. *Adding information about a practice*

If you click the Impact tab, you come to the view shown in Figure 5-23. Here you can add your own discussion points for the impact discussion, including any observations you might have and also the benefits of this practice. I use this tab as an input during discussions with my customer so that we both can agree on the maturity level they are at presently, and the impact this particular practice has on the organization.

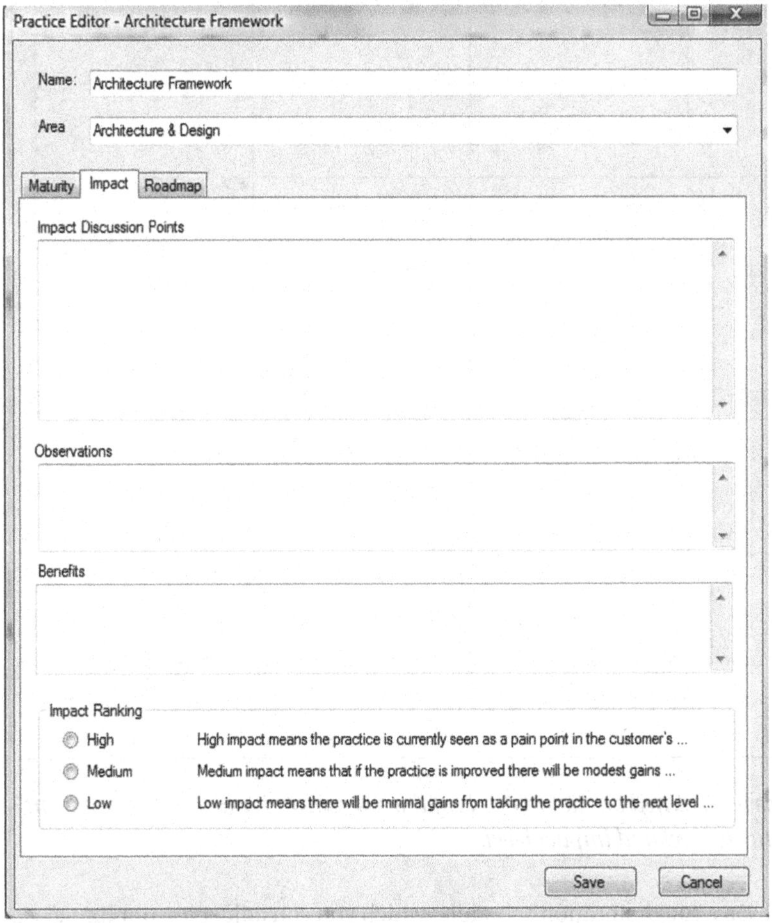

Figure 5-23. *Adding information about the impact of a practice*

When you are finished, press Save to get back to the first screen. The maturity level and the impact ranking are used by the Assessment Builder to position the practice in the right-hand diagram on the web page, as you can see in Figure 5-24.

Here you can see that Architecture Framework is at the Dynamic maturity level and that its impact is Medium. When you add information about another practice, the diagram updates. You then continue this work until all practices have had their impact level determined. Then you click Roadmap at the top-left corner to open a new window. On the left side of this window are all the practices collected below their classifications. (You can see this classification in each quadrant in Figure 5-24.)

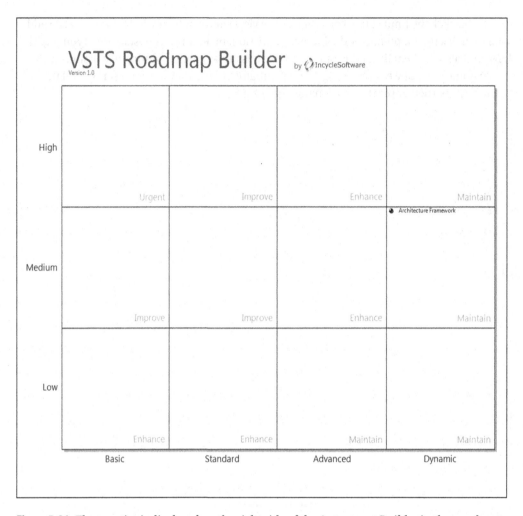

Figure 5-24. *The practice is displayed on the right side of the Assessment Builder in the quadrant determined by the maturity level and impact level.*

To the right you'll see a rough iteration schedule, which you can adjust to your liking. You can add start and finish dates for each iteration and can add or remove iterations if you want. This is the timeline you use to decide which practices you need to be working on directly (the low-hanging fruits) and which can wait for a while. You must base this decision on discussions with the customer, so the organization feels like it is ready to take the steps necessary.

By using drag-and-drop, you use the Assessment Builder to place the practices in the iteration you decide upon. You then continue working through the practices, and the iteration schedule is slowly filled with items (see Figure 5-25).

Some practices don't have to be added to the roadmap. I don't think it is a good idea, or that it is even necessary, to add all practices. When we start implementing the changes necessary to solve the lowest hanging fruits, we will soon see that other issues are solved automatically. So go easy and carefully discuss which practices you want to add to the iteration plan.

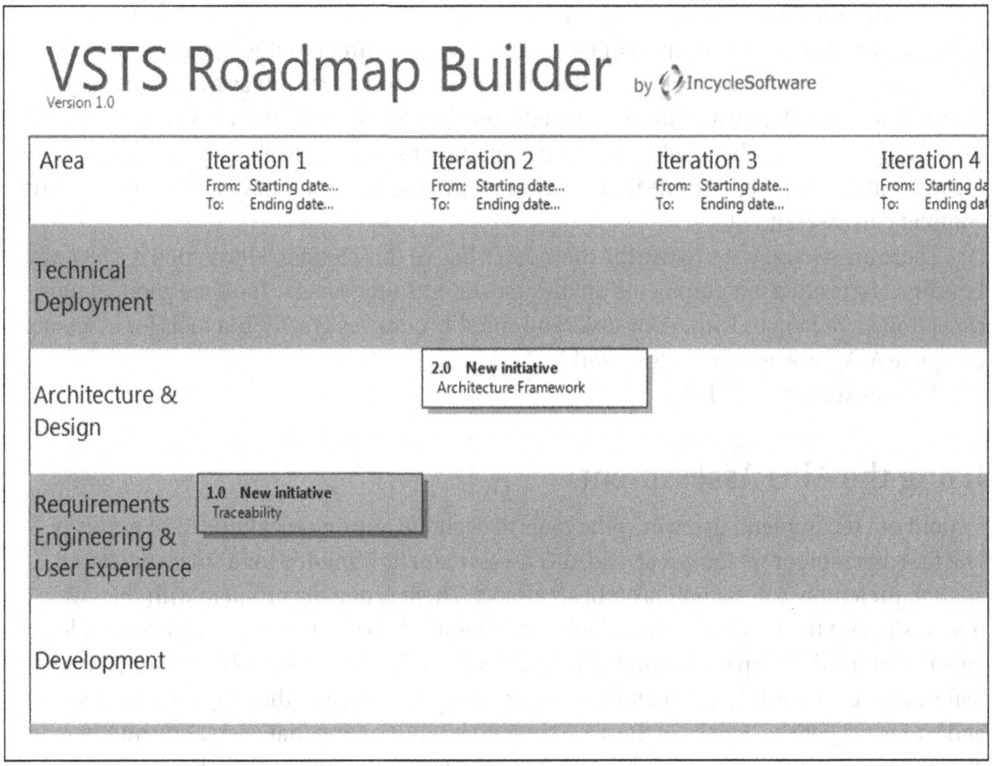

Figure 5-25. *Building up the roadmap ahead*

When you have finished, you have a rough schedule you can use as an input to plan an ALM process change project, with each iteration filled with tasks. Because neither the Assessment Builder itself nor the assessments tell you *how* to solve the issues you find, the next step is to dive deeper into the issues and see how to do that. But that is the problem of the implementation project, of course. What you now have is a nice project plan that you can take to the decision makers, and then ask them for money to go ahead, and that is a good start.

How to Use These Tools

When I assess an organization's ALM process, I need to gather as much information as possible about my client and the client's organization. This is hard work if done manually. I would say it is close to impossible to collect that amount of information from so many people in the organization in a cost-effective way, without the use of a tool.

In my earlier days, when studying psychology at the University of Gothenburg, I learned to conduct different types of interviews. The sheer amount of information given to the interviewer can be pretty overwhelming even from just one interview subject. To conduct the same interview with several subjects and then combine these answers manually would be tough. That is the reason I started to look into using a tool to help me in the process while not stopping me from getting the results and the information I needed.

I have used the questions from Microsoft's assessment tools as a basis for conducting interviews with people from ALM organizations. I have gathered people from all aspects of the ALM process, making sure both the business side and the IT side have been represented (see Chapter 2 for information on this topic). Then we have spent an hour to an hour and a half discussing these questions in one-on-one meetings. After conducting all interviews, I have completed the assessment myself and used the interview result as a basis for answering the questions. This way, I have obtained a pretty realistic view of the organizations and their ALM processes. The results have also been better and have been more accepted by the organizations when I have done it this way as compared to when I have let only one person complete an assessment.

There are several ways to use the tools described in this chapter. I have tried it a few ways. Let's first start with a few comments on the assessments themselves. Tools are good, in most cases. Tools can help us with many tasks and simplify our lives greatly, but tools for assessing a complete ALM process? Could that work?

The answer is yes, and no.

Using the APO Assessment

I would not recommend using only the tools to evaluate any organization's ALM maturity. The first assessment we looked at, the APO assessment, is intended for a single person to answer, preferably a decision maker of some sort. There is one big problem with that: we humans have a tendency to want to look a little better than we do. So the error you could get here is that the decision maker probably will answer a little too positively as compared to the reality. I have seen this happen many times, trust me. In this case, the answers will be wrong and you won't get the benefit of the assessment. I am not saying that everybody out there is giving overly optimistic answers, but the chances that that you will get a false result are greater if you trust only one person's verdict by letting that person complete the assessment alone. For this reason, I recommend an independent person doing both the assessments in the form of interviews with several persons in the organization instead of having only one person answering the web assessment.

A tool cannot get what is said between the lines, nuances that only an observer can pick up. The tool in itself is very good if we use it as a basis for discussion, but the results lack value if we let only one person speak. The financial figures we get as a result are perhaps good to have in a first discussion with the person paying for a change project, but I don't see their immediate value because the assessment itself is a bit flaky.

Using the Application Platform Capability Assessment

The second assessment, however, dives down deep. The detailing is very good in many cases, so it's miles away from the APO assessment. Some of the same problems from the preceding discussion are still valid, however. A tool cannot get all the nuances that an observer can. Hence I have the same approach here. I use the Application Platform Capability Assessment questions as a basis for interviews, and make sure that I interview people about their special field only. Architects answer architect questions, project managers answer project management questions, and so on. This approach has worked very well.

I would strongly recommend using an external partner for the assessments. It is often easier to look at an organization when there are no strings attached, and no manager to answer to.

Using the Assessment Builder

After having completed both assessments, I have used the XML file from the second assessment as an input to the Assessment Builder. I have then conducted a workshop with the customer and a few customer representatives, going through the results of the assessment. We have together gone over all issues found and prioritized them in the Assessment Builder, generating the road ahead for the organization. So when we are finished, we have a good as-is analysis and also a to-be analysis. After this, we are ready to discuss how we can take the next step(s).

Following a Schedule

Each meeting has been one or two days depending on the number of people I have to interview. I usually work with a coworker so we can get as many interviews completed in the first day as possible, and use the second day as a backup.

When doing such an ALM assessment, I have followed the schedule outlined in the rest of this section.

Meeting 1

The first meeting, held with all participants, has the following components:

- A one-hour presentation of ALM by myself or my coworker. We go over ALM at an overview level so that everybody has an understanding of the subject. Basically, we present an introduction similar to Chapters 1 and 2 of this book, covering why it is important to take control of the ALM process and what problems we try to solve.

- A half-hour presentation of the whole assessment process. I want the participants to be aware of what we are going to do and how we are going to do it. They must feel secure in talking to the interviewer and not feel intimidated by the situation.

- At least one-hour interviews with all participants. I make a schedule for the day(s) so that everybody knows where and when the interview starts. The interviews usually take longer to conduct than we expect. At first I used only a half-hour, but that soon proved to be too little. Now we are using one hour, with a half-hour break in between, giving us time if an interview goes over its scheduled time.

Between Meetings 1 and 2

After the first meeting, I have at least one week's worth of work, performing the following tasks:

- Perform the assessment based on the interviews. My coworker and I sit down and spend about a day going over the questions and answers, and discussing our own reflections. After this, we are ready to use the assessment form to input the answers.

- Complete a short presentation and report for the customer, which is handed out at meeting 2. We try to summarize the results of the assessment in a report and as a PowerPoint presentation with our own reflections included. We will also give the customer the whole output of the assessment, but this is included in the final report, after meeting 3.

Meeting 2

The second meeting with participants follows this plan:

- A one-hour presentation of the results from the first day. Discussion is allowed, to get feedback from participants. I want this presentation to trigger discussions among the participants. I have found that this is a good way to get them thinking in new directions. It is also valuable for them to question the results. Many times people who disagree with the results have been silenced by another participant giving information as to why the result is the way it is. The whole process is a start for better collaboration and openness in the organization. After such discussions, many have felt that it was a great exercise.

  I use these discussions to get more information about how open the participants are to improvements in the organization. When I am about to summarize the results of meeting 2 and propose a way ahead, I already know a little about how much the customer can swallow in terms of changes to the process. This sets the level on how many changes I can suggest as first steps, and how comprehensive these changes should be. An organization that is not as open to change will need an eye-opener—by this, I mean that I will need to suggest something that gives participants immediate return on their change efforts. That way, I can show them by example that there is lots to gain from taking control of the ALM process, and this helps them take a bigger step toward process change after that.

- A half-hour presentation of the next assessment. As with the first assessment presentation on day 1, I want participants to be aware of the process and to be at ease. It is essential that the participants feel comfortable with the interview situation and with why we are conducting the assessment.

- At least one-hour interviews with all participants. I make a schedule for the day(s) so that everybody knows where and when the interview starts. Allow plenty of room for discussions. If you have several interview subjects, you need more time than if you are interviewing only one person.

Between Meetings 2 and 3

After the second meeting, I take at least another week to do the following work:

- Perform the assessment based on the interviews. My coworker and I allow at least one day for discussing the findings of the assessment and our own reflections. This is more work than after the first assessment, and we have a lot of information at our disposal. Take your time, discuss, and reflect. To get the best result, you cannot rush. (The best result might be a low score; I mean *best* as in most true to the actual situation in the organization.) As learned earlier in this chapter, many of the questions can provide deeper information about the organization than we might believe at first glance. I try to use the information that I have gathered on one question to help me better understand the answer to a related question. For instance, a discussion about code analysis gives me information about the use of tools to automate different tasks in the development process. When my coworker and I have conducted separate interviews, we collaborate by comparing our discussions and this way get a better (more realistic) answer.

- Complete the Assessment Builder. My coworker and I use the Assessment Builder to analyze the results of the assessment, and to select the issues we would prioritize when starting a change process in the organization. We prioritize based on our experiences and come up with suggestions on how the customer should continue. We try to pick the lowest-hanging fruits, because just picking these often results in improving other issues as well. The issues are all connected, and one thing depends on another, so when something is solved, something else often improves in the process. We don't try to implement changes in all aspects of the ALM process, even if it should be required.

- Complete the presentation and report for meeting 3. As before, we create a report with the results of the assessment combined with our own reflections. We also summarize our own suggestions for how to follow the change process.

Meeting 3

The third meeting with the client follows this plan:

- At least a one-hour presentation of results from meeting 2. This time it is even more essential to allow discussions and to encourage everyone to participate. On many occasions, these discussions have been eye-openers to participants, giving them energy to move on. This sets the level on how many changes I can suggest as the first steps, and how comprehensive those changes can be. As I mentioned earlier, an organization that is not as open to change will need me to show them by example that there is lots to gain from taking control of the ALM process. This then helps them take a bigger step on the way to process change.

- A presentation(s) of areas that the organization scored low on. We allow at least one hour for this, depending on the subject(s) and number of subjects. When necessary I, or one of the Know IT experts, gives a presentation of an area we think the customer needs more input on. For example, if the customer is weak in the architect area, we let an architect give a presentation. If we need to dive into Scrum, we do that, and so on. Having a better understanding of the weak areas will help the customer see the benefits of doing something to strengthen them. I want them to be able to prioritize better in the workshop that follows these presentations. If a change is to be successful, I need the project members to feel that they have suggested the changes, not that I (or the managers) have pushed it in their faces. If you are convinced about the benefits of a change, you will more likely regard that change positively, thus giving management better feedback on their investment. We also try to look at the aggregated assessment results on the web site. Microsoft provides an aggregated view on how other companies have scored on these assessments. This provides valuable input for selecting the next steps.

- A three- to four-hour workshop prioritizing actions from Assessment Builder. This is important. My coworker and I have already presented our recommendations. Now it is time for the customer to start planning ahead. Based on the customer's needs and their resources for a change project, we select the best prioritization order for them. Then we start discussing the next steps based on that prioritization. How should they continue? Which actions give the best return on investment (lowest-hanging fruits)? Are any actions connected? In which order should they be carried out?

In a true agile manner, I have always been ready for changes or suggestions from the customer. This enables the customer to feel that they get the most value out of the time and money spent on the assessment. Sometimes questions and discussions carry on for a while, especially on day 3, and these discussions are important for the customer as well as for me to take into consideration when planning the road ahead. There is usually a tremendous amount of knowledge in the organizations that we should use.

Note Decision makers need to understand that if they do an assessment, they might need to make changes to their organization. Always make sure that your customers are ready to take steps to implement these potential changes. If they are not committed to this, the assessment is a waste of time and money for them.

Doing the assessment as a three-meeting suite has worked very well for me. The customers seem to appreciate it and say they get great value out of it. Personally I think it is a far better approach than just doing the web assessments alone and trusting their results.

Why Do an Assessment?

Why should you spend the time and money doing an ALM assessment? I think the best reason is that before implementing VSTS (or any other ALM tool for that matter), you need to know what the potential pitfalls in the ALM process really are. Every process has room for improvement, and the assessment is a very good way of finding out where improvements are best suited. You need to have as clear a picture as possible of the organization's maturity level so that you can better anticipate what actions are needed for the organization to improve and thus be more effective.

You can help your customers prioritize better if you know where the real problem is. It is easy to be home blind. You think you know where the problem is, but before doing a proper analysis, it is hard to say. Making changes to the wrong thing(s) ultimately costs a lot of money—money better spent on correcting the real problem, which in the end could save money.

An ALM process is not something to implement all at once, as you saw in the Shinsei Bank example in Chapter 4. You do it best little by little, piece by piece, starting with the lowest hanging fruits. If you just can show the decision makers the improvements of smaller actions, it becomes easier to get them to fund the rest as well.

Summary

This chapter has discussed the value of doing an ALM assessment of the ALM process before implementing VSTS (or any other ALM tool of your liking). The ALM assessments Microsoft offers are good but are best used in collaboration with an external partner carrying out the process in the form of interviews.

I have shown one way of using the assessments and the Microsoft Assessment Builder. Feel free to use it if you want, or use it as a foundation for your own methodology.

In the next chapter, we will get down to business. You will have a look at Visual Studio Team System and see how you can use this tool to enhance your ALM process.

CHAPTER 6

■■■

Application Lifecycle Management Using Visual Studio Team System

Application Lifecycle Management is an important process for organizations with IT development. A good implementation of ALM will help the organization deliver better business value to fulfill the business needs. Automating tasks by using tools such as Visual Studio Team System can support this process.

In this chapter, you'll learn how VSTS can be used to fulfill the three main pillars of ALM and the issues addressed by ALM 2.0. You'll start with an overview of ALM and of VSTS and then move on to the specifics of using VSTS for ALM.

Application Lifecycle Management Overview

As you may recall from Chapter 2, there are three main pillars of an ALM process:

- *Traceability of relationships between artifacts*: Traceability can be a major cost driver in any enterprise if not done correctly. There must be a way of tracing the requirements all the way to delivered code—through architect models, design models, build scripts, unit tests, test cases, and so on. Practices such as test-driven development and configuration management can help, and these can be automated and supported by VSTS.

- *Automation of high-level processes*: There are approval processes to control handoffs between analysis and design. There are other handoffs between build, deployment, testing, and so on. Much of this is done manually in many projects, and ALM stresses the importance of automating these tasks for a more effective and less-time-consuming process.

- *Visibility into the progress of development efforts*: Many managers and stakeholders have limited visibility into the progress of development projects. Their visibility often comes from steering group meetings during which the project manager goes over the current situation. Other interest groups such as project members may also have limited visibility of the whole project even though they are part of it. This often occurs because reporting is hard to do and can involve a lot of manual work. Daily status reports can quite simply take too much time and effort to produce, for example, especially when we have information in many repositories.

Other important topics that ALM 2.0 addresses are as follows:

- *Improving collaboration*: Collaboration is needed between teams, team members, stakeholders, and users, just to mention a few relationships. When development is spread around the world in different locations, collaboration can be hard to manage without the help of a proper tool.

- *Closing the gap between IT and business*: The big gap between IT and the business side of an organization is another big problem for organizations, preventing us from delivering the greatest business value we can achieve in our projects.

- *Using one tool*: The complexity of using several tools for solving project issues as a team member can be tough and costly as well. Switching between tools can be a cost driver. Using one tool enabling us to add plug-ins and to use more features directly in our ordinary GUI instead of switching between applications is preferable. So if you have several roles in a project, you can still use one tool to get the job done.

- *Enhancing role switching*: ALM also addresses the potential to use one tool when switching among different roles in a project. In many cases, project members play several roles in projects. A developer, for instance, might also work with tests or databases. If that person can use the same GUI for all tasks, there will be minimum overhead for switching between these roles.

Visual Studio Team System Overview

VSTS has come a long way in fulfilling the ALM 2.0 vision but it does not (yet) cover all practices. And that's okay. The most important thing is knowing that VSTS is an open and extensible product that will let us adjust its features to our needs and add the things it might lack at this point. It is also important to know that Microsoft is spending a lot of time, energy, and money on developing this product further. It is not a toolset that will go away; it is one of the most important toolsets in the Microsoft ecosystem.

There are several parts of Visual Studio Team System. If you look beneath the surface, you can see that VSTS consists of a server, Team Foundation Server, and a suite of client product editions.

Team Foundation Server

You can see that the heart of VSTS is *Team Foundation Server (TFS)*, as shown in Figure 6-1.

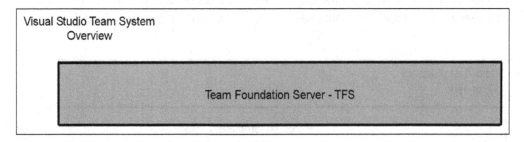

Figure 6-1. *Visual Studio Team System—an overview*

TFS exposes different functions and services for project managers, version control, reporting, build and work item tracking (see Figure 6-2). You will soon take a look at all of these in more detail. Not shown in this picture is that VSTS and TFS use Microsoft SQL Server 2005 as its data repository.

■**Note** *Work items* are tasks of different kinds in VSTS. We have work items for requirements, bugs, general tasks, and so on. To put it simply, a work item is a piece of work that must be completed in a project. The work item tracking system is one of the core parts of VSTS for our ALM process implementation.

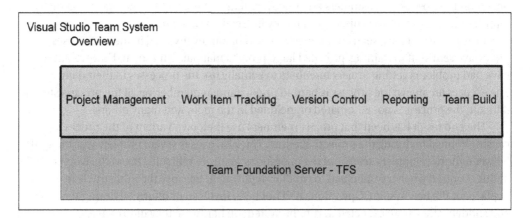

Figure 6-2. *The heart of VSTS*

Process Template

What keeps all of these services together is the *process template* (see Figure 6-3). This is a very interesting part of VSTS. The template helps us visualize and automate tasks and steps that the process includes. It helps us by providing document templates for requirements specs, test cases, scenarios, handoffs, and other artifacts we should produce.

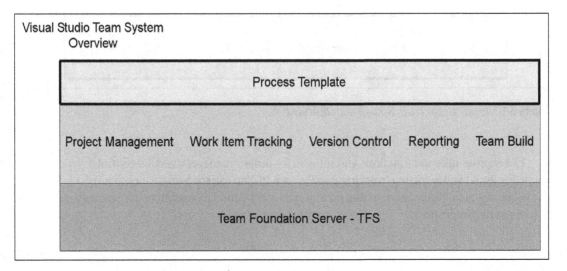

Figure 6-3. *The process template*

Most companies use some kind of process for their development or ALM. Even though some companies don't think they have a process, they do. The process might not be written down, but the company still has ways of doing things that in reality are the process—for instance, naming conventions, where to store builds, how to handle change requests, and so on. When I sit down with customers and uncover all these little habits that together actually represent their process, they discover that they in fact do have a process.

In many cases I have seen companies with lots of money invested in their processes. They have sent staff to training, provided large process manuals, and so on. However, they have had problems getting project members to actually use the processes in their daily work. The excuses are many: the process is hard to understand, remembering all the process steps is difficult, the process is not automated or included in the tools, and many others.

The end result has been that project members use their own variant of the process, causing confusion during the project's lifetime. This also causes severe problems, as handoffs between the development team and the operations team are difficult. One of the worst cases of this occurred when a system had to wait for deployment because the infrastructure wasn't in place for the new system. Operations had not been involved or informed during the project and suddenly they were expected to run the system on hardware they didn't have.

In VSTS, we can implement our development process as a template that will be mandatory for all new projects. When we create a new project, we also create a new instance of the process template. And we don't have to stop at the development project level either. We can implement most parts of our ALM cycle in the template as well, enabling us to take advantage of VSTS all along the way. The template helps us visualize and automate tasks and steps that the process includes. It helps us by providing document templates for requirements specs, test cases, scenarios, handoffs, and other artifacts we should produce.

The template also provides information about which reports we have available for each new project—reports that we use to retrieve information about the status of our projects and many other things. The template also contains information about one of the most important core parts of VSTS: the work items. These can be adjusted as needed so we can make sure they contain the information the organization must have included with them. This information could be state information for a bug, for instance, such as Active, Resolved, or Closed.

This template is so flexible that we can develop and implement our own process, we can choose to use the two versions of Microsoft Solutions Framework that Microsoft supplies, we can use a third-party template such as Scrum for Team System from Conchango, or we can choose to customize the MSF templates to our own liking. We can also have several process templates in TFS so we can use different templates for different projects. Because VSTS really is not used to its full potential without the process templates, I cannot stress enough that you should consider which templates you want to use and the information you want them to include.

VSTS Editions

Our technical team members can use one of the Visual Studio Team System editions. There are currently four of these, with a fifth version called Visual Studio Team System Suite incorporating all of the others (see Figure 6-4). The four editions are as follows:

- *Visual Studio Team System Architecture Edition*: This is specifically made for architects of various kinds.

- *Visual Studio Team System Development Edition*: This is the edition that developers use.

- *Visual Studio Team System Test Edition*: This is intended for testers and has great tools covering most aspects of testing in a modern environment.

- *Visual Studio Team System Database Edition*: This is the latest addition to the team suite. The target group for this edition is database developers as well as other developers needing access to the database functionality in a smooth way.

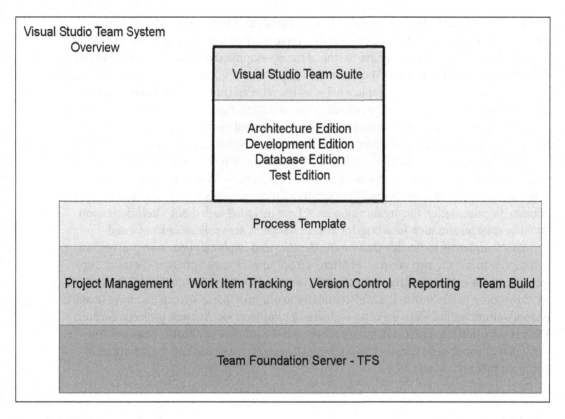

Figure 6-4. *VSTS team suite*

Web Access

All projects in VSTS have their own web sites available. By using Windows SharePoint Services, a *team project portal* is created when the project itself is created. By using this portal, we can access some of the functionality in TFS. An alternative is available as a free download from Microsoft: *Team System Web Access*. This gives us much better support for all features in TFS. Web Access lets us access the parts of VSTS that are available from inside Visual Studio, but from an easier-to-use interface, especially for nontechnical project members. Figure 6-5 shows how Web Access is related to the other parts of VSTS.

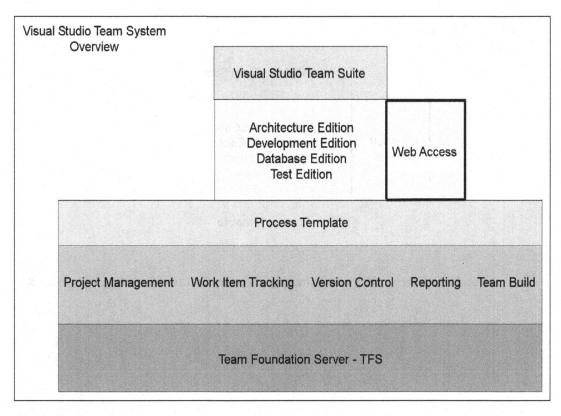

Figure 6-5. *VSTS web access through a project portal and Web Access*

My customers use a team project portal primarily to provide access to reports and documents for nontechnical people not used to the Visual Studio interface. When we want to give an external user (such as a customer or remote stakeholder) access to work item creation and editing, or another more advanced task, we usually use Web Access.

Microsoft Office

Microsoft Office (see Figure 6-6) can be used by project managers, for example, wishing to use tools that are familiar to them, such as Microsoft Project and Microsoft Office Excel, during a project. Basic integration with Office tools is included in VSTS 2008, and this will improve over time.

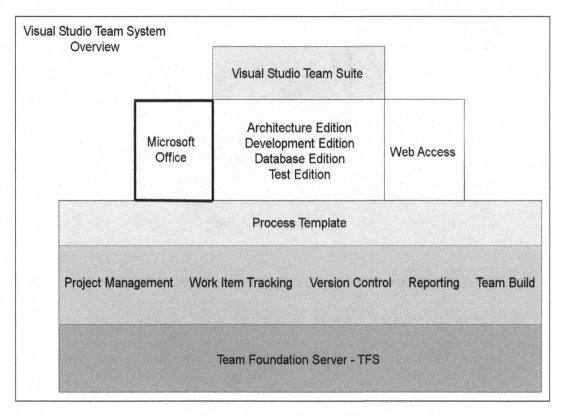

Figure 6-6. *VSTS integrates with Microsoft Office.*

Add-Ins

One thing I should mention that is not included in Figure 6-6 is *Team Explorer*. This tool can be used as an add-in to Visual Studio, and gives access to TFS directly from within Visual Studio. From here you can open reports, add new tasks (called *work items* in VSTS), and run queries against the TFS database.

VSTS is a flexible tool, as I have mentioned. It is also very *extensible* (see Figure 6-7) as all functionality can be accessed via web services. This is a very nice feature that enables us to build our own support for VSTS in other applications as well. Many third-party vendors have done this, and a wide array of add-ins and tools are available. My favorites come from Teamprise, a company that has built add-ins to Eclipse so that we can use TFS features in our Java development environment as well. Teamprise also provides Team Explorer for the Mac, which is helpful to me when I travel around carrying only my MacBook Air but still need access to our TFS servers.

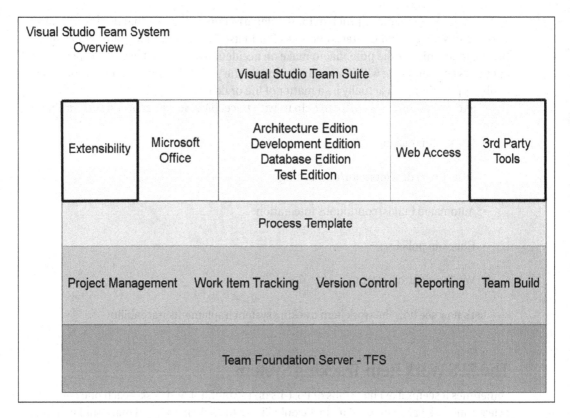

Figure 6-7. *VSTS is extensible.*

Traceability

Having traceability in our ALM processes is key to the successful delivery and maintenance of our applications and systems. In Chapter 1, I told you about a company that stopped making changes to its systems just because no one ever knew where a change (or bug fix) might have its impact. We don't have to have such a situation.

At the Swedish Road Administration, a new version of our system suddenly made old bug fixes disappear. The vendor of that piece of software did not have control over its different versions and did not have a good testing strategy. If the vendor had used automated tests, for instance, they would have discovered broken tests for the bug fix when the fix itself was not included in the next release. By checking which work items were associated with the failed test(s), the vendor would have been able to see which of these contained the problem. This would have indicated why they created the test in the first place, so they could have more easily fixed the problem. This traceability would greatly improve their code.

And if they had used a good configuration management process, they would also have had the capability to trace all versions where the bug fix needed to be inserted, so they wouldn't forget to include it in the coming releases.

This has been a serious problem for the departments of the SRA that use the software. The Traffic Management Center sometimes found itself with no working phones because of the upgrade. This has the potential to make an accident worse than it already is, because the operators communicate with the rescue team and the police. Having communications suddenly stop working can actually be a matter of life or death.

There are several ways VSTS can help us with traceability so we can avoid such problems:

- Work item tracking

- Test-driven development/unit testing

- Automated builds/continuous integration

- Check-in policies

- Version-control system

Let's now see how the work item tracking system implements traceability.

The TFS Work Item Tracking System

Sometimes it seems like I have tons of Post-its on my monitor and desk—each one containing at least one task I am supposed to do. I would like to track them in a tool that could help me, but often it just isn't possible. It could be that some tasks are connected with one project, others with another. I have tried writing them all down in an Excel sheet and saving that to my computer. But soon I have found that this spreadsheet is located at my laptop, my customer computer, my desktop, at another customer computer, and so on. And I have no idea which one is the current version.

I know, I know. Maybe I should have better structure in my life, but things are as they are, and I try to get by anyway. But the problem exists for me and it can be a real problem sometimes when I have no clue as to which version I should trust.

The same thing is often visible in projects. Project managers have their to-do lists for a project, and they all have their own way of keeping them updated. Let's say a PM uses Excel to keep track of the tasks—the status of tasks, whom they are assigned to, and so on. How can the PM keep the team updated with the latest to-do list? If the PM chooses to e-mail it, chances are that some won't save the new version to disk or will just miss it in the endless stream of e-mails coming into the mailbox. Soon there are various versions floating around, and things are generally a mess.

One way to solve this could be to use a project web site running on Microsoft Office SharePoint Server or some other tool like that. This could help, although we could still be in trouble if people forget to save changes or check in the document after they have updated it.

Another problem may occur if, for example, an Excel sheet is updated by a tester who discovers a bug and changes the status of one entry in the task list to indicate that a developer should look at the task again and solve the bug. How can we alert the developer that the bug exists? We would want this action to take place automatically, right? That would be hard if we used only an Excel sheet. The same thing occurs the other way around. When a developer has fixed a bug, we want the tester to be alerted that the problem has been resolved, so the tester can then check whether the bug can be closed.

What about requirements traceability? If the only place we keep track of the connection between requirements and the code is in a document, how do we know that the document is really updated? Can we trust that information?

Even if we purchase a separate tool to help us keep track of tasks, it would still be a separate tool for all categories of team members. There are tools for bug tracking, requirements management, test management, and so on—the list can go on for a while. Chances are that someone will forget to update the tool because it takes too long to open or is too difficult to work in or any other excuse for not doing the update. This could cost the project lots of money and time.

Work Items

In TFS we have a task-tracking system at our service. The core of this system is represented by the tasks themselves, which as I said earlier are called *work items*. A work item can be pretty much what we want it to be. It can be a bug, a requirement of some sort, a general to-do item, and so on. All work items have a unique ID that helps us keep track of the places it is referenced (see Figure 6-8). The ID lets us follow one work item, let's say a requirement, from its creation to its implementation as a piece of executable software (component).

Work items provide a great way for us to simplify our task management in a project while at the same time enabling traceability. No more confusion as to which version of the task list is the current one. No more manual labor for gathering status reports on work progress that are used only at steering group meetings. Now we have a solution that lets us collaborate more easily with our teams and enables all members and stakeholders to view status reports whenever they want. We can also more easily collaborate with people outside the project group by adding work items via the Web.

Query Results: 16 results found

ID	Work...Type	Rank	State	Assigned To	Title
2509	Bug		Active	Mikael Waltersson	Nytt modem med IDREG VALUE ="" kan inte
2383	Task		Active	Joachim Rossberg	Set up: Set Permissions
2384	Task		Active	Joachim Rossberg	Set up: Migration of Source Code
2385	Task		Active	Joachim Rossberg	Set up: Migration of Work Items
2386	Task		Active	Joachim Rossberg	Set up: Set Check-in Policies
2387	Task		Active	Joachim Rossberg	Set up: Configure Build
2388	Task		Active	Joachim Rossberg	Set up: Send Mail to Users for Installation ar
2389	Task		Active	Joachim Rossberg	Create Vision Statement
2390	Task		Active	Joachim Rossberg	Set up: Create Project Description on Team
2391	Task		Active	Joachim Rossberg	Create Personas
2392	Task		Active	Joachim Rossberg	Define Iteration Length
2393	Task		Active	Joachim Rossberg	Create Test Approach Worksheet including
2394	Task		Active	Joachim Rossberg	Brainstorm and Prioritize Scenarios List
2395	Task		Active	Joachim Rossberg	Brainstorm and Prioritize Quality of Service
2396	Task		Active	Joachim Rossberg	Set up: Create Project Structure
2397	Task		Active	Joachim Rossberg	Create Iteration Plan

Figure 6-8. *Each work item has a unique ID.*

TFS is so flexible in this regard that it lets us tailor the work items as we want them to be. The work items can contain information in different *fields* that define the data to be stored in the work item. This means that each field will have a name and a data type. Data types supported in fields are the primitive data types such as string, integer, and double, as well as some complex types such as DateTime, PlainText, HTML, and others. System fields are one example of a field (or more correct, a label for a group of fields) that must be present in every work item type, and represent the minimal recommended subset of fields that any custom work item template should contain. Having such a common subset allows reusing basic Work Item Query Language (WIQL) queries or reports from predefined templates for your custom templates.

All work items can have different information attached to them. We can have information about whom the work item is assigned to and the status of the work at the moment (for example, a bug could be open, closed, under investigation, resolved, and so on). The State field can be modified so that each work item type can have its own state mechanism. This is logical because a bug probably goes through other states than a general task goes through, for instance. We can also attach documents to the work item and link one work item to other work items. We can create a hierarchy of work items if we want. Let's say that we implement a requirement as a work item and this requirement contains many smaller tasks. Then we can have the requirement itself at the top and nest the other requirements below that so we know which work items belong to which requirement.

When a bug is discovered, for instance, we can quickly follow the original requirement by its work item ID and see in which places of the code we might have to make some fixes. We can also see the associated work items so that we can evaluate whether other parts of the code need to be changed as a result of this bug fix.

Because TFS saves information about the work item on the data tier, we can see the history of the work item. We can see who created it, who resolved it, who closed it, and so on. The information in the databases can be used for display on reports, allowing us to tailor these depending on our needs. One report could show the status of all bugs, for instance. Stakeholders can see how many open bugs exist, how many are resolved, and much, much more. It is completely up to us how we choose to use the work items.

For those of us familiar with and used to working with pivot tables, we can use Excel as well to drill down into the information in the VSTS data warehouse. I have coworkers who think it is better to use Excel to directly connect to these tables and who use very detailed information in their reports.

The Work Item Form

The work items are defined in the project template in VSTS. The template and thus the work item types are defined in a set of XML files stored on the TFS server. The XML file(s) for our work items define what information the work item will include on its form in VSTS (see Figure 6-9).

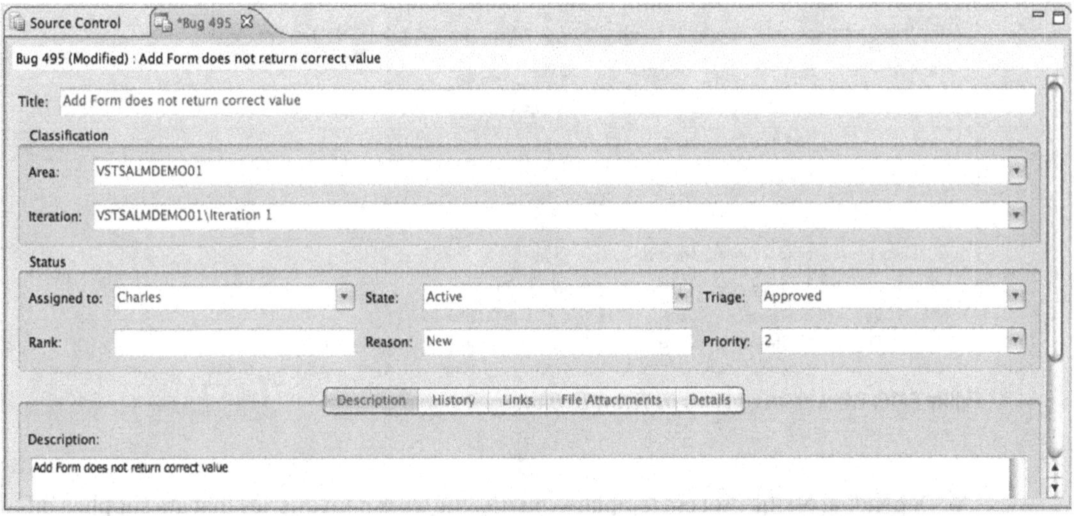

Figure 6-9. *The Bug form in MSF for Agile*

As you can see in Figure 6-9, the Bug work item type in MSF for Agile includes fields for many aspects of the bug. We can assign the bug to a specific person, set state (status), set triage, set priority, and much more. We can also add a description of the problem and attach files such as screenshots of the bug. There are other options as well, but I will not cover them here.

The fields on the work item form can have properties set for them. We can let a field be read-only, required, automatically populated, and so on. Because we can also change what information is included on this form by editing the XML, we can make it include the information that we want.

I have heard some customers say that they have had problems using the process templates that Microsoft provides because the information required to fill in the forms is not the information they want to track or record. Instead of changing the work item types, they have tried to adapt to the work items. Don't make this mistake! If you need other information besides what is included in the templates, or if you need the information in another way, change the template. That's the whole point of having an open and flexible solution such as TFS. We can adjust the tool to fit our needs. I have, for instance, seen the Bug work item that Microsoft uses, and it looks nothing like what is included in any of the templates you get with VSTS. Instead Microsoft encourages us to adjust the tool to our needs. This includes adjusting the work items.

Work Item Queries

In Team Explorer, we can query the work item databases (see Figure 6-10) by using a new query language Microsoft provides: Work Item Query Language (WIQL), which has a SQL-like construct. Figure 6-10 shows an example of a query returning all active bugs, for instance. From Team Explorer we can create new queries or modify existing ones.

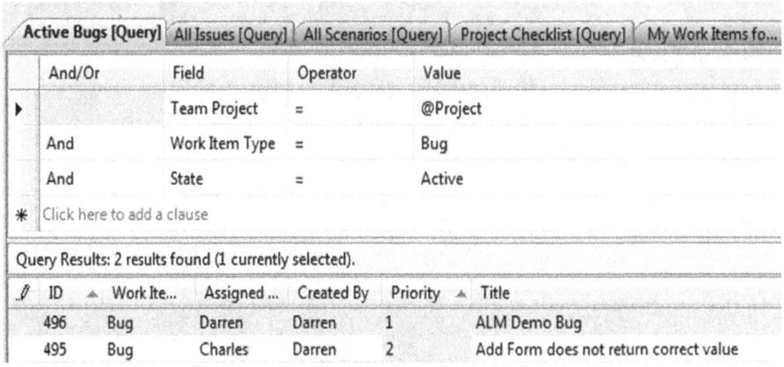

Figure 6-10. *Work item queries in Team Explorer*

Depending on the process template you use, the work item queries that are supplied differ quite a bit. Conchango's Scrum for Team System has different work item queries than MSF for Agile, for instance. When we have used the Scrum template in some of my projects, we have found it necessary to add new work item types because the organization needed these for their ALM process. Queries to get information about these new work item types naturally don't exist, so we have had to make these queries ourselves. Some of these queries have been built during the projects when the need arose, and many of these have later been included in the process template so they are now part of all new projects.

Conclusions on the Work Item Tracking System

The work item tracking system is one of the core components of VSTS. This system enables us to create work items, or units of work, and can be used to enable traceability. We can use the work items included with VSTS from the beginning, or we can choose to adjust these to our needs, or even create our own work item types. Each work item instance has a unique ID (as you saw earlier in Figure 6-8) that we can attach to the things we do in VSTS. This enables us to follow one work item—let's say a requirement, for example—from its creation to its implementation as a piece of executable software (component). We can also associate one work item with others and build a hierarchy of work items.

When a bug is discovered, we can quickly follow the original requirement by its work item ID and see in which places of the code we might have to make some fixes. We can also see the associated work items so that we can evaluate whether other parts of the code also need to be changed as a result of this bug fix.

If we implement a requirement as a work item, we can use the work item ID to track this requirement through source code and to the final build of the executable system. By requiring all developers to add one or more work item IDs to the check-in using a check-in policy, we can enable this traceability.

My suggestion is that you look closely at the work item types supplied by Microsoft. Then you can decide which of these you can use for yourself and which you might adjust to suit your organization's needs. If none of the ones supplied can be used, you have the capability to create your own work item types. Use this opportunity! Don't adjust your way of working to the MSF template. Adjust VSTS to your needs instead.

Configuration Management Using VSTS

In any (development) organization, we need to have control of the versions of our systems we have in production. If we don't have that, the overall ALM process will suffer, because we will suddenly lose traceability. This will make it harder to implement changes and bug fixes, because we won't know which versions we need to update. One example of this is the Swedish Road Administration, as mentioned earlier.

Without the help of a proper tool, we soon will get lost in the variety of applications we have. VSTS can help us with this in many ways. After a brief description of software configuration management, I will cover three of the most important concepts that have great support in TFS and Visual Studio tools:

- Version control

- Release management

- Build management

What Is Software Configuration Management (SCM)?

In software engineering, software configuration management (SCM) is the task of tracking and controlling changes in the software. This is exactly what the vendor described in the preceding section did not have. Configuration management practices include revision control and the establishment of baselines, and are very important.

The more complex our solutions become, the more important it is to make sure we have control of the versions of the applications we have in our organization.

There are several goals of SCM, including the following:

- *Configuration identification*: Ensuring that we know what code we are we working with

- *Configuration control*: Controlling the release of a product and its changes (version control)

- *Build management*: Managing the process and tools used for builds

- *Defect tracking*: Making sure every defect has traceability back to the source

If these issues are not covered by our ALM process, we could very soon find ourselves in a much worse situation than what the SRA finds itself in from time to time. It is crucial for the development teams to have full control over which versions of the applications exist, which are in production, and where. This topic is closely related to the portfolio management team, and generally a big company has one or more persons devoted to keeping track of this. The SRA has no other option but to keep working with the vendor mentioned earlier because no replacement application is available on the market today. But the reputation of the vendor is going down. Because the vendor is involved in many other development efforts at the SRA, the reputation slowly but steadily affects their ability to remain as a supplier. We don't want that to happen to our own companies.

Version Control and Release Management in VSTS

As I have said, it is common when we develop software to have multiple versions of the same software at different places. Software developers often work on the same code base doing updates to the code simultaneously. This is probably one of the problems with the software vendor I mentioned earlier. When this vendor performs bug fixes, they make the fix to one version of the code and forget to add it to the application's main code base. Thus they find themselves with one version of the code that is the main code base, but without the hot fixes the developers produce. If we are unlucky, we can have multiple versions of the system at multiple customers, but only some of these versions have the bug fix. As you can see, it is important to have a way to retrieve and run different versions of the software to determine in which version(s) the bug exists. It is also desirable to be able to merge a fix into the other versions when necessary.

Using the version-control system in VSTS, we can manage and control multiple revisions of the same information in our projects. This information can be source code, documents, work items, and other important information that we want to add version control to. When we want to work on an item under source control, we check it out to our local computer so we can start working on it. When work is done and tested, we check in our changes so the version on the server is updated.

There are some important concepts I want to address before moving on:

- Workspace

- Changeset

- Branching

- Merging

- Shelving

Workspace

When we check out code from source control, we retrieve a client-side copy of the files and folders from a specific path on the server. They are placed in what is called a *workspace*, an area on our hard drive that is used for editing, adding new items, deleting, moving, and managing the checked-out items. The workspace is not accessible to anybody else in the project, only to its creator.

No change is uploaded to the server until we check it in again. This means that the developer can do what he or she wants to these items without affecting the version on the server. The developer keeps the items in the workspace until they are tested by the developer. Then the developer can check them in so that everybody else can retrieve the updated files.

Sometimes we need to test a specific solution to our code. Say someone discovers that a bug might exist in the code we are working on, for example, but wants the bug verified before any attempts are made to fix it. We can create a new workspace, download the same code you have in your first workspace, and start looking for the bug. This does not affect the code in the first workspace, because it is in a separate location on the hard drive. (Just don't forget which workspace you are working in; that might create some problems.)

After verifying that the bug is real, you can let the other developer fix the bug. After the bug is fixed, you can update the first workspace by running a Get Latest command from the Version Control menu in Visual Studio to retrieve the other developer's changes If the changes affect the code you were working on, you can merge the changes into your files. If any changes to the same lines of code have been made, they will be highlighted with a warning from the TFS version-control system. You can then compare the two versions of code and choose whether you want to complete the merge.

Changeset

A *changeset* is a logical container for everything that is related to a single check-in. You will find files and folder versions, links to related work items, check-in notes, and much, much more information here (see Figure 6-11). All changesets get a unique ID from the TFS server so that you can find them later. The combination of a work item ID and the changeset ID that occurs when a developer associates a check-in with a work item improves traceability. You can immediately see which changesets were included in the development of a specific work item. And in turn, you can see which work items a specific changeset was associated with.

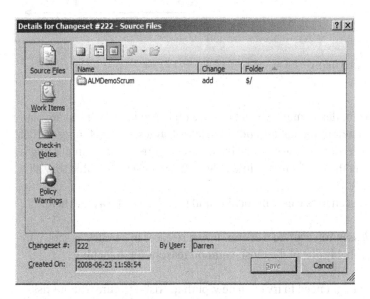

Figure 6-11. *Changeset in VSTS*

Branching

Branching lets us have two or more parallel versions of a source control project. I already covered one example briefly. Here's another: Let's say that you have an application that reaches Release 1 (see Figure 6-12). This application will continue to live on in production, but management wants the development team to start working on Release 2. You branch a copy of Release 1 and name that *Release 2*, so you have two parallel main lines of the code: Release 1 and the branch, Release 2.

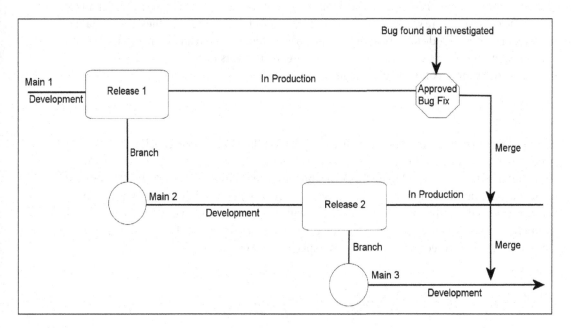

Figure 6-12. *Branching version-controlled items*

When Release 2 is ready for deployment, you let this live on in production. If you are planning a Release 3, you make a new branch of the code in Release 2 and start developing on that. Now you have three parallel versions of the code, all having some parts in common. If a bug is found in Release 1, you can let the bug fix merge into Release 2 and Release 3 so that they all have this fix.

Let's take a look at some scenarios where branching and merging can be a great help:

- *Isolating different releases:* You want to work on several releases in parallel, as shown in Figure 6-12. This is probably one of the most common reasons for branching.

- *Isolating features:* You might need to try out a new, perhaps risky, feature without risking the stability of current release. Branching can allow the developers working on this feature to work on their own branch.

- *Isolating teams:* Some companies let teams have their own branch of the code so that they won't interfere with each other during development.

- *Isolating integration*: If you merge source code from one branch into another, there's always a risk that you will create a new bug or make the code unstable in some way. By first trying the merge on an integration branch, you can make sure that you don't do this (if you do, problems will show up on the integration branch). After you have a stable branch, you can merge the changes from the integration branch back into the source branch and the other branches. The integration branch is more or less a staging area where you can try out the changes first.

This is a simple example of branching just to introduce this area to those of you who have not had the opportunity to dive into this yourselves. Branching can get really complex and is something that should be thought of in the ALM process. Make sure that a good branching strategy is in place.

Branching involves a few things:

- When we create a new branch, we take a snapshot (at a certain point in time, or at a certain state of the code) of the code so that we have an isolated version of it. This is called a *child branch*. The source is hence called the *parent branch*.

- It also involves containing and stabilizing changes in the isolated snapshot of the parent branch.

- We merge changes to code between branches. We can merge in all directions: from parent to child and from child to parent.

Merging

In Figure 6-12, you saw that a fix merged from Release 1 to Release 2 and 3. But a merge doesn't have to be just the merging of a fix. You can also take all things that have changed in one branch and merge those into other branches or the main line. These changes can include name changes, file edits, file additions and deletes, undeletes, and so on. TFS keeps track of all changes in all branches so that this can work.

Shelving

Let's say that you are working on some code when your child's day care calls and says that you need to come by early to pick up your child because of the flu. The code you are working is by no means finished when you need to rush off, so you don't want to check it in because that would ruin the nightly build. You need a place where you can securely store the code until you can continue working on it: you can use shelving. *Shelving* means that you store what you are working on as a *shelveset* (compare this to changeset) on the TFS server. This means that you get all the security of your server, so you don't have to worry about your development environment. Shelvesets are not versioned, however, so you have only the version that is saved. This means that you shouldn't work too long on a shelveset before checking in the code. When you arrive the next day, you can unshelve the shelveset and continue working again. If you can't return the next day, one of the other developers can retrieve the shelveset and continue working on your code. Then this developer checks the code in when it is done.

Shelving is also great for code reviews, when a developer reviews another developer's code. You can use it for fixing a bug as well, enabling you to hold current work on something else while you fix the bug. Microsoft states the following scenarios for shelving:[1]

- *Interrupt*: When you have pending changes that are not ready for check-in but you need to work on a different task, you can shelve your pending changes to set them aside.

- *Integration*: When you have pending changes that are not ready for check-in but you need to share them with another team member, you can shelve your pending changes and ask your team member to unshelve them.

- *Review*: When you have pending changes that are ready for check-in and have to be code-reviewed, you can shelve your changes and inform the code reviewer of the shelveset.

- *Backup*: When you have work in progress that you want to back up but are not ready to check in, you can shelve your changes to have them preserved on the Team Foundation Server.

- *Handoff*: When you have work in progress that is to be completed by another team member, you can shelve your changes to make a handoff easier.

Visual Studio includes a tool for working with source control called *Source Control Explorer* (see Figure 6-13). From here you can check in and check out the version-controlled items easily. The Source Control Explorer is completely integrated into the Visual Studio (VS) GUI.

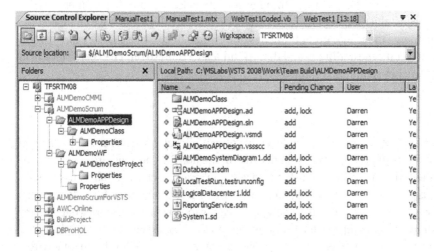

Figure 6-13. *Source Control Explorer*

---

1. Microsoft, "Team Foundation Server Branching Guide," www.codeplex.com/BranchingGuidance.

In the Source Control Explorer, you can perform all the tasks included in the version-control system of VSTS:

- Browse team projects and workspaces. By doing this, you can easily see what is under source control.

- See whether all items are synchronized. If not, you can synchronize with the server so your local workspace is updated. The synchronization is done by issuing the Get Latest command from the menu.

- View pending changes that have not been checked in. You can also check in or undo a check-in from here.

- Check out files or folders for edit.

- Lock a checked-out item so no one can edit it at the same time as you do.

- Delete, undelete, rename, and move folders or files.

- Resolve conflicts when, for example, two developers have updated the same code.

- Shelve and unshelve source code.

- Look at the history of items under source control. You can also compare versions of the same file or folder. If you need to, you can retrieve a specific version for closer examination.

- Branch and merge source control team projects, files, and folders.

- Apply labels to changesets. For instance, you could label a changeset with the name *Release 1*. Later you can search for all items included in the label Release 1 if you need to. A label is a marker that you can attach to a set of unrelated files and folders in the Team Foundation version-control server. You can use the label to simplify their retrieval to a workspace for either development or build purposes. Therefore, a label is like a changeset or date/time to which and from which you can add and remove files and folders or change the versions of the items therein.

The version-control features of Visual Studio Team System are powerful. They are fully integrated into the GUI, which is something that ALM 2.0 prescribes as well. If you want to, you can access some of the features from Web Access as well. Many people want to use the command line for their work, and VSTS enables them to use the command line for working with version control as well.

However, if you do want to use Visual Studio to access the TFS version-control system, you can do that. The extensibility of VSTS makes this possible. One example of this is the Teamprise suite of client applications that can access TFS, including the version-control system. Teamprise has developed an Eclipse plug-in that lets users access TFS from Eclipse instead. Teamprise also lets you access TFS from Mac OS X and Linux command lines. This way, you can more easily integrate different development platforms in a TFS project. You still will use the TFS repository, and have the ability to get reports and other information directly from TFS.

Build Management

A *build* is basically the process of taking the source code and all other items necessary in an application and building it into executable software. Team Foundation Build is the build engine in VSTS and executes the build process as defined by the VSTS settings. Team Foundation Build is built on the Microsoft build engine (MSBuild), which is the build platform for Microsoft and Visual Studio. You can attach unit tests to a build process so that you automatically run these every time the build process kicks off. Team Foundation Build is fully integrated into the Visual Studio GUI so you don't have to use separate tools for handling these tasks.

Team Foundation Build supports several types of builds:

- *Full builds*: We build everything in our project. This can be resource- and time-consuming.

- *Partial builds*: We build only one or more parts of the system.

- *Nightly builds*: Many projects build the system during nighttime. Especially if the build process takes a long time, this might be very handy.

- *Custom builds*: We can use the extensibility of VSTS to create our own build types, or edit any of the existing ones.

- *Incremental builds*: We build only the components that have been changed since the last build.

You can also add a number of tasks that you want to be executed when running the build:

- Get the latest source code from the version-control system

- Compile sources

- Run static analysis tool

- Execute unit tests

- Update work items

- Perform code coverage

- Calculate code churn (how many rows of code have been modified or added since last count)

- Produce build reports

- Drop exe/output into predefined location

Using the build features of Team Foundation Build, you can set up your own build lab, separate from the development environment and the TFS server (see Figure 6-14). You do this so you won't drown the development environment or the TFS during builds. This is especially important if you choose to use continuous integration.

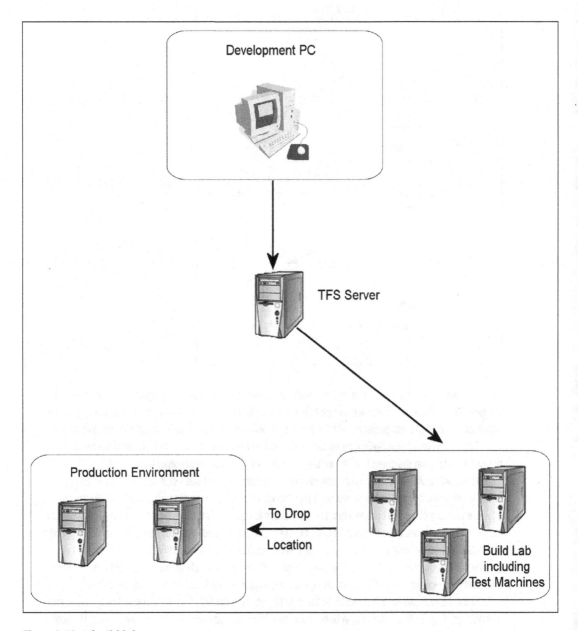

Figure 6-14. *A build lab*

OVERVIEW OF TEAM FOUNDATION BUILD

From the Team Explorer, you can work with Team Foundation Build's *definition creation and build reports*. The build definitions provide an interface you can use to define your build steps and the parameters necessary for your builds. The builds can be defined to be on demand, rolling, or continuous integration, which we talked about earlier.

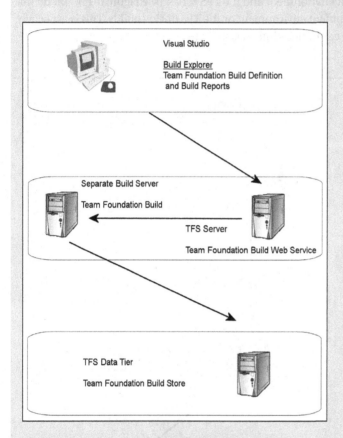

You can view the build reports and see build progress information in Visual Studio through the *Build Explorer*. The build components are completely integrated with VS. Team Foundation Build associates build definitions as part of team projects, and the build definitions are listed in Team Explorer in the Builds folder.

The *Team Foundation Build web service* is located on the application tier and accepts the requests from the Build Explorer on the client tier. The web service coordinates the execution of build steps.

The *build service* is running on a separate build computer in your build lab. It doesn't have to be on a separate machine but it is preferable so the build process won't take too many resources on the computer and interfere with any other TFS components. The build process can be resource-intensive and long-running. This component accepts the instructions sent from the build web service and executes them. This is the component that actually does the build process for you. The build execution takes your build definition(s), builds the executable code, and generates the output in your specified drop-location. All build steps are run here, and if you have unit tests you want to run, or work items you need to update, the build service does all that for you.

In the *Team Foundation Build store* on the data tier, you find the SQL Server database that stores all information regarding the Team Foundation Build processes. From here you get all data for your reports. The reports list the status of your builds. You can also see detailed information about the build steps. There is also information about work items resolved, what code has changed, and a summary of the results of included tests.

Automation of High-Level Processes

Without one or more templates, VSTS will not be used to its full potential, as you saw earlier in this chapter. You could still use its version-control system and some other tools, but the real value comes from using it to automate your ALM process. In the process template, your whole ALM process is defined.

The template defines the following (and more—Chapter 7 provides additional information about this):

- *Work items types*: Which work item types are necessary and what information should they have attached to them. You can also define the workflow for a work item. For a bug, you might have different states the item flows through, such as Active, Resolved, Closed, and so on.

- *Project phases*: By using areas and iterations, you can define the initial project phase setup of your projects. If you use RUP, you can define the process phases in that model, or you can create the first sprints of a Scrum project. Areas and iterations are flexible, and you can create your own way of working through these concepts.

- *Document structure and templates*: The number of documents that should be produced during a project will differ depending on your process model. In the process template, you define the document structure you need and the templates you should use. For instance, you can add templates for requirements specifications or acceptance testing here.

- *Reports and queries*: In the process template, you can specify which reports and work item queries you need to have as defaults in your projects. You probably want reports and queries showing the progress of your project, such as the status of bugs or work remaining. You can create your own reports by using SQL Server reporting services or Excel, and add them to all projects by adjusting the process template.

- *Security*: The template also adds information about which users or user groups have access to what information. You can connect TFS groups to your Active Directory accounts, for instance.

The process template is the overall process for our ALM implementation. Many of my customers create different templates for different kinds of projects. They also create templates for operations, so that when a development project is finished and deployed, the operations staff can use their template to run the system until the system dies. A few customers have started creating a template for ITIL, for instance, and I am looking forward to seeing the result of that work.

What is important to remember is that you can adjust the process to your needs. You should change the default MSF templates or even replace them, and not adjust your own way of working to the templates coming with VSTS out of the box. Microsoft enables this flexibility by letting you easily access the process templates to adjust them or to add new templates. Microsoft also has a Power Tool called the Process Template Editor (http://msdn.microsoft. com/en-us/tfs2008/bb980963.aspx) that integrates well with Visual Studio and lets you work with the template definition files (XML files) in a GUI. Use the flexibility and extensibility to make VSTS work for you.

Visibility

Information about project status is important to all participants of a project—and I don't mean team members only, I mean stakeholders and decision makers as well. As a project manager, I have spent too much time chasing down information to answer questions about the status of projects, how much work remains, and what the latest bug status is.

VSTS provides two primary ways of enabling visibility:

- *Reports*: Reports are created by using SQL Server Reporting Services and accessing the TFS data tier directly. You can define and adjust these as you want. You can also use Excel to create reports if you prefer. Reports can show various kinds of information. The Remaining Work report in Figure 6-15, for example, shows the numbers of active, resolved, and closed work items in a project.

- *Queries*: Queries are used to ask questions of the work item tracking service. One question might be how many bug work items you have. How many and which are dedicated to me? How many bugs are there? And so on. You can create new queries when necessary.

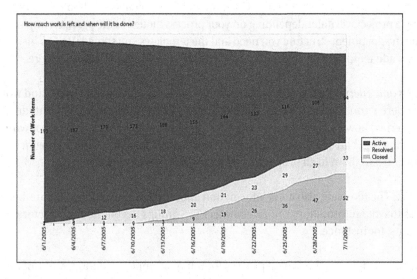

Figure 6-15. *The Remaining Work report*

By using these two components, it will be easier to gather the information you need for your status reports for a steering group meeting or project meeting. You won't have to look around at several places and in several applications for this information anymore, but instead can use the automated reports and queries from inside VSTS.

In my role as a project manager, I am responsible for reporting project status to the steering group. Many times I have struggled to gather the information needed to generate some nice and hopefully informative reports for these meetings. Usually, I need to chase down information from several separate sources: the work item system, the test system, the build system, and so on. And once gathered, the information must be processed and combined so the data for the reports is useful. This is tedious work, and it is easy to make a mistake. For most projects, I need to answer some or all of the following questions—if not every day, at least once a week:

- How much work is left?

- When will that work be done?

- How much of the work is unplanned?

- How good are we at handling bugs—finding, fixing, closing them?

- Are we actually finding the right bugs?

- How productive are the teams of the project?

- How are we using the resources on the team?

Is it really optimal that I should have to chase down this information every time I need it? Shouldn't I instead just be able to generate the reports, preferably automatically, so I can focus on more-important tasks? And wouldn't it be better if reports were available on the Web or intranet so the steering group or other stakeholders could more easily access this information when they want it? That way, the steering group meeting could be spent in a more productive manner, using time to discuss important things such as prioritization of requirements.

Another way VSTS can help projects and managers/stakeholders is by providing the ability to see the real status of the project, and not hear the covered-up version the project manager's report. This is unfortunately a problem that I have heard from both customers and coworkers. Sometimes when problems occur in a project, the project manager still wants to look as if he has absolute control in front of the steering group, so he produces favorable charts and reports instead of revealing the actual status. If the project manager regains control before the next steering group meeting, all is fine, but sometimes things get out of control and the project suffers. The worst part here is that if the stakeholders knew about problems early on, they could take actions to solve them before they became real problems. They could give more power to the project manager or do something else that would help.

Project managers will certainly benefit from VSTS. Because VSTS has all data in the same repository, you can more easily retrieve the correct information when you want it. The flexibility of the SQL Server database that stores all information is great. You can work with the data warehouse information just as you would with any other database.

Depending on which process template you use, you can access various reports that can answer the questions asked earlier, and many others. If you want to and have the skills to do it, you can also create your own reports by using SQL Server Reporting Services and adding them to the process template. If you'd rather work with Excel, you can do that as well and create pivot tables from the data in the warehouse. This is the way many of my coworkers do it.

By using the project portal (see Figure 6-16) or Web Access, you can publish the reports so that everybody who has privileges can see them. This is an easy way to make sure that information is available all the time. Just this little, relatively nontechnical improvement will off-load work from the project manager, freeing some of the PM's time for better things.

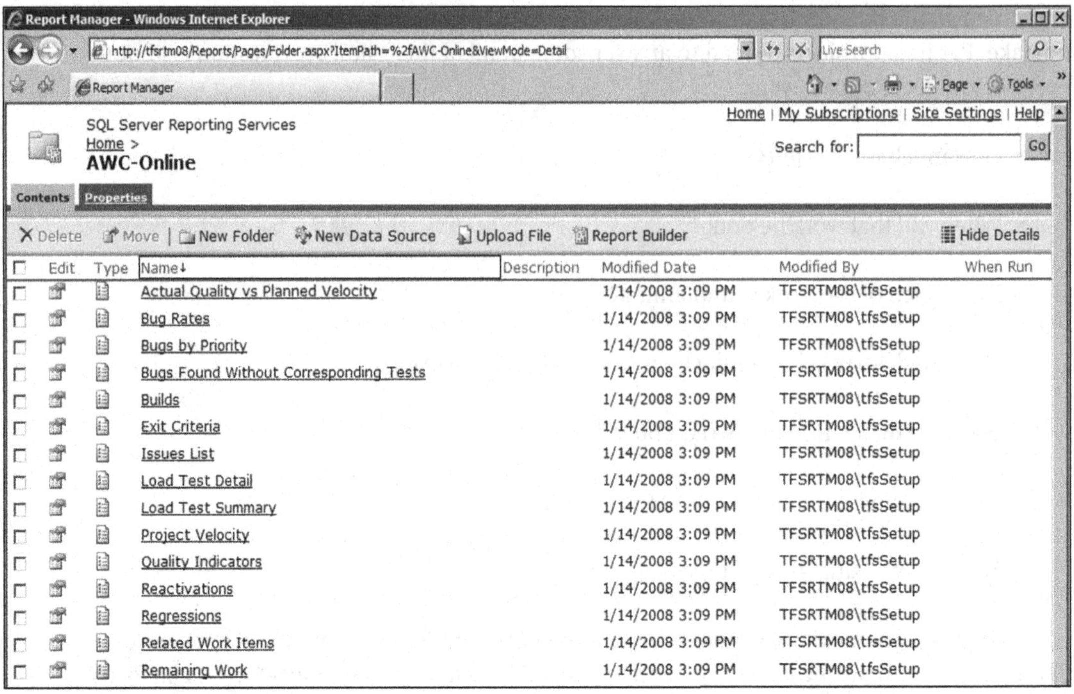

Figure 6-16. *Viewing reports from the project portal*

Let's take a look at what we get with the default reports in VSTS. We'll use the MSF for Agile template for this walk-through. Let's start with some of the questions presented earlier, so you can see the power of the standard reports.

How much work is left? This is a crucial question that all project stakeholders and participants ask themselves regularly. One way to answer this is look at the state of our work items. If you look at the Scenarios work item type, you can see that it has three states: Active, Resolved (coded, waiting for test), and Closed. By opening a report such as the one in Figure 6-17, called Remaining Work, you can get a pretty good overview. I suggest you look at this report for the duration of an iteration.

This report shows how many scenarios are active (the dark-colored field), how many scenarios are resolved (light-colored field), and how many are closed (the color in between). During the project, Active scenarios should decrease steadily.

If the Resolved work items increase drastically, something is wrong. The reason is probably that testing has a problem and is creating a bottleneck. As a project manager, I would then have to take some action. Are the resources for testing adequate? Do they need more staff? Or has anything else happened?

If the top line decreases (total number of scenarios), you can suspect that work has moved from this iteration into another. This shouldn't happen because the number of items to include in the iteration would have already been decided.

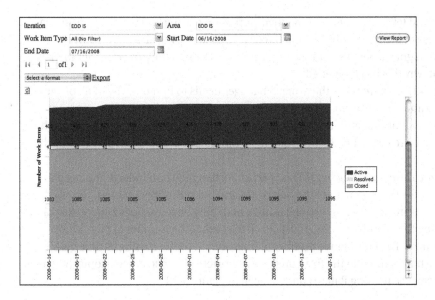

Figure 6-17. *Remaining Work report*

If the top line increases, more work is being added to the iteration. Unless you have planned extra resources to handle increasing work during the iteration, having much unplanned work can cause problems.

How much of the work is unplanned? You can use a report called Unplanned Work to answer this question (see Figure 6-18). Because no one knows everything that will happen during a project, it is necessary to keep good track of unplanned work. If you are using Scrum, for instance, you should really not have any unplanned work during an iteration because the sprint backlog is fixed. This report shows the total number of work items, divided into categories of planned and unplanned.

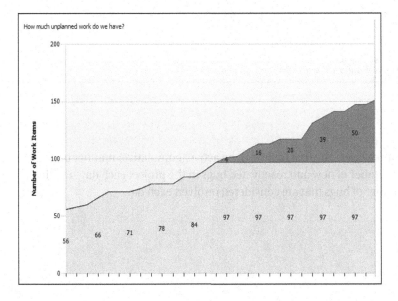

Figure 6-18. *Unplanned work*

This report will tell you whether unplanned work is increasing and whether it is increasing at the expense of planned work. If unplanned work is increasing and planned work is decreasing, you might suspect that this is the case. Then it's up to the project leader to make decisions about why this has happened.

If planned work is decreasing, the project manager needs to find out why (if he or she doesn't already know). The reason might very well be that some work is not necessary anymore (which is good) or that ambitious estimations were made during sprint planning, which turned out not to be realistic, and so work had to be moved out of the sprint and back to the project backlog.

How good are we at handling bugs? This is an important question indeed. You need to have control over the development of the bug count and the status of your bugs. You need to make sure that you are finding bugs (which is not a bad thing because bugs always exist) and that you are fixing them. However, you must check to see that the number of bugs is not increasing over time. The cumulative number of bugs should be decreasing as time goes by. You also need to make sure that the fixed bugs are not reactivated because of sloppy bug fixes. To do this, you can use the Bug Rates report, as seen in Figure 6-19.

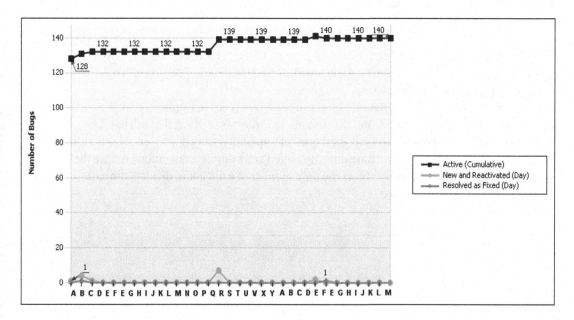

Figure 6-19. *Bug rates*

This diagram has three lines. The first indicates the active (cumulative) number of bugs. The second shows the number of new and reactivated bugs in the project each day, and finally the third shows the number of bugs that are considered resolved each day.

If you combine this diagram with the Quality Indicators report (see Figure 6-20), you can really get some useful information about how the project is going. This diagram is one of the ones I like to show on the project portal. It is rather complex, but after you have studied it for a while, you can get some really nice information about how tests are going (tests passed, failed, or inconclusive).

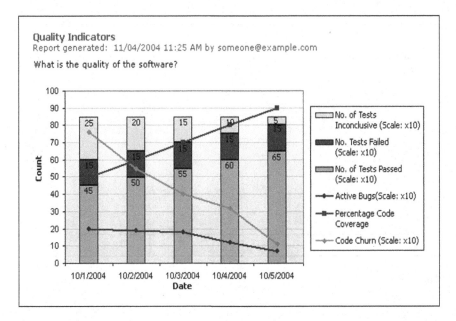

Figure 6-20. *Quality indicators*

If you look at the *code churn* (the number of code lines changed or added since the last count), you can see whether there have been a large number of changes to the code base. As the project or iteration moves on, this number should decrease together with the number of active bugs, indicating that better and better code is being written. At the same time, you should see that the code coverage line should increase, as you write more and more unit tests in the project. You also want to see that the number of closed bugs increases over time as bug fixing goes on, and that reactivations are kept at a low number. The Reactivations report tells a little more about the reactivated bugs (see Figure 6-21).

This report shows the cumulative number of reactivated and not reactivated bugs. The number of reactivated bugs should naturally decrease over time. You can also see the number of reactivations per day. If this suddenly increases, something is wrong, and you need to investigate why this happened.

The strength of the reports is that they give you an overview of the project status without you having to chase the information from different repositories. Because they are always up-to-date, you can easily share this information so that the team and stakeholders alike can access it when they want.

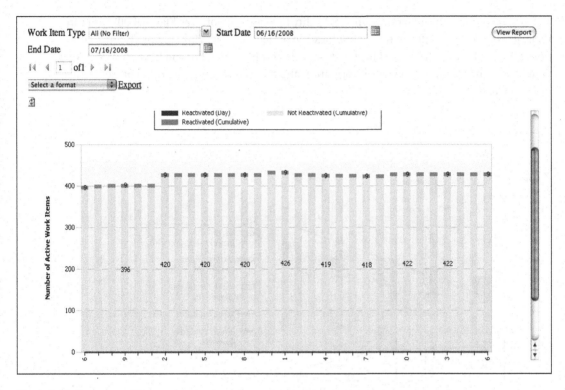

Figure 6-21. *Reactivated bugs*

I think the reports that are included in MSF for Agile and MSF for CMMI are good. You can get most information from them. On one of my first projects with VSTS, I was called to a meeting with the stakeholders who wanted to know the current status of the project. This was an unplanned meeting, and I had little time to prepare. I took the Quality Indicators diagram and the Remaining Work diagram and talked about these. The stakeholders were impressed with the diagrams and that I was able to produce them so fast. When I told them that they could also visit the project portal for any updates to these reports, they were satisfied.

Because I am part of the advisory council for the process team for the coming version of VSTS, I can say that we have exciting things ahead as well in regards to reports and the capabilities to share the reports. A number of interesting features are coming that will improve our capabilities to share project-related information in the team and with stakeholders. I am pleased with Microsoft's efforts in this area as I can directly see their benefits in my own projects.

The reports and queries are great, but of little value in terms of visibility if you cannot share them with the people who want to see them. This is where the collaboration features of VSTS come into the picture.

Collaboration

As you know, VSTS comes with Team Explorer, which is an add-in to Visual Studio. With this tool, the developer can access every aspect of a TFS project. The developer can view reports and queries, for instance, as well as access the document in the project. The developer can access the version-control system, build system, tests, and so on as well.

The Team Explorer is full featured but is still a tool for people used to working in Visual Studio. For me that is no problem, but for most project managers and stakeholders, the GUI is confusing. They want to have an easier-to-use tool to access the relevant information.

Each project that is created with VSTS has a *project portal* created as well. This portal gives us access to reports, documents, project process guidance, and other project-related information through a web interface. This enables people who are not used to the VS interface to easily retrieve the information they need.

The Project Portal and the VSTS Web Access

When you create a TFS project, a project portal is also created. This web site is created by using Windows SharePoint Services or, if you prefer, Microsoft Office SharePoint Server. This means you get all features of the two SharePoint versions, such as document version control and workflow. It is important to remember that the documents on the SharePoint site are not stored and version-controlled from the TFS version-control system, but from SharePoint. You can configure the setup so that all documents from the portal are version-controlled by TFS instead, but you have to do this manually if you want that functionality.

In Figure 6-22, you can see what the default project site looks like in a web browser. You have access to reports, queries, and documents just as you do from within Team Explorer.

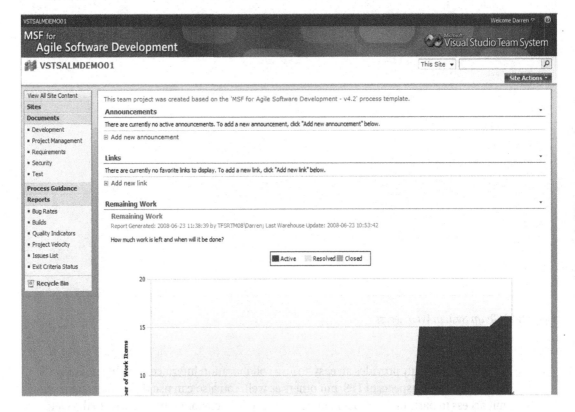

Figure 6-22. *The default project portal*

This site is useful because it provides one place for all information that you want the project team to have access to. You can also make it available to stakeholders and decision makers so they can track the progress of projects—a good way to let them have access to information so that they feel like they are the important part of the project that they are. This way, they can directly check status and won't have to wait for a steering group meeting two weeks away.

The project portal has some limitations, however. You cannot create, modify, or view any work items, for instance. Nor can you access the version-control system, the build system, or a few other parts of TFS. If you want to enable nontechnical users to work with these, you should not have to force them into using Visual Studio. That would be too much of a hassle for most of them. What you want instead is an easy-to-use tool that lets them access all features of TFS without having to rely on using VS.

Microsoft has solved this problem by purchasing a third-party web-based product and provides this as a free download to anyone having a TFS license. This tool is called Team System Web Access and can be seen in Figure 6-23.

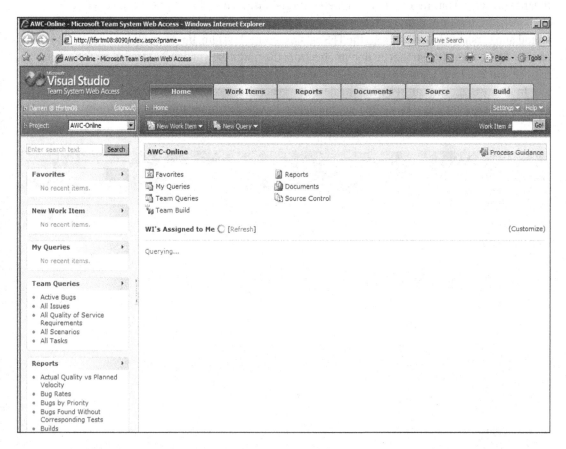

Figure 6-23. *Team System Web Access*

Web Access truly provides an easy-to-use collaboration interface enabling not only VS users to access all aspects of TFS, but others as well. You also can use rights management to limit access to parts of the TFS functionality. If you let a customer have access to the Web Access web site, for instance, you don't want that person seeing projects other than the one(s) they are involved in.

Collaboration, of course, does not only mean giving access to information, even though this is as important as any other means of collaboration. Collaboration also means that we should be able to work together to fulfill one or more goals.

Work Items for Collaboration

You can use the *work item* features of VSTS to enable your process workflows. Let's say a project manager, or anybody responsible for inputting requirements as work items into VSTS, creates a new work item of the Scenario type. This scenario should probably be assigned to a developer to implement. The project manager uses the work item system to assign (see Figure 6-24) the scenario to a specific developer, in this case Darren. Darren continues to work on the scenario until it is ready for testing. Darren then assigns the work item to a tester who performs the testing. When the testing is done, the work item is perhaps closed. If a bug is found, either the tester or anyone finding the bug can use the work item tracking system to see who developed the scenario implementation and reassign it to, in this case, Darren again. VSTS keeps track of who has worked on the work item so that you don't have to manually keep track of this.

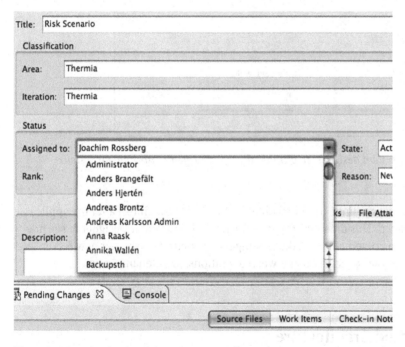

Figure 6-24. *Assigning work items to a specific person*

System Designers in the Architect Edition for Collaboration

Another way to use VSTS to enhance collaboration is through the *system designers* of the VSTS architect version. These designers are graphical interfaces illustrating how a new system should be implemented.

Starting with the Application Designer, business architects and IT architects can use this GUI to collaborate in drawing a big, yet amazingly detailed, picture of how the system will integrate with the existing IT infrastructure (see Figure 6-25). If you have a SOA approach, the existing services and the business processes they implement can be connected to the new service(es) and you can relatively easily see the problems and possibilities. The best thing is that they don't have to look at technical drawings or code to solve this problem. They use a GUI that is simple to use and easy for the business experts to understand; the architects can minimize confusion by not having to speak in only technical terms.

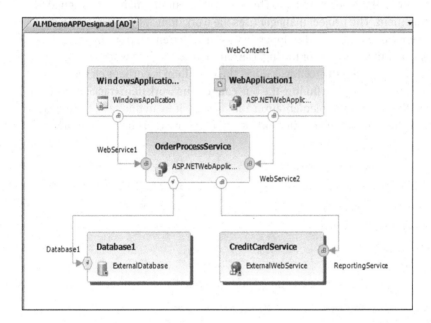

Figure 6-25. *Using the system designers to graphically collaborate in building our systems*

The IT architect will continue to work with the infrastructure architect after the application design is completed. This time they may use the Logical Datacenter Designer to see how the new system can be implemented on the existing infrastructure or whether new servers are necessary. This will enable collaboration between operations, maintenance, and development.

Service-Oriented Architecture

Using service-oriented architecture is another way to enable automation of business processes with the help of IT systems. As you saw in Chapter 4, SOA can enable you to more easily orchestrate the processes and adjust the IT systems to changes in the business processes.

IT and Business Gap

Closing the gap between IT and business is obviously a very tough problem to solve. VSTS won't get us all the way, that's for sure. I don't think any tool ever will, which is an important consideration. But tools can help us bridge the gap, so you should carefully consider how you can use them for this. That is the reason I showed you the benefits of SOA. It is also the reason that I suggested you start considering the architect roles in your organization. We need to improve on our ALM process and way of working to start solving this. When we have a new way of working, VSTS can support much of our efforts using, for instance, the process template to implement this new way of working.

What is also important is the support we have from the system designers in creating a SOA and maintaining a map of our business processes (implemented in the SOA) as template system diagrams for use in all projects. By using the system diagrams, different architects can work at different levels of the architecture, directly seeing the results of their efforts.

This enables us to enhance collaboration as mentioned earlier, and collaboration is key if we really want the gap to start closing.

Visual Studio in itself also has good support for writing services for a SOA. Windows Communication Foundation (WCF), for instance, is included in recent releases of Visual Studio, enabling developers to write effective services inside the tool of their choice.

Still the gap between IT and the business sides is a question of work process. It requires considering many things, and when you have a solution or start working toward a solution, you must evaluate what parts of this work process you can automate and use tools for solving. One thing worth mentioning here is the use of the Visual Studio Team System Project Server 2007 Connector with VSTS that lets you integrate VSTS with Microsoft Office Project Server. Having this integration will allow you to better control your resources and better automate this process as well. This way, you can align your portfolio management process better so that you can choose which things to work on more effectively.

I suggest that no matter whether you come from the IT or the business side, start by talking to the other side. That's where closing the gap really starts.

Office/MS Project Integration

When I have run projects in the past, I have mostly used Microsoft Office Project to handle project planning, especially the Gantt diagram. I suspect this is the case for many of my fellow project managers as well. In many cases, I have used this product not primarily because of the tool itself but because so many of my customers use Microsoft Office that it becomes natural for them to also use Project. Project has its strengths and weaknesses, as all tools do, and I cannot say that I don't like it, but I have never become friends with it. Sometimes it does things that I don't expect, and even though I know this is because I am too unfamiliar with its features, I still blame the product from time to time—unfair, but that's life sometimes.

Excel and Project are two tools that most companies use on both the business and the IT sides of the company. By being able to use these tools, business people can more easily be a part of the ALM process, because they can use a tool they are already used to working with.

But because Project is the tool that I use and that my customers favor, I expected Microsoft to have integrated it with VSTS out of the box. And as you have seen, there is some integration. We can work with work items from both Project and Excel (another favorite tool with most companies). We can start working with our requirements in Excel or Project and sync these over to VSTS, making work items out of them. Nice!

But (there's always one of these, isn't there?) I expected more. I wanted full integration with Microsoft Office Project Server. This is the tool of choice for many customers as they try to handle their resource management. Many often use the whole Enterprise Project Management (EPM) suite Microsoft offers, and are thirsty for integration with their VSTS servers.

So what can we do until Microsoft adds out-of-the-box integration with Microsoft Project Server to VSTS? We can use the Project Connector from CodePlex that Microsoft offers in the meantime. This is a very nice tool that can help us a lot. The main problems I've encountered are that it is so far unsupported, and that has been a drawback for some of my customers. Those who have been curious have not taken the step because there are few official reference cases for this tool. I've asked Microsoft for reference cases, and they have told me that several companies in the financial sector use the integrator, but no one is stepping out as the official reference.

The VSTS connector integrates the data across VSTS and Project Server, and helps us synchronize work items (tasks) between these two applications. Managers can use the connector to monitor workflow between the two and have the option to approve or deny the activities concerned.

We can get a good tracking of tasks and assignments by using the connector, and it integrates work items on the assignment level. The connector provides the following:

- A single tool in VSTS to track project progress. Even though Project Server offers the Web Access site for tracking information, we can see the same in VSTS.

- Synchronized updates of development tasks in real time.

- Less manual work in tracking the progress of our projects on a day-to-day basis.

- Updates and notifications to users. If a work item update occurs, the project manager can be notified.

The connector is integrated with VSTS, as shown in Figure 6-26. The Project Server event handlers are responsible for reporting the changes occurring on the project server side to the ProjectEventHandler web service at the connector side. The Project Server event handlers are installed with the Project Connector.

The ProjectEventHandler web service speaks with the synchronization web service responsible for integration with the connector core.

TFS in turn integrates with the WorkItemChangedHandler web service on the connector side. This in turn speaks with the synchronization web service just as the ProjectEventHandler web service does.

The connector has been developed to provide extensibility: so far we can synchronize work items, assignments, project plans and timelines, and other entities, and by using the extensibility, we can tailor it to our needs.

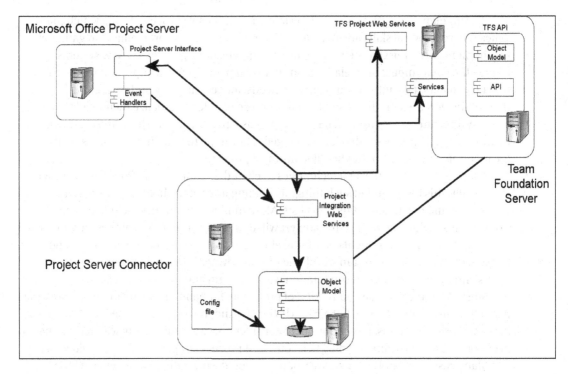

Figure 6-26. *Project Server connector*

Requirements Analysis in VSTS

The process of gathering and documenting requirements is an art form in itself. This documentation takes skills and is important for any project. It is also essential for the ALM process to have a good methodology for handling the requirements process.

Conceptually, requirements management includes three types of activities:

- *Eliciting requirements*: This is the task of determining the requirements of users, stakeholders, customers and so on. This is sometimes also called *requirements gathering*.

- *Analyzing requirements*: After the requirements are gathered, they need to be analyzed so you can determine whether they are unclear, incomplete, ambiguous, or contradictory. If they are, these issues need to be resolved. Analysis is done for impact and planning purposes as well as for organizing requirements into reasonably actionable buckets.

- *Recording requirements*: Requirements can be documented in various forms, such as plain text in Word documents, use cases, user stories, or process specifications.

Requirements analysis is often a long and work-intensive process during which many delicate psychological skills are involved. You have seen that it is problematic to gather all requirements from the start because so much happens during a project. New systems change the environment and relationships between people, so it is important to identify all the stakeholders, take into account all their needs, and ensure they understand the implications of the new systems. It is also difficult for these people to verbalize their needs because a new system often exists only on paper and not as a prototype yet. This is the reason for many of the agile processes that have emerged. They hope to help in this process, so that the requirements can be better handled during a project.

Analysts can employ several techniques to elicit the requirements from the customer. Historically, this has included such things as holding interviews, holding requirements workshops, and creating requirements lists. More modern techniques include prototyping and use cases. Where necessary, the analyst will employ a combination of these methods to establish the exact requirements of the stakeholders, so a system that meets the business needs is produced. In the Scrum world, the product owner is responsible for the requirements and prioritizes these in cooperation with the team and the scrum master.

Most ALM processes have some kind of procedure for handling the requirements analysis part. I have mentioned Scrum, but MSF, RUP/EssUp, and the others described in Chapter 3 all have their process for this. It is important to consider how we want to work with requirements in our organizations before deciding what our ALM process template in VSTS should look like.

Many customers and coworkers ask how we should work with requirements in VSTS. Requirements are one of the most important aspects in tying together the business side with the IT side in the ALM process. This is a tricky question. The area is something that could improve in VSTS, in my opinion. By using MSF for Agile, we can use the work item types of Scenario (functional requirement) or Quality of Service (nonfunctional requirement) and add them to the work item tracking system. In MSF for CMMI, we find the Requirements work item type. What I would like to have is a better tool helping us gather the requirements from the beginning—a tool that we can use with our stakeholders when we start planning. This might hopefully come in future versions of VSTS.

The extensibility of VSTS makes it possible to write your own integration with the requirements tool you like. There are also third-party vendors such as stpsoft (`www.stpsoft.co.uk/vsts/`) providing requirements add-ins and tools for VSTS. Stpsoft has developed two tools that are worth taking a look at:

- *ReqSheet for Microsoft Visual Studio Team System*: A lightweight environment for working with requirements in Team System projects. Requirements are stored hierarchically in documents, which can be e-mailed as attachments and shared by using Microsoft SharePoint. ReqSheet can be used as a stand-alone product or integrated with stpsoft Storyboarding for Microsoft Visual Studio Team System.

- *Storyboarding for Microsoft Visual Studio Team System*: A Microsoft Visio-based requirements definition tool for Team System projects to visually define and validate requirements through GUI and workflow storyboarding. Generates scenario screen flow diagrams, HTML storyboards, reader-friendly UI specifications, test scripts, and Team System work items. Can be used alone or integrated with stpsoft ReqSheet for Microsoft Visual Studio Team System.

We have started to evaluate these for one of my recent projects, and they look interesting.

Microsoft recently published a document describing how requirements should be handled in VSTS. Take a look at it at `www.microsoft.com/downloads/details.aspx?FamilyId= EEF7BB41-C686-4C9F-990B-F78ACE01C191&displaylang=en` because it contains a lot of interesting thoughts.[2]

The Scenario work item can be used to input functional requirements (see Figure 6-27). You write these as a description of the single interaction path that a user performs to reach a certain goal. One example is that a customer should be able to place an order. Such a high-level scenario will probably be divided into several smaller, more manageable work items later, when iteration planning starts. By linking these work items together, you can make a hierarchy of work items so you can follow the high-level requirement through the project to the executable code.

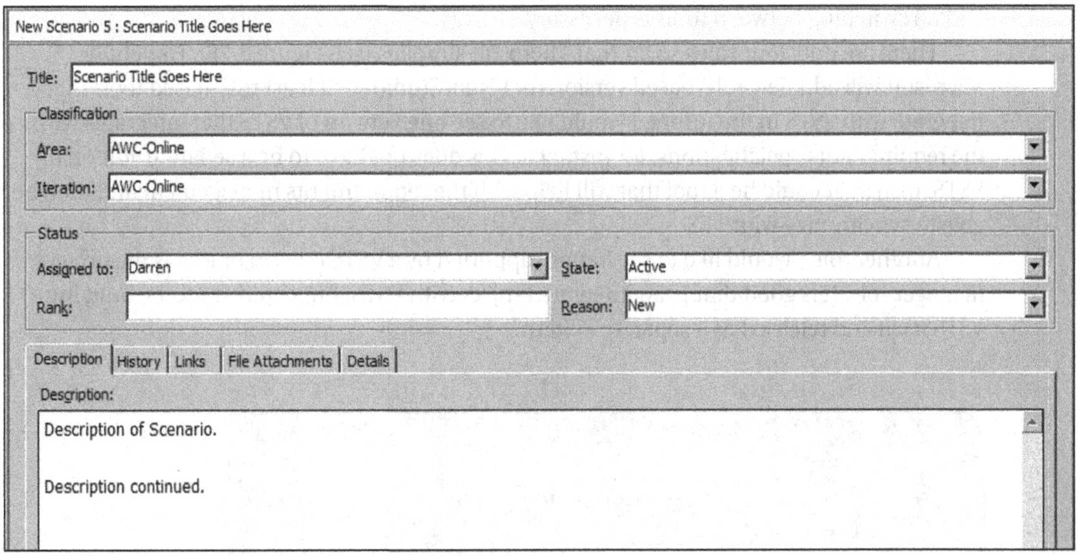

Figure 6-27. *The Scenario work item*

Nonfunctional requirements are added by using the Quality of Service work item type. Nonfunctional requirements can include the availability we should have for a solution, the load it should handle, and so on.

If you use Scrum, the Scrum for Team System, or eScrum, there are work item types for backlog and sprint items that you can use to input your requirements. Many scrum masters don't favor tools, except for maybe Excel, but you can use that as well if you want, because many will probably use it to collect requirements anyway. By using the Office integration, you can then add the requirements to the TFS and produce work items out of them. In Chapter 7 we will have a closer look at requirements in VSTS.

---

2. Microsoft, "Requirements Management with Visual Studio Team System White Paper," March 2008.

Use of One Tool/Role Based

A good ALM tool should enable you to use add-ins that will provide new features inside one interface. If a developer needs testing features, these should be possible to integrate into the development tool. The developer should not have to switch tools to do testing tasks. VSTS is extensible and lets you create your own add-ins as well as purchase third-party add-ins that will be accessible from inside of VSTS.

VSTS is also role based, so project members shouldn't have to switch between different versions of VSTS in order to perform other roles. VSTS has four editions: the Architect Edition, the Developer Edition, the Test Edition, and the Database Edition. They can be installed separately, but as soon as you install one version on a machine where another edition is already installed, they integrate and the new edition adds on to the old, giving access to its features from the same interface as was already on the machine. This is pretty much how the add-ins work. You get more and more functionality in the same GUI when you add this functionality, and no switching between tools is necessary.

There are only four roles so far that Microsoft supplies (see Figure 6-28). Hopefully, Microsoft will add new role-based versions of Visual Studio or at least role-based tools that integrate with VSTS in the future. I would like to see one version of VSTS that integrates with the requirements specifications, for instance. This does not have to be a separate edition of VSTS; instead it could be a tool that will help with the requirements management and then be able to synchronize with TFS.

Another role I would like to see better supported by a VSTS edition or tool is the project manager role. It is good that I can integrate Project with VSTS, but couldn't this be built into VSTS itself and released as a separate edition?

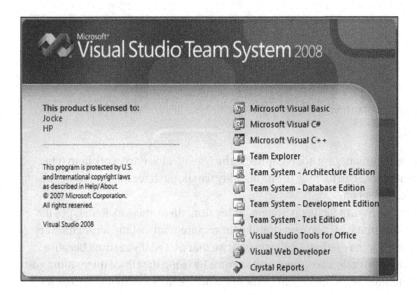

Figure 6-28. *My version of VSTS includes all roles of VSTS.*

As a project manager, I am not used to the interface of Visual Studio and will probably want to use tools that I am familiar with for my tasks. So far, I use Excel or Project and like these tools. Maybe in the future Microsoft will add similar tools into a Project Manager edition of VSTS, but that remains to be seen. So far I can use the integration between Office and TFS for my basic needs. This enables me to work with work items in the Office tools, and then sync this information over to VSTS. The integration works well as long as I work with only one project. I would think that the Enterprise Project Management team would like better integration with TFS from Project Server as well. This integration exists today, but only as a download (unsupported) from CodePlex. I would like this integrated into VSTS, and have been told that this will happen.

Extensibility

When the built-in features of VSTS are not enough, you can use the extensibility features to expand and enhance it. VSTS is often seen as a closed black box that Microsoft ships, when it's more like an enterprise resource planning (ERP) system for ALM. Any ALM environment must be customized for an organization's processes and the existing applications and services.

Many of my customers have been a bit reluctant to customize VSTS. They have instead tried to squeeze their way of working into the templates Microsoft provides with VSTS. I think this is the wrong way to do it. My suggestion is that you start the other way around. Start by asking yourself how your organization wants to work. This process involves all parts of the organization, from the business side to operations. Try to find agreement on how to work in the ALM process. By doing so, you will see that this also is a good start for collaboration in the company.

For instance, consider the work items and the information in them. If the fields and information in the MSF templates are not enough, extend or edit them. VSTS lets us do this by changing the process template. You can choose to add the information that you need, and it will be stored in the TFS databases, so you can have access to it from within your reports and queries. Don't forget to change the reports or queries as well; otherwise, you will not see your information.

Some of my customers have changed the workflow of a work item by adding more states to them, when the ones supplied have not been enough. Often we have used the VSTS Power Tools to do this.

When you have an initial idea of how you want to conduct the ALM process, start looking into what VSTS gives you out of the box. Use what can be used, change other things, and build your own solution where needed.

The best thing about VSTS is its extensibility and flexibility. You can adjust the whole tool to fit most parts of your ALM process. If you want to, you can develop your own add-ins by giving support to roles not included from the start. I can only strongly encourage you to use these extensibility features, but in the end it is your choice.

Some customers have started by using the extensibility features to push information into TFS from their own systems. This way, they have been able to slowly replace the old systems one by one, and in the meantime still have access to the information in these tools from VSTS.

The extensibility can also be used to build other tools that integrate with VSTS. The best example is probably the Teamprise collection of tools that integrates Eclipse with VSTS. From my MacBook Air I can access all my projects by using the Teamprise Team Explorer (see Figure 6-29).

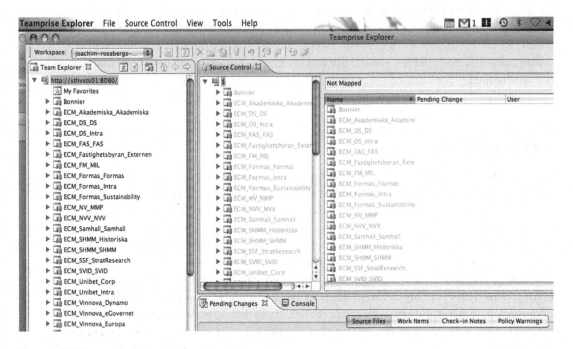

Figure 6-29. *Teamprise Team Explorer*

Summary

VSTS has impressed me a great deal during the time I have used it. There are always things you want to improve, but that is the case with all tools.

In my opinion, VSTS can help us implement a good, automated, and robust ALM process. There are features for all aspects of ALM 2.0. Correctly used, these features will help us improve our ALM process, which in the end will give us better business value and more-successful projects.

The three pillars of ALM—traceability, process automation, and visibility—are all important for any organization to have. Visual Studio Team System is a great foundation on which to build our ALM solutions. VSTS has work item tracking for traceability, process template implementation in the tool itself for process automation, and reports and queries for visibility. Through a project portal, Web Access, and system designers in VSTS, you can improve collaboration between all parties having an interest in your projects.

VSTS is role based in the sense that it supports four project roles. It has an architect edition, a development edition, a database edition, and a test edition. They are not separate tools, so when, for instance, a developer installs the test edition, the test features are added to that developer's existing GUI. You can also add custom add-ins to the GUI and do not have to use several tools to get the job done.

You can also use the architect edition to enhance collaboration between the business side of the organization, operations, and the IT side. I would like to see a better way to gather requirements directly into VSTS so that the integration would be even better. This would truly be a better step in bridging the gap between these different parts of the organization.

Project managers have the capability to use tools they are already familiar with. Most use Excel or Project for project planning, and there is integration between these tools and VSTS. We can easily sync information between these tools. I would like to see better integration with Project Server so we can sync information into our Enterprise Project Management systems (talking Microsoft here, I mean Microsoft Office Project Server and Portfolio Management Server).

The extensibility of VSTS makes it fairly easy to write your own code integrating VSTS with other applications. Teamprise, for instance, has applications using this extensibility to add Team Foundation Server integration into Eclipse. I use Teamprise Team Explorer on my MacBook Air, enabling me to access the VSTS projects I need to from Mac OS X. This is an incredible strength of VSTS, and something we should give Microsoft credit for. There are also other solutions integrating, among others, Microsoft Outlook with VSTS, letting us convert e-mails to work items with just a click.

So all in all, Visual Studio Team System is a great foundation on which to build our Application Lifecycle Management process.

The next chapter will dive deeper into how we can customize VSTS to even further enhance the ALM process. After that I want to show you an example from real life. In Chapter 8, you'll see how my coworkers and I have implemented VSTS in several companies, which is working out very well.

■ ■ ■

CHAPTER 7

Working with VSTS Customization to Further Enhance the ALM Process

In this chapter, we will take a deeper look at some more features of Visual Studio Team System that can help us improve our Application Lifecycle Management process. I cover the concepts of VSTS without going into too much technical detail. In some cases, I cannot avoid being technical, but the focus is always on how VSTS can help us improve and automate the ALM process.

There are very good books providing more-detailed information about VSTS on the market today, so if you want to dive down into it, purchase any of those. One that I particularly like is *Pro Visual Studio 2005 Team System* by Jeff Levinson and David Nelson (Apress, 2006). Even though this book is about the 2005 version, I really think you can find some nice insight in it.

I use VSTS 2008 for most demonstrations in this chapter, but I try to not be version specific, because most topics I cover are general issues, not restricted to a specific version of TFS. If I deviate from this, I will let you know.

We will discuss these topics with the following ALM cornerstones from Chapter 2 in mind:

- Automation of high-level processes

- Traceability

- Extensibility

- Collaboration

Let's first start with a deeper drill-down into the different parts of VSTS. I think it is important to know a little bit about the architecture of VSTS to better understand the potential of its extensibility features for our ALM process.

The Overall Architecture of Visual Studio Team System

Let's take a closer look at the architecture of VSTS. For better deployment, it is essential to have knowledge of this. Chapter 6 showed the condensed overview of this, but now we will take a slightly deeper look.

Architecture of Team Foundation Server

Team Foundation Server uses a three-tiered architecture under the covers (see Figure 7-1). It has a client tier, an application tier, and a data tier. All clients interact with the application tier by using web services or the Team Foundation Server Client API. This is also what enables us to develop our own clients or integrated TFS support in our own applications. The application tier uses services from the data tier, where several databases exist.

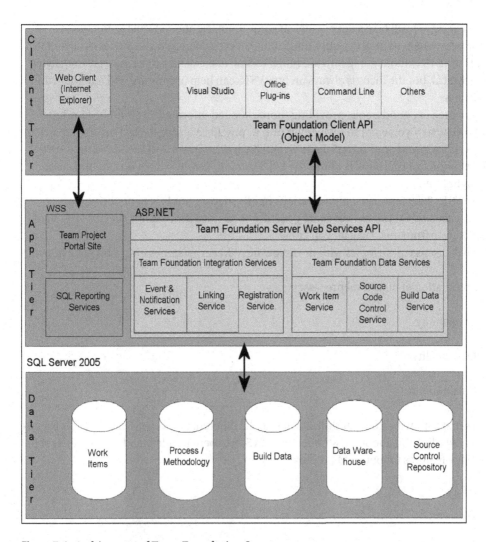

Figure 7-1. *Architecture of Team Foundation Server*

Client Tier

There are several important components in the client tier. The Visual Studio integrated development environment (IDE) is of course one of them because that is our development environment, including Team Explorer. In Visual Studio, we have access to the version-control system and of course the work item tracking system.

There is also a check-in policy framework. In VSTS, we can set policies on the check-ins. This enables us to make it mandatory that, for instance, a developer must have written information about the check-in or connected the check-in with a work item, in order to complete the check-in procedure.

There are plug-ins for Microsoft Office as well, enabling us to use Microsoft Office Excel or Microsoft Office Project to access some of the TFS functionality. We can synchronize work items between Office and TFS, enabling the project manager to work in Excel or Project and then synching the updated information to TFS. This way, the project manager can work in the tool he or she is already familiar with.

If we want to, we can use command-line tools to manage the different TFS tools. Many of the command-line tools are aimed at the version-control system and enable us to automate tasks and also schedule them. I have used the command-line tools to retrieve a list of workspaces I have created on a computer, for instance. This list has been built into a script enabling me to create a new workspace through the command line without using a name of an already-existing workspace, add some source code files to this new workspace, and then check them in.

All these tools use the Team Foundation Client API (object model) to access the TFS functionality. It is by using this API that Microsoft wants us to write our own TFS integration tools. For instance, plug-ins to Visual Studio developed by Visual Studio Industry Partners (VSIP) should use this API.

The project portals are accessed by a web browser, the same way the Web Access site is. The difference is that the standard portal is much more limited in its features, whereas Web Access allows us to work with all aspects of VSTS. The client tier also provides Work Item Web Access (WIWA), which we can use to allow partners and customers (among others) to access some of the functionality in TFS—for example, to create and edit work items and see work items that a particular user has created. WIWA is great when you want to be able to allow certain users the ability to add change requests or bug reports, for instance, without having to have a Client Access License (CAL) for TFS.

Application Tier

The application tier contains the logic of VSTS. You can see in Figure 7-1 that the services and functions from this tier are exposed as ASP.NET web services. Microsoft has not intended third-party integrators to program against these services, but they exist and hence we will reference them here. There is nothing stopping us from using them either, so we can reference them from our own applications or plug-ins if we want to.

Two collections of web services are available to VSTS:

- Team Foundation data services

- Team Foundation integration services

Let's start with the *data services*. These web services are primarily used to access the data in the data tier. We have services for accessing the version-control system here (shown in Figure 7-1 as *Source Code Control service*). When we perform a source code operation of some kind in Visual Studio, for example, our requests are routed through these services. When we create, update, delete, or query work items, we use the services from the *Work Item service*. All build operations we use are accessed through the *Build Data service*. The MSBuild framework, which we can programmatically access from our own code, will be routed through this service as well.

The Team Foundation *integration services* let us access integration and automation services. The integration services include the following:

- *Registration web service*: This is used to register various other TFS services. The information stored in this service database is used by the services so they can discover each other and determine how they can interact.

- *Security services*: This category is divided into two services: the Group security service and the Authorization service. The Group security service manages requests about TFS users and group security, and is used to create TFS users and groups. The Authorization service handles access control for TFS. We can integrate TFS security with Active Directory (AD) as well. Most VSTS implementations I have seen create TFS groups with certain TFS rights and then add AD users and groups to these TFS groups.

- *Linking service*: In VSTS, we can link information from different tools to each other. A Defect work item can be linked to the source code that was changed to fix the bug, for instance. All information about links is routed through this service.

- *Event and Notification services*: We can use events in VSTS in a way that enables us to get notifications when things change. For instance, we can set up an event that will notify us if a build fails, or we can use an event to automatically start a continuous integration build when somebody checks in source code. These services help us implement such events and notifications.

- *Classification web service*: To help us with cross-tool reporting for artifacts that do not share a common taxonomy, the Classification web service collaborates with the Linking web service. If we typically organize work items by teams and organize tests by component, for example, we might want to report on tests alongside work items by team.

If you look at Figure 7-1 again, you can see that the application tier also has two other parts: the reporting services that use *SQL Server Reporting Services*, and the *Team Project Portal site* implemented on Windows SharePoint Services. All reports in SQL Server are created by using SQL Server Reporting Services, which means we can also add our own reports or modify the ones Microsoft provides.

Data Tier

Let's start with the data tier and work our way up. There is no support in VSTS for accessing the data in this tier directly from the client applications. VSTS uses a web service architecture, and if you want access to the services it exposes, you need to send a request to one of the web services. As you may recall from the SOA discussion in Chapter 4, we recognize that this is in line with a good SOA implementation. A service should always protect its data.

The data tier has five databases. One of them stores information about the work items in VSTS. Another database stores information about the methodology we use—that means information about the process template(s) we have accessible. There is also a database for information regarding the build system—that is, information about all things included in a VSTS build such as build results, scheduled builds, drop locations for builds, and so on.

The data warehouse stores information related to all TFS tools and the features in them. TFS stores all information about test results, for instance, so we can publish this information to all team members and other interested parties. The last database is the version-control database or the source repository. As you will see later, all source code is stored in the database, and not as files as it was in Visual Source Safe. We also have information about branching and other version-control information here.

VSTS uses Microsoft SQL Server 2005 as a data repository.

Visual Studio Team System Deployment

There are basically two ways to deploy our Team Foundation Server: we can use a single-server deployment strategy or a dual-server model.

Single-Server Deployment

Single-server deployment is the simplest way of implementing TFS in your organization. Microsoft recommends this setup for smaller organizations with up to 400 users. In this setup, the data tier and application tier are installed on the same server. Figure 7-2 shows a model of single-server deployment.

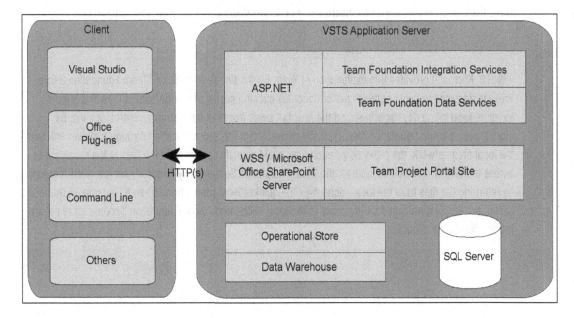

Figure 7-2. *Single-server deployment*

Dual-Server Deployment

Dual-server deployment, on the other hand, means that we install the data tier and the application tier on different servers. This deployment model, shown in Figure 7-3, is most useful for larger development teams and a total number of users around 2,000. Microsoft also recommends that we install TFS build services on a separate server as well, so that the build process doesn't affect development.

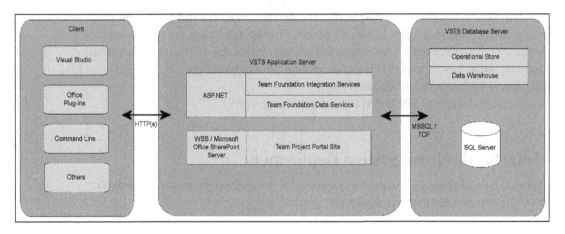

Figure 7-3. *Dual-server deployment*

If we have a very complex environment with development at different locations, we can also use a separate TFS proxy, which helps boost version control at the remote locations. In Figure 7-4, you can see that we have included a proxy, but more important, we have added a standby application tier so we can have fail-over if anything happens. You can also see that we have included several separate build servers so we don't overload the application tier.

■**Note** Microsoft provides this explanation of Team Foundation Server Proxy: "Team Foundation Server Proxy is designed to boost network performance by caching copies of source control files in a remote location, local to the developer needing the files but away from the main source control location. By storing copies in the remote location, typically connected to the source location through a slower link than the local area network, the proxy helps each user avoid a costly download of the files to their workspace across the slower connection. Instead, the Team Foundation Server Proxy generally serves client requests by returning the files from the local cache over the quicker local connection. When a file is not in the local cache, the file is downloaded by the proxy to the local cache from Team Foundation Server, before returning the files to the client."

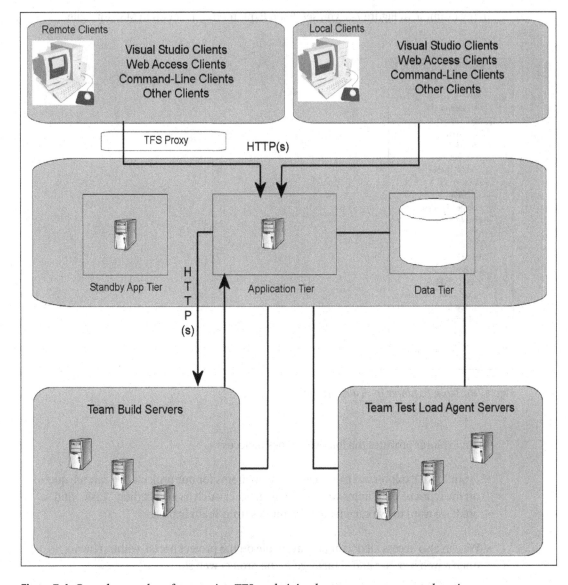

Figure 7-4. *Complex topology for securing TFS and giving better access to remote locations*

Team Explorer

You will soon see which versions of Visual Studio (VS) are available for Visual Studio Team System. Before that, however, I want to tell you about a tool that is available in all of the Team editions of VS. This tool is called *Team Explorer* and is the primary connection into the Team Foundation Server and its functionality. This is the client tier part of the TFS. Remember that the things you see in Team Explorer are defined in the process template for the project and can differ from project to project.

In my example in Figure 7-5, you see Team Explorer as it is set up in MSF for Agile.

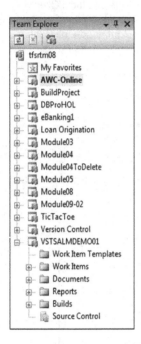

Figure 7-5. *Team Explorer in Visual Studio*

Team Explorer provides the following types of access:

- From Team Explorer, we can access the work items for our projects. We can see queries on the types of work items we have in the project, such as Defect (bug), Tasks, and so on. If we want to, we can create new queries from Team Explorer.

- We can also access all documents available on the project portal, without having to open a web browser and actually go to the project web site.

- Reports created with SQL Server Reporting Services can be added to the project template. We can then run these reports from Team Explorer and see the result from within Visual Studio.

- For team builds, we can access build information, and automate and run builds from Team Explorer.

- We can also access the source control system from the Team Explorer interface.

Visual Studio Professional

The core tool for developers is the Visual Studio IDE. This is the foundation of all the VSTS editions. The difference is that the editions have additional tools included, specific to the developer role they are intended for. Visual Studio Professional (VS Pro) provides an extensive core functionality pack, which I will cover briefly here.

The following tools or features are included in VS Pro, and hence also in all Team editions of Visual Studio:

- *.NET Framework*: VS Pro 2008 includes .NET Frameworks 3.5 and 3.0, and .NET Compact Framework. We can also use 2.0 and 1.1 in VS Pro if we install them separately.

- *Unit testing*: Unit testing is included in VS Pro.

- *Windows Presentation Foundation*: We can use this framework to create the visual appearance of Windows client applications.

- *Windows Communication Foundation*: This is a runtime and API that will enable us to create easier communication between services and consumers.

- *Windows Workflow Foundation*: By using this programming model, we can build workflow-enabled applications.

- *Windows Forms*: This is the standard Microsoft way to build Windows applications.

- *ASP.NET*: This is the framework for building web applications and services.

- *Programming languages*: VS Pro includes the programming languages Visual Basic .NET (VB.NET), Visual C#, Visual C++, and JScript.

There are other tools as well, but these are the most important ones and will give an understanding of what VS is.

VS Pro is a great tool, but it will not give access to TFS out of the box. What we can do, however, is purchase a CAL to TFS and install Team Explorer on our computer. This will provide access to basic functions in TFS such as version control, work items, and so on. It will not provide any additional tools like the ones you will see in the Team Editions of VS, but it will let us use our development environment in a TFS project without purchasing a Team Edition. If the developer has no use for the extra tools in the role-specific Team Editions, it might be cost-effective to just purchase the CAL for the VS Pro edition and start working in a project.

Editions of Visual Studio Team System

Visual Studio Team Editions are available in four versions:

- Visual Studio Team System Architecture Edition

- Visual Studio Team System Database Edition

- Visual Studio Team System Development Edition

- Visual Studio Team System Test Edition

You can also buy all the editions in one package through the purchase of Visual Studio Team System Team Suite.

The different editions are, as their names indicate, designed for the specific roles that project members can have in a development project. Let's say a developer needs to have the features of the Test edition as well as the features of the Development edition. If that developer is working on the Development edition and later installs the Test edition, he or she will have access to both editions from the same GUI. The developer does not have to use two different tools, but can continue using an expanded version of the tool he or she is familiar with. This is in line with the ALM 2.0 requirements on ALM toolsets.

So what differs between the versions? First we can look at the tools of VS that all the versions have in common.

Features That All Editions Have in Common

No matter which edition you purchase, you will still have access to these features:

- *Process framework and guidance*: You will always have access to the Team Explorer window so you can access the project's implementation of the process you have chosen. You can also access process guidance from VS (if this is created for your process).

- *Class Designer*: The Class Designer is a tool that helps design the structure of applications in a graphical representation. This is perfect to use in discussions with people who don't need to see the code itself so design discussions can be kept at a higher level (see Figure 7-6).

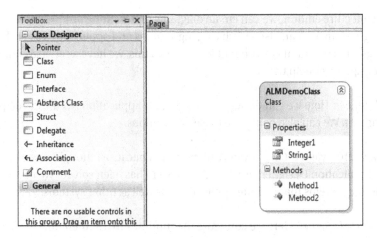

Figure 7-6. *The Class Designer in Visual Studio Team System*

- *Visio and UML modeling*: Microsoft Office Visio for Enterprise Architects is supplied as a separate installation, and separate application once installed. You can use this for modeling a system and creating Unified Modeling Language (UML) diagrams. As you will see, many of the same features provided here are available from inside VSTS Architecture Edition. To me, Visio is a great tool when I do system or architectural design during the planning of a project. Visio can be used to create great-looking representations of how we plan the system. However, after development starts and reality kicks in, we tend to forget to update these diagrams, and they soon lose their value. If I use Visio these days, I do it to design systems at a pre-study phase or early in the project before getting the go-ahead to start the project. Then I create Visio diagrams to explain how the system will be designed, based on the information available at that point. But as soon as the project starts and the real architecture is created, I use the VSTS Architecture Edition instead. You will soon see why.

- *Unit testing*: Unit testing is a technique coming from the Extreme Programming camp and basically means that we write code to test the functions that we have programmed. You'll learn about this in more detail later in this chapter. Unit testing has been seen as a success factor in development over the last few years, and I have had very good experiences with it myself. Microsoft now has support for this in all editions, which is a great initiative. When VSTS first came out, only the Development and Test editions had support for unit testing.

Visual Studio Team System Architecture Edition

This edition is intended for people doing architecture. To me, this is one of the most exciting editions in the family. If this had been available when I worked most extensively with architecture, I would have been ecstatic.

By using the Architecture edition, we can create diagrams representing our proposed system or our existing system. We can also attach existing systems and applications as well and configure settings and constraints at different levels. To do this, we have a set of graphical distributed system designers to help us:

- *Application Designer*: Here we can design, in a visual way, applications in the development environment. We can also configure these applications.

- *System Designer*: This was a bit of a mystery to me at first because I thought it was very similar to the Application Designer, but now this mystery has been solved. We use this designer to design systems that include applications as well as other systems.

- *Logical Datacenter Designer*: Here we configure the runtime environment in a logical datacenter.

- *Deployment Designer*: By using this, we can define and even validate system design against the logical data design. We can use it to make sure that what we build will be able to be deployed in our infrastructure.

I will come back to these designers when we talk about architecture with VSTS later in this chapter. For now, it is enough to say that using these tools enables us to enhance collaboration between business, solution, and infrastructure architects in a great way.

Visual Studio Team System Database Edition

Finally, Microsoft has provided a set of tools for database developers that are as easy to use as Visual Studio itself. We now have the capability to version-control our database scripts and other database items just as we can do with developer items in the other versions of VS.

The Database edition is fully integrated with VS (see Figure 7-7), which helps database developers in their development process while at the same time improving collaboration with other developers in the team. In my view, this is an important step in integrating the database team with the rest of the development team.

In the Database edition, each database project is an offline representation of a database. It exists within the scope of a VS solution, and we can perform tasks such as builds and deployments on it. Because this edition is fully integrated with VS, we can work in it much as we can work with all development. The difference is that we focus on database development and can configure database settings instead of other application settings. We can use this edition to create and validate databases, tables, views, stored procedures, and so on in design time.

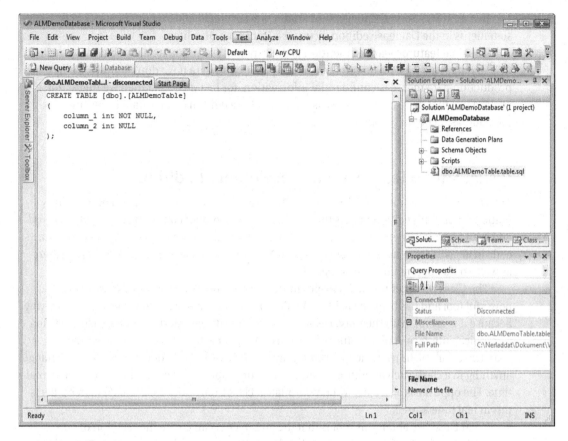

Figure 7-7. *Visual Studio Team System Database Edition*

If we want to, we can import existing database schemas into the tool, reverse-engineer them, and put them under source control. It is not the entire database we version-control in VSTS; it's the database schema. If we have already deployed a database, we can compare the design-time database with the production database and see whether any modifications have been made to it in the production environment by using a schema-comparison tool. If changes have occurred, we can import these changes so that the design-time database is up-to-date. And the other way around: If the design-time database has changed, we can get the update scripts created so we can bring the production environment up-to-date.

When we are finished designing a database, we create a build script, including database object creation scripts and deployment scripts so we can deploy the database into production. If the database exists, we can have the update scripts generated for us.

If we have two databases with matching schemas, we can compare the data in the two databases. We can also generate scripts to get the data in the target database to match the source. This can come in handy when retrieving data into a test environment from the production server.

We can also get unit testing of our databases in design time. We can generate unit tests for stored procedures or functions, or we can choose to create our own unit tests. This is a feature I know many of my database-specialized coworkers have been waiting for.

Just as in SQL Server Management Studio, we can create and execute Transact-SQL statements in the Database edition by using a Transact-SQL editor.

The final feature I want to mention is the capability to populate a database with realistic test data. This way, we do not have to use production data if we don't want to. Sometimes production data includes confidential information, for instance, and then we might not want to use that data. If that is the case, the Database edition creates data for us, matching the database schema.

Visual Studio Team System Development Edition

The Development edition of VSTS is probably the most widely spread version of the Team Edition family. This edition targets the large .NET development community around the world and is an enormous step forward for developers, in my view. With this edition, we can write code in all .NET languages such as C# and VB.NET (although you can do that with the others as well, so it's not unique to this version).

The Class Designer that a developer most likely will use is not new in any way. It is a powerful tool and has been available in VS Pro for a while. I just want to show it to you anyway because it is useful. With the Class Designer, we can create and modify classes easily by using a graphical interface. A nice feature of the Class Designer is that it is connected with the source code all the time. In fact, you could say that it *is* the source code—because if we change anything in a class, such as adding a new method or property, the code will be updated in real time. The opposite is also true: when we update a class from code, the Class Designer reflects this in real time as well.

What I also like about this tool is that the architect(s) can create the skeleton of our classes during their architect work and then leave those to the solution designer to continue working on. So we can let the architects design the interfaces of not only the participating parts of the system, but also the classes if we like. The implementation of the logic in the classes is still the solution developer's responsibility to develop, which is good because that is not architecture, as you saw in Chapter 4.

At first my coworkers and I thought that the idea of a graphical class designer made programming a little bit too much like building a toy or something—a "real programmers write code, we don't use tools" kind of thinking. We started trying it out, however, and realized we liked it a lot. The connection between code and the Class Designer in real time was something that especially appealed to us. By having the graphical interface, we discovered that we could more easily discuss and share our thoughts with the not-so-technical team members, which improved collaboration a great deal. Things are not as abstract when you see them in the Class Designer, as they might be when you see only code. My recommendation is that you at least try it out if you haven't done so already. If you don't program, ask a developer to show you and see whether you feel the same way as we do about its collaboration possibilities.

The GUI of the Development edition does not differ much from the other editions, as you can see in Figure 7-8.

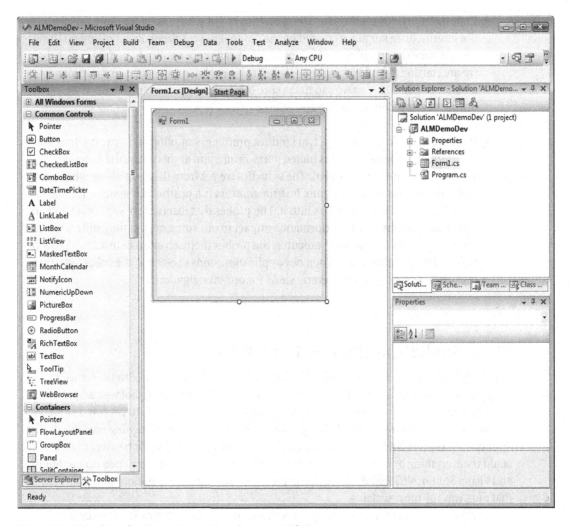

Figure 7-8. *Visual Studio Team System Development Edition*

There are three sets of tools I want to mention here:

- *Code analysis*: Code analysis is a useful tool. When many developers are working on
  a project, they often have their own habits of writing code. Variable declarations,
  naming conventions, and so on can differ. At the Swedish Road Administration (SRA),
  I currently work with public procurement of IT services and development projects. We
  use a lot of consultants who often continue writing code in existing applications. This
  makes it hard for me to really know whether they follow the development guidelines
  we have at the SRA. By using code analysis, I can run checks on the code, making sure
  it follows the rules I have set up. I can force the developers to follow these guidelines
  by not allowing a check-in without having run a successful code analysis. We can use
  code analysis to turn our habits into rules so we get a higher quality in our code.
  Microsoft supplies a lot of industry standards best practices with VS, but we can also
  add our own.

- *Code metrics*: Code metrics are useful metrics of our source code (or more precisely of the intermediate language created by the compiler at runtime). By reporting on these, we can trace the complexity of our code so we can more easily adjust if we notice that we are starting to build a spaghetti plate. This is useful for managers, project managers, and developers alike, so we can make sure our code won't cause problems later, either during development or during operations.

- *Profiling tools*: These tools use two kinds of profiling: sampling and instrumentation. In s*ampling*, code execution is halted periodically, and at this pause the functions that are being executed are recorded. The statistics we get from this help us see which methods consume the most CPU time. *Instrumentation* is a postbuild operation that takes our software and inserts probes into it. The probes that inserted are very small and are designed to minimize the performance impact to our software, but they still can have a slight impact. As our software executes, the probes themselves execute and VSTS gathers the data that they emit. When our application stops executing, the collected data is processed and displayed in several views for our investigation.

Visual Studio Team System Test Edition

When my former coauthor Rickard Redler and I first started using Visual Studio, we were happy to see that the functionality of the Web Application Stress (WAS) tool we had previously used for stress-testing web sites was integrated into Visual Studio .NET. To get some confirmation on our proposed way of architecting software in our first book, *Designing Scalable .NET Applications* (Apress 2003), we convinced Dell to lend us their test lab for two weeks so we could try everything out. Happily, we set off to Stockholm with our source code on our laptops and Visual Studio .NET installed. We wanted to stress-test different solutions and point out that ours was the most scalable.

Once there with everything set up, we started configuring Application Center Test (ACT), which was the tool Microsoft provided in VS at that time. To our surprise, we could not use multiple test clients and we really needed that. ACT was limited to one client only while WAS gave us the capability to use many clients. We had to come up with a solution, and after several hours of discussions with Microsoft Sweden, we came up with a complicated setup. (I refer you to the previously mentioned book if you want to know how we really did it in the end. It worked but it was a lot of effort.)

When I started trying the tools in VSTS Test Edition, I was pleasantly surprised. It seemed like all I had wanted before was included. We finally have testing tools that compete well with Mercury/HP's QuickTest Professional and other big tools on the market. And they are all integrated in VS so we don't have to use several tools to run or set up our tests.

The Test edition has several test types available:

- *Unit tests*: Well, as I have said, all editions of VS have them now, and the Test edition is no exception.

- *Web tests*: We can record and play back tests of web sites and mimic user behavior of different kinds.

- *Load tests*: We can use these to stress-test not only web sites but also application logic—pretty much what my former coauthor and I wanted to do in the Dell test lab. We created web tests and used them for load-testing the solution.

- *Manual tests*: Sometimes we cannot automate all tests, so we need to have testers doing manual tests. We can create and run manual tests directly from within VS.

- *Generic tests*: A generic test wraps external programs and tests that were not originally made for use as VS test tools.

- *Ordered tests*: We can sort our tests so that they are run in a certain order.

From within the Test edition, we can create, modify, and run all of these tests. We can automate them and connect them to our build process if we want to. It is also possible to run tests from the command line. VS collects the test results and saves them to the database so we can see reports on them later.

Testing with VSTS

Visual Studio Team System Test Edition provides a suite of testing tools that can help us test both web applications and services. These tools are integrated into the VS environment. With these tools, testers can author, execute, and manage tests directly from VS. Many of the test competitors offer stand-alone tools that are not integrated into VS, and having as many tests as possible accessible from the same tool is something that ALM 2.0 promotes.

I think it is great that Microsoft has provided a testing tool that has the potential to fight with the big actors on the market such as Mercury (now part of Business Technology Optimization, or BTO, Software from HP) and others. What makes it even more interesting is that compared to many of its competitors, the price of VSTS Test Edition is significantly lower. Many of my coworkers specializing in testing have been very impressed with Microsoft's test suite. It might not have all the advanced features of Mercury/HP QuickTest Professional, but is more attractive because of the price tag. At Know IT Sweden, we have started to use the Test edition a lot for stress-testing web sites.

In VSTS Test Edition, we find the following test types:

- Web tests

- Manual tests

- Generic tests

- Ordered tests

- Load tests

Let's take a look at how these tests work and how we can use them.

Web Tests

When Rickard Redler and I wrote our first book about scalable .NET application architecture a few years ago, we presented an example web application in the book. When we tested the scalability, we used ACT, which shipped with the early versions of Visual Studio .NET. In ACT, we recorded a user interacting with the web site in a typical way, and then let ACT replay the interaction, simulating an increasing load of users. What we did was run web tests against the test environment that Dell lent us.

A *web test* consists of a series of HTTP requests, which in our case was the user interaction. The test tool sends a series of HTTP requests at the protocol layer and records response times and other testing information.

In Figure 7-9, you can see the results of a web test in the Web Test Viewer inside VSTS Test Edition.

Note Web tests are also called *declarative web tests*.

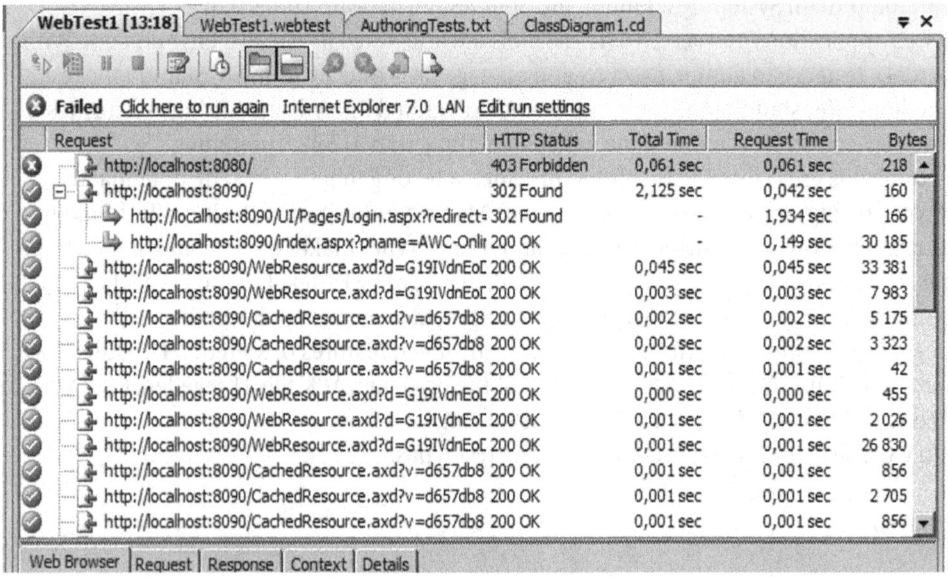

Figure 7-9. *Web test results in the Web Test Viewer*

VSTS Test Edition has some limitations, however. We cannot run JavaScript, for instance. If we want that functionality, we must simulate it in some way. Fortunately, we can do that by using several methods: use a web test plug-in, code the web test (more about this in a moment), or use some other methods as well.

There are two ways to create the web tests:

- *Record user interaction in a web browser*: This is fairly simple to perform. We start recording our own fake user interaction directly from VS. VS then starts a browser, and everything we do is recorded so we can replay it later. If we need to extend this recorded web test, we can convert it to code (C# or VB.NET, for instance) and have a coded web test instead.

- *Code the web test*: This means that we create the web tests manually in the Web Test Editor (see Figure 7-10) or that we have converted a recorded web test to code. A recorded web test includes powerful web-testing abilities but lacks the features of advanced programming languages. Coded web tests should be used when advanced flow-control or looping constructs are required. We will probably most often start with a recorded web test, convert it to code, and then extend it.

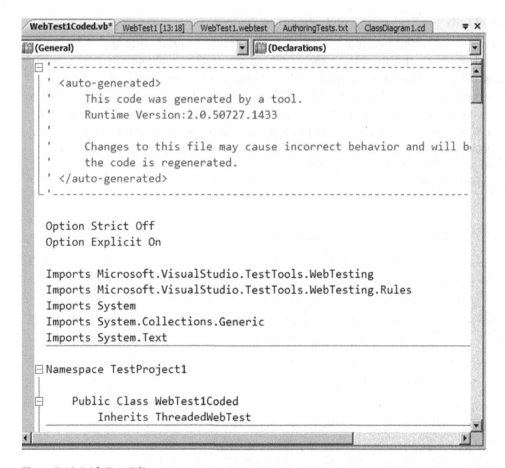

Figure 7-10. *Web Test Editor*

When should we use web tests? There are a number of reasons for using web tests. Web tests are, among other things, used to test how our web applications perform under a heavy load so we can determine whether we have chosen the right scalability and performance model. We can let the tool simulate an increasing number of users so we can determine when the site actually stops responding. Web tests are also used to test the functionality of the web site.

A user generally supplies information to a web site. If we test an e-commerce site, for instance, we would probably want to record the user placing items in the shopping cart and then purchasing these using a credit card. To simulate different users, we can create data-driven tests that fetch user information (address, phone, name, credit card number, and so on) from a data source. We can hard-code this if we want, but most likely we want to have this information in SQL Server (or any other data store, such as an XML file). In VSTS Test Edition, this is possible to accomplish, giving us greater flexibility in the way we perform the tests than we could do in the old ACT.

All results from the web tests are stored in the TFS database for easy retrieval later for our reports.

Manual Tests

It is not always possible to automate all tests. In some cases, we need a user to perform the test and decide whether the test was successful—in other words, a *manual test*. As an example, we might need to test user interface behavior or details in the user interface. We can create our own test cases by using a Microsoft Word document as a template (see Figure 7-11).

In the template, we write down the steps necessary to execute the test and the expected result. When the user later runs the manual test from within VS, the tester is presented with this document and follows the steps listed. The tester can then indicate whether the test passed or failed by clicking a button. The result is stored in the TFS database so we can report on the results later.

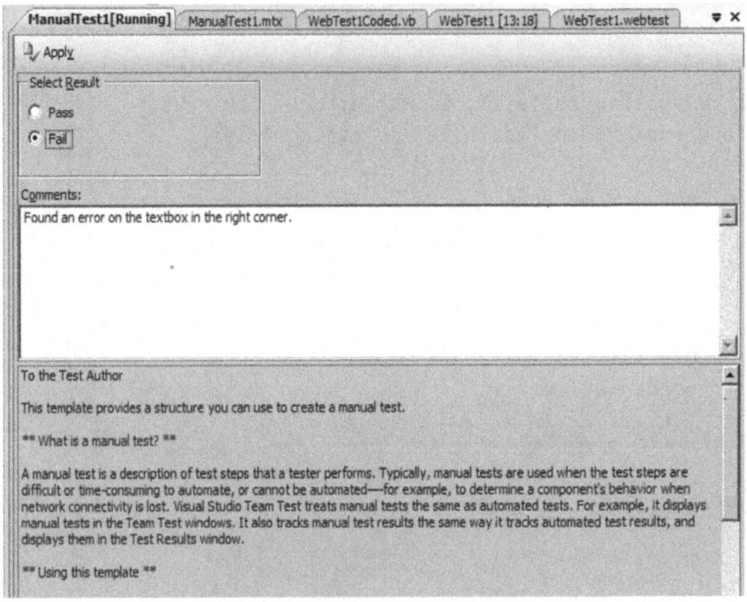

Figure 7-11. *A manual test template from MSF for Agile*

Generic Tests

If we have invested money to create tests in other test tools, we don't want to lose that invest-ment by redoing these tests in VSTS Test Edition. This is one of the reasons Microsoft has included a *generic test*. By using a generic test, we can create a wrapper around the third-party tool and still use VSTS to run the tests in the other tool. We can also use generic tests to run programs and existing tests.

However, this works only if the wrapped tool can be run from the command line and returns a Pass or Fail value. Optionally, the generic test also returns detailed results for the "inner" tests that it contains.

We can use VS to run and manage these tests from within the Visual Studio interface. This also allows us to store and publish the results just like any other test result. VS treats these tests just like its own tests.

Ordered Tests

Sometimes we might want to run a series of tests in a specific order. In this case, we can use an *ordered test*. We can create an ordered test of all test types except load tests. In VS we can arrange the tests in any order we want. We can also run the same test multiple times if neces-sary, by including it several times. An ordered test appears as a single test in the Test List Editor and the Test View window.

The results of an ordered test appear in a single row in the Test Results window. The results can also be viewed for each individual test in the ordered test by drilling down from the ordered test results.

■**Note** By using the Test List Editor, we can organize tests into test lists. We can also run tests, and filter and group the display of tests we have loaded, and also import additional tests into a currently loaded set. If we want to, we can export tests as well.

Load Tests

A *load test* is primarily used to evaluate the performance of a server by simulating multiple users at the same time. The web tests we create can be used in load tests to simulate multiple users accessing our web site so we can then evaluate the performance of the site. As you have seen, this is done by simulating a series of HTTP requests. A load test can simulate several users by opening multiple connections simultaneously. To further increase the load on the server, we can use multiple client computers simulating a heavy load.

But not all applications are web applications. And because not only web applications are dependent on good performance and scalability, we can also use load tests to test other com-ponents. This can be done, for example, by running unit tests from a load test.

Load tests consist of a series of web tests or unit tests that operate under multiple simulated users over a period of time. Load tests are created with the Load Test Wizard (see Figure 7-12). There is also a Load Test Editor we can use to edit our load test configurations.

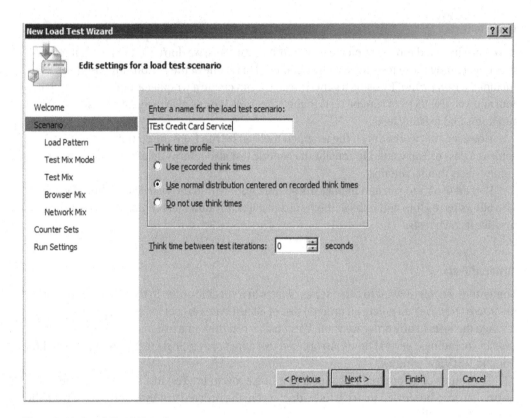

Figure 7-12. *Load Test Wizard*

Load tests are used for several types of testing:

- *Smoke tests*: These are a collection of tests aimed at identifying any obvious problems before conducting further testing. They evaluate how the application performs under a relatively light load, so we can see whether there is an immediate problem (compare this to looking for smoke in a forest to catch a forest fire early).

- *Stress tests*: This is what we already covered; we evaluate how well the application performs under stress for a specific time period.

- *Performance tests*: These tests determine how responsive the application is under heavy load.

- *Capacity planning tests*: These determine how the application performs at various capacities. We use this type of test to evaluate which hardware we might need to handle the load we expect on the system.

Automation of High-Level Processes

As you have seen throughout this book, it is essential to automate the ALM process to fully realize the benefits of taking control of it. VSTS can help us quite a lot by letting us have one or more process templates on the TFS server that define the way we work with the ALM process.

In this section, you'll take a look at the VSTS process template as well as the two instances of Microsoft Solutions Framework templates that Microsoft provides us with out of the box. You'll learn about a template based on Scrum that is developed by a third-party vendor (Scrum for Team System), and about another template that is not available out of the box with VSTS but can be downloaded from Microsoft's website (eScrum). Finally, I'll tell you briefly about three other templates: EssUp, Lightweight Scrum, and XP for Team System.

Project Process Template

What is the process template, really? Well, it's nothing magic at all. The template helps us visualize and automate the tasks and steps that the process includes. It helps us by providing templates for documents such as requirements specs, test cases, scenarios, handoffs, and other artifacts we should produce. We even get a web page including help and description for the steps in the process. And it's completely configurable.

In VSTS, the process template is in fact a set of XML files that are stored on the TFS server. We can have one or more process templates on the server, and when a project is created, we can choose which template we want to base our project on (see Figure 7-13). The Project Creation Wizard creates a new TFS project based on the XML files for the process we have selected.

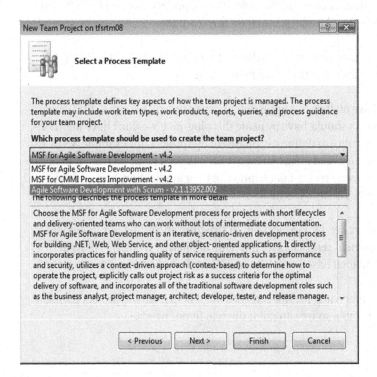

Figure 7-13. *Choosing the project template during project creation in VSTS*

The process template has three key parts that I think are essential to understand in order to be able to determine which adjustments we need and can make to VSTS so that it suits our needs:

- Process template plug-ins

- XML process definition files

- Project Creation Wizard

Process Template Plug-Ins

The template plug-ins are components that are executed when a new team project is created on the TFS server. They set up the required files and configure data for a specific area of the process template. TFS includes the following plug-ins:

- *Version control*: This part defines the initial version-control system's security permissions and check-in notes.

- *Groups and permissions*: This plug-in defines the initial security groups and the permissions for these.

- *Work item tracking*: Here we get the definitions of the work item types that the process includes: which work item queries are the defaults for a project, and the default work item instances we have for all projects based on this template.

- *Reports*: All reports we have access to by default in a project are defined by using this plug-in. We also define the structure of the reports here.

- *Classification*: If we have an iterative approach to development, we can define which initial iterations a project should have by using this plug-in. If we don't have iterations, we can use this functionality to define the phases of our project, for example. VSTS also has another classification called *areas*. An area is pretty much what we want it to be. One customer of mine uses one area per window in their application, and others use them in some other way. The usage is up to us.

- *Windows SharePoint Services*: Our project portal structure, including our document structure and the document templates we have, are defined by using this plug-in. The project portal is defined based on a Windows SharePoint Services site template.

As you can see from the preceding list, we can get a lot of help from the project template. All these plug-ins are customizable so we can tailor them to fit our needs.

XML Definition Files

The plug-ins discussed in the preceding paragraphs use XML files to create our team project. When we run the Project Creation Wizard from VSTS and create a new project, the plug-ins read these files and look at what is defined in them. The plug-ins implement what we have specified in these files, creating the structure we want for our project. To fully understand how much we really can control the process template, take a closer look at these files:

- *Work Item Tracking XML*: In this XML file (`WorkItems.xml`), there are three types of tasks the plug-in must do:

  - *Work item types* indicate rules, fields, states, and transitions for an item of work that will be tracked on a team project. All our work item types are specified here, such as bugs, tasks, requirements, and so on.

  - *Work item queries* specify the queries we can run on our work items. The WIQL definitions themselves are saved in separate files, and these are pointed out in this file.

  - *Work item instances* define which work items will be present by default when a new project is created.

- *Classifications XML*: In the file `Classification.xml`, we find all definitions for our *iterations* and *areas*. We can specify which iterations and areas will be present by default.

- *Windows SharePoint Services XML*: This file is named `WssTasks.xml` and defines three tasks:

  - *Site templates* indicate the template on which the project portal is based in WSS. The site template itself is not part of the process template.

  - *Document libraries* define how our document structure will be on the project portal.

  - *Folders and files* specify any additional folders we need, and which files we want to use as templates for our project documents.

- *Version Control XML*: In the file `VersionControl.xml`, we define a team project's initial version-control *security permissions* (what actions can security groups and individuals perform on version-controlled items?), *check-in notes* (are they required or not?) and whether *exclusive check-out* is required (this controls whether multiple users can check out the same file at the same time).

- *Reports XML*: The file ReportTasks.xml specifies the project's initial reports for our projects. *The reports site* task defines the link to the reports on the project portal. *Folders* has information about which report folders will be available under the reports folder in the Team Explorer. *Reports* specifies which report files will be available in the report folders.

- *Groups and Permissions XML*: The initial security groups in a project are defined by the file GroupsandPermissions.xml. Here we find information about groups (TFS security groups, not Active Directory groups) and the permissions they each have.

Project Creation Wizard

When we want to create a new project in TFS, we right-click on the server in TFS and choose New Team Project, as shown in Figure 7-14. This starts the Project Creation Wizard.

Figure 7-14. *Creating a new project in Team Explorer*

As with all Microsoft wizards, this one helps us through the process, which in this case is creating a new team project on the TFS server. This wizard uses the plug-ins in the preceding list, which in turn use all the XML files we have covered. It's pretty simple and works very well.

Microsoft Solutions Framework

What process templates does Microsoft provide us with out of the box? Well, I have mentioned them before: Microsoft provides two instances of the Microsoft Solutions Framework (MSF), and they differ from each other. They are targeted at two different styles of development, really.

MSF for Agile builds on the agile values you read about in Chapter 4, and MSF for CMMI follows the Capability Maturity Model Integration methodology from the Software Engineering Institute (SEI). The latter is a more formal model aimed at improving existing development processes. The difference is visible not only in its documentation, but also in the greater number of work items and reports that MSF for CMMI has as compared to MSF for Agile.

Table 7-1 lists the work items that Microsoft supplies for the two instances of MSF that ship with TFS.

Table 7-1. *Work Items in MSF*

MSF for Agile	MSF for CMMI
Bug	Bug
Quality of Service (Nonfunctional requirement.)	Requirement
Risk	Risk
Task (Generic, we can use it as we want.)	Task
Scenario (An example of how the end user will use the system. Compare this with an extended use case.)	Review (Identifies the result of an in-depth look into the code or design of the application.)
	Change request
	Issue

As you can see in Table 7-1, the two instances of MSF differ in the work item sets they offer. MSF for CMMI has two more work item types than MSF for Agile. The information on the work items also differs a bit.

When it comes to reports, there are also a lot of differences (see Figures 7-15 and 7-16).

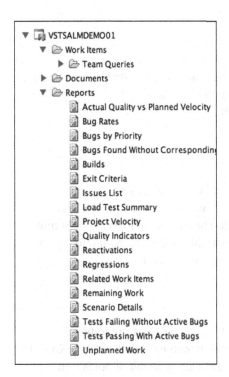

Figure 7-15. *The reports differ between MSF for Agile . . .*

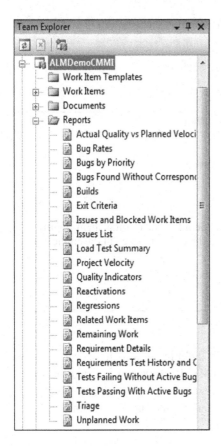

Figure 7-16. *. . . and MSF for CMMI*

The document structure is also different. We will come back to these reports and queries later in this chapter when we talk about project management using VSTS. We'll leave them for now and jump into the agile templates based on Scrum.

Scrum for Team System

One of the most exciting Scrum templates for VSTS is Scrum for Team System from Conchango (www.scrumforteamsystem.com). It is a free, downloadable template we can use to run our projects in a true agile spirit. This is by far the best implementation of a Scrum process in VSTS, even though Microsoft's eScrum doesn't fall far behind. Scrum for Team System is easier to install than eScrum, which definitely is to its favor.

Features

Most Scrum features are supported in Scrum for Team System, and there are some extra artifacts as well helping us run our projects. Scrum for Team System is used widely at Know IT, and feedback has been good from my coworkers, even those most fanatic about Scrum practices.

Scrum for Team System includes the following features:

- Work items for sprint, product backlog, sprint backlog, sprint retrospectives, and impediments

- Reports for sprint and product burndown, and many more to help you monitor your project

- Process guidance, which explains all the rules, roles, and artifacts of Scrum

- Multimedia guidance from Ken Schwaber, the co-creator of Scrum

Artifacts

As you saw in Chapter 4, Scrum uses several artifacts, or tools, to help us support the development process and track progress. Simplicity is the name of the game in Scrum and is thought to support face-to-face communication. These tools should never replace this communication, though. This is also the reason why tools are used scarcely in many Scrum projects.

But tools such as VSTS can help us in many ways. We can capture the necessary data, formulate the artifacts, and expose them digitally by using a tool. In most of the Scrum teams using Scrum for Team System at Know IT, we still use printed or sketched versions of the artifacts anyway because we want to encourage communication. In many cases, we print reports from VSTS and hang them on the wall. These are sometimes referred to as *information radiators* and are used to contribute to the team's sense of purpose and motivation.

We will now have a look at some of the work items, reports, and queries in Scrum for Team System. This overview is provided to help you decide whether this is a template you can benefit from. Keep in mind that Scrum for Team System focuses on the development process. If we want to extend the template to cover the other aspects of ALM, we need to do this manually. I will show some examples of the work items in Scrum for Team System so that you can understand just how much we can change in TFS. We don't need to use the MSF work items if we don't want to. I thank Conchango for their help in supplying examples for these work items and reports.

- *Product Backlog*: This is a work item for maintaining product backlog items (see Figure 7-17). The Product Backlog work item is the most fundamental artifact in Scrum. The backlog is a prioritized list of functional and nonfunctional requirements. We also can add information about high-level estimates for the amount of work it will take to turn each item into a completed part of the system. Conchango recommends that backlog items be added, modified, and viewed through either Team Explorer or the Microsoft Excel 2003/2007 Team System plug-in. Microsoft Project 2003 isn't a tool that fits well with a Scrum approach, according to Conchango, and is therefore not supported in Scrum for Team System.

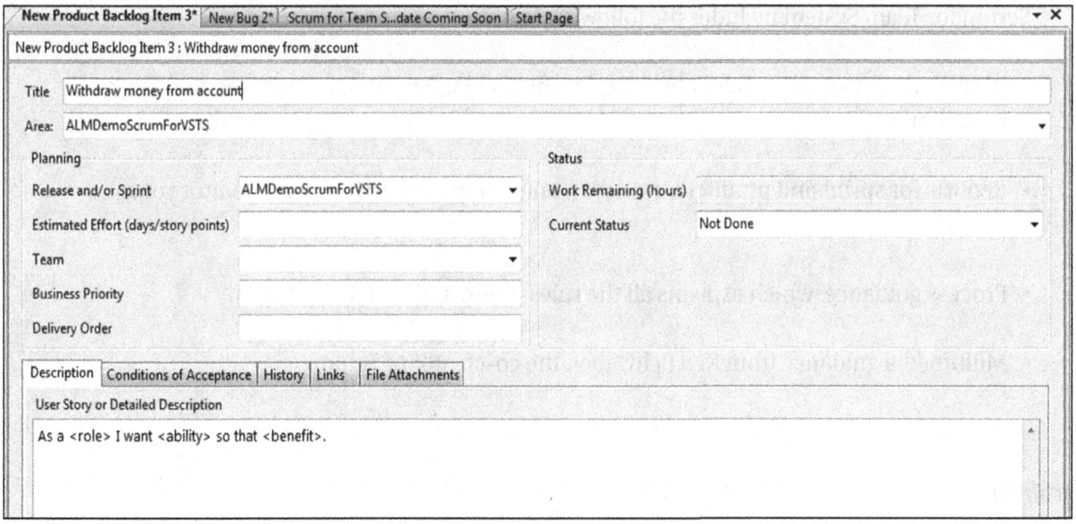

Figure 7-17. *The Product Backlog work item in Scrum for Team System*

- *Sprint Backlog*: This is a work item (see Figure 7-18) for maintaining sprint backlogs. The Sprint Backlog is a list of tasks that defines a team's work for a sprint. The list is created during the sprint planning meeting. The team defines what is required to turn each committed Product Backlog item into system functionality. For each Sprint Backlog item, the team identifies who is responsible for doing the work and also estimates the amount of work it will take to develop.

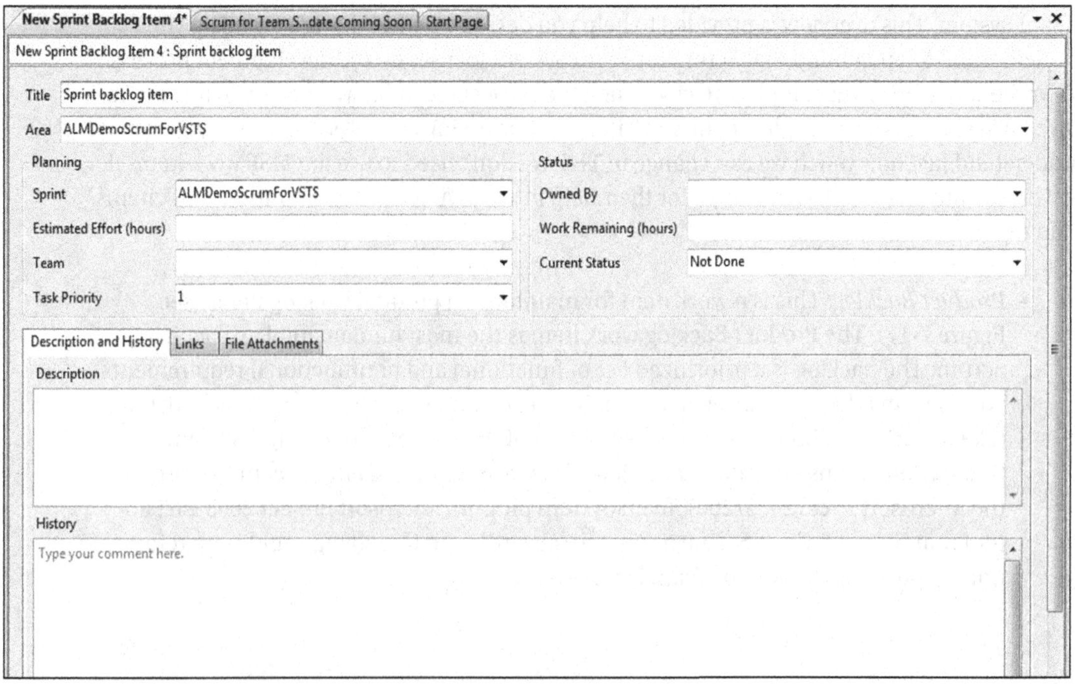

Figure 7-18. *The Sprint Backlog work item in Scrum for Team System*

- *Bug work item*: This is a work item type in Scrum for Team System used for reporting bugs (see Figure 7-19).

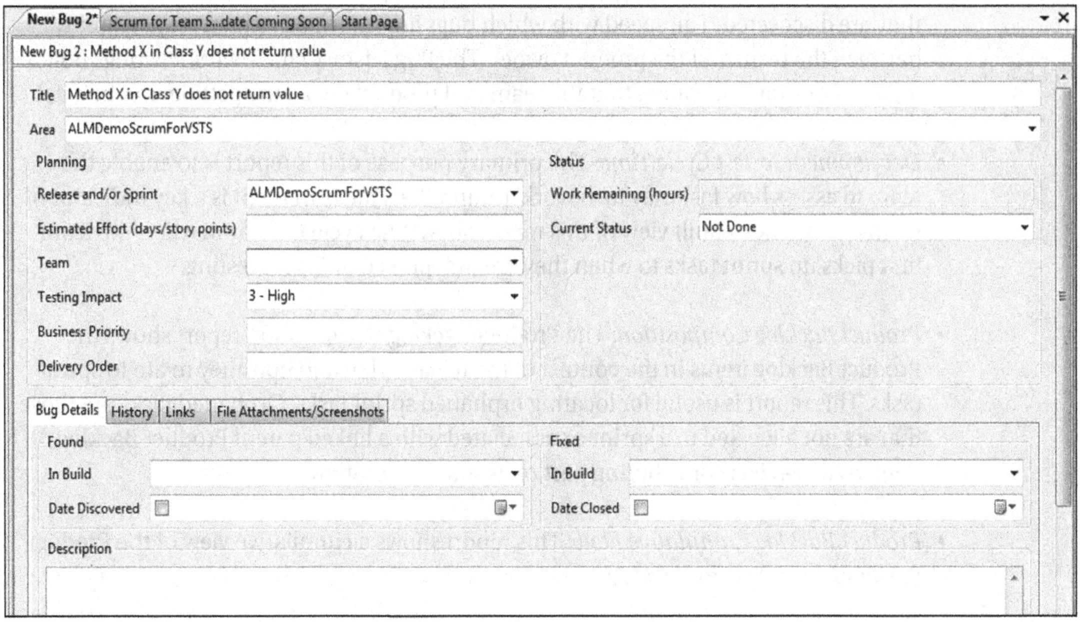

Figure 7-19. *The Bug work item in Scrum for Team System*

Scrum for Team System also provides some reports that are not described or defined by Scrum. At www.scrumforteamsystem.com/processguidance/v2/Artefacts/Reports.aspx, you can find these described in more detail. The reports are useful in supporting the Scrum development process, so even the most hard-core Scrum user should like them. Conchango has provided these to promote good development and testing practices that are intended to improve the overall quality and speed of team output. My coworkers like most of these reports. So here's a list of some of the most important ones:

- *Bug Count*: The Bug Count report shows the numbers of bugs by their state, with drill-down revealing a breakdown by testing impact on a given date. Visual indicators also show whether the number of bugs in a given state is increasing, stable, or decreasing.

- *Bug Found and Fixed*: This chart shows the comparative rate at which bugs are found and fixed in a selected time window. The time window defaults to the current sprint start and end dates, but other sprints can be chosen.

- *Bug History*: The Bug History report is a chart showing how the number of open bugs, categorized by testing impact, has changed over time. This provides a clear indication of the build up of *bug debt*.

- *Bug Priority*: The Bug Priority report shows a chart of bugs outstanding, grouped by their testing impact. A testing impact of Blocking is the most severe and indicates that the bug is preventing further testing of functionality.

- *Bug Resolution Time*: This report shows how fast bugs are being resolved from the date they are discovered. The speed with which bugs are resolved is a joint responsibility between the team and the product owner. The Bug History chart will show bugs building up over time, indicating that the team and product owner are getting into bug debt.

- *Development to Test Cycle Time*: The primary purpose of this report is to enable the team to assess how fast they turn work around. This measurement is a key indicator of team agility. The default view of this report shows the cycle time from when the team first picks up sprint tasks to when they are first passed to QA for testing.

- *Product Backlog Composition*: The Product Backlog Composition report shows the Product Backlog items in the context of the release plan and how they relate to sprint tasks. This report is useful for locating orphaned sprint tasks. Orphaned tasks are those that are not allocated to a sprint or associated with a linked parent Product Backlog item for which it is contributing part of its implementation.

- *Product Backlog Cumulative Flow*: This report shows a cumulative view of the Product Backlog item over time by state.

- *Product Burndown by Day*: This day-by-day version of the Product Burndown chart shows how the team is performing on a daily basis. It also shows how new work and bugs are adding to the total amount of work and hence whether the team will be able to finish by the intended release date.

- *Product Burndown by Sprint*: This sprint-by-sprint version of the Product Burndown chart illustrates how the team is performing on a sprint-to-sprint basis. It also shows how new work and bugs are adding to the total amount of work and hence whether the team will be able to finish by the intended release date.

- *Sprint Backlog Cumulative Flow*: This report shows a cumulative view of the Sprint Backlog items over time by state.

- *Sprint Burndown*: The Sprint Burndown chart gives the team members a daily indication of their velocity and progress against the work they have committed to for the current sprint. Even early on in a sprint, the burndown chart gives the team a good idea of how they're progressing against their sprint tasks and whether they will complete them by the end of the sprint.

- *Sprint View*: The Sprint View report shows a matrix of the Sprint Backlog items allocated to a sprint, against the working days included in the sprint. The report may be physically quite large, and is intended to be printed out on A3 paper or larger, or projected onto a wall or whiteboard.

- *Team Project Portal*: This provides a simple dashboard giving an overview of project progress at a glance. In addition, the portal includes links to the full Scrum for Team System reports through a web browser. There is also a team wiki for capturing and communicating dynamic, ad hoc information, and a document repository for formal documentation. An overall picture of project progress is provided by parameterless versions of the Sprint Burndown and Product Burndown charts.

Scrum for Team System also has a query called All Impediments. Anything that impedes the team's productivity and quality is an impediment. The scrum master is responsible for removing any impediment that is stopping the team from producing quality code. The impediment list is simply a set of tasks that the scrum master uses to track the impediments that need to be solved. In Figure 7-20, you can see the Impediment work item type.

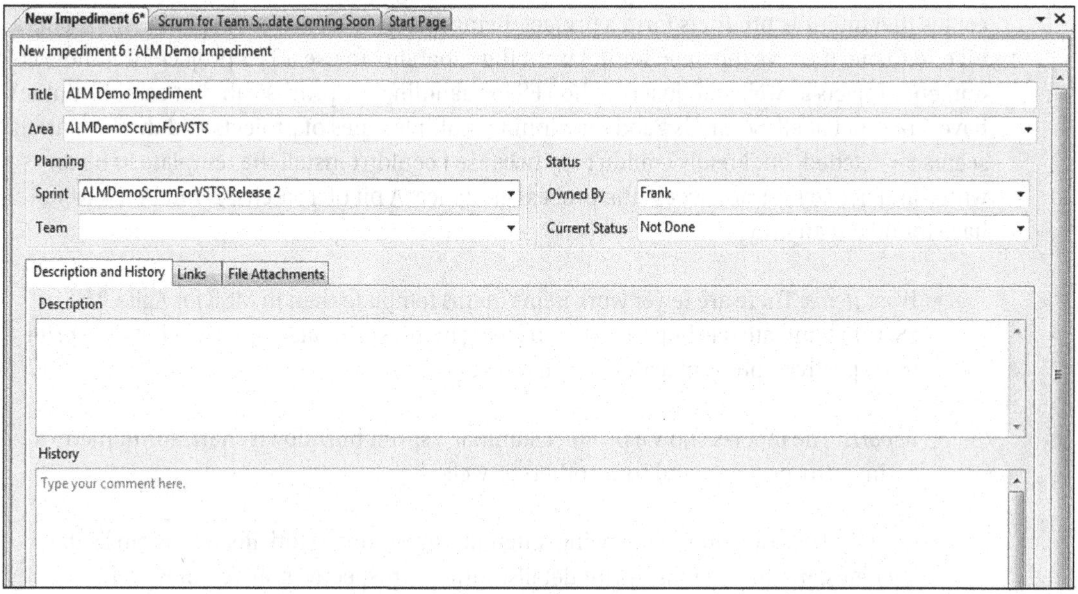

Figure 7-20. *The Impediment work item in Scrum for Team System*

In my opinion, Scrum for Team System works very well. My coworkers seem to be very happy using it, and no real worries have arisen with them. There are other implementations of Scrum for VSTS as well. Let's have a brief look at Microsoft's own version.

eScrum

The eScrum template is Microsoft's own version of a Scrum process. It is more agile than MSF for Agile, and more true to the agile values. It has a nice dashboard for tracking your sprint, lets you keep on top of the daily Scrum electronically, and offers a wide array of Scrum reports such as burndowns, metrics, and a product summary. You can download eScrum for free from http://msdn.microsoft.com and give it a try. Remember that it is not supported by Microsoft in any way and is provided as is.

The downside of the eScrum template is that it seems to be a bit difficult to install. For this book, I tried to install it on two different virtual computers using Microsoft Virtual PC (VPCs), but none of them succeeded. Scrum for Team System installed without problems on both of these VPCs. This is unfortunately a common problem. When I looked around on the Internet for a solution, I discovered that many had similar problems. So Microsoft, you have a good implementation of Scrum here, and a template offering more agility than MSF for Agile. Why is it so hard to install?

What do we have in the package after it is installed? Because my own VPCs obviously didn't work, I turned to my friend and Microsoft employee Dag König and asked him to provide some screenshots so that I at least could write about it. As far as I understand, there is a concept in eScrum called *product*. The thing with Scrum is that it's adaptable; that's the whole point. There is no golden rule of how it actually works. There are guidelines that people generally follow, but in eScrum you must have something called a product. The eScrum project you create isn't good enough; it needs something actually called a product. The concept is that multiple products form a project. Being forced to have a concept like this seems a bit odd to me. If I have the need for it, I want the capability to use a TFS project for nondevelopment projects as well, and just use the TFS for handling my process. In that case, I wouldn't have a product at all. Scrum is good for running multiple types of projects and this limitation seems far-fetched, but I really couldn't say because I couldn't install the template to begin with—and hence I cannot access the process guidance. A bit of a catch-22, but here's what I have found out anyway:

- *Work items*: There are fewer work items in this template than in MSF for Agile. The eScrum template has bugs, product backlog items, sprint tasks, product details, sprint retrospectives, product features, and more.

- *Reports*: The reports show a product summary, sprint burndown chart, sprint metrics, sprint retrospectives, and some others as well.

- *Queries*: There are queries showing different aspects of all work items. We can list backlog items, product details, sprint details, sprint retrospectives, all features of the product, and a few others.

It's a shame that Microsoft has not spent more time on this template, or at least its installation. I really wanted to have a go at it, but because the installation problems stopped me, it will have to be another time.

Other Process Templates

There are other VSTS templates as well. At http://msdn.microsoft.com/en-us/vsts2008/
aa718795.aspx, we can find many more. There we will also find news about everything regarding templates in VSTS. Just to mention some of the other templates, here are three to consider:

- *EssUp*: This template from Ivar Jacobson International is one of the most talked about
  but least seen, I would say. The reason for this is that Ivar Jacobson International
  requires us to attend a course or buy consulting hours from them before we can use it.
  Together with the customer, IVC looks at the needs of the organization and then they
  together produce the process template for use in VSTS. I like the idea of this because it
  makes the organization think about their needs and how to implement these in VSTS,
  and not just buy a new version-control system. But just sneaking a glance at the template is not possible yet.

- *Lightweight Scrum*: This template, from the Scrum Community Process project, is
  another one I want to promote. You can find it at CodePlex (www.codeplex.com/
  VSTSScrum). The Scrum community project has been created to generate a Scrum
  process template that takes advantage of the features of VSTS. The template is available
  for Visual Studio 2005 and 2008 at the time of this writing. This template is a free download, so just go ahead and try it out.

- *XP for Team System*: If you are a fan of Extreme Programming, there is also a template
  for that on CodePlex (www.codeplex.com/XPForTeamSystem). This template extends the
  existing MSF for Agile template. For instance, it removes the Quality of Service work
  item type and adds a Story work item type.

Visibility

There are different ways to enable visibility in our projects. You have seen in Chapter 6 that
reports and queries can provide access to all the information we have in the TFS server regarding our projects.

Information about the status of our code is essential for project members to have access
to through a project. Even managers and stakeholders might need information without having
to chase the project manager to get it. Automating data generation for reports and queries is
essential to off-load the project manager, and VSTS can help us with this.

Code Metrics

Code metrics are used to trace the complexity of our code so we more easily can adjust if we
notice that we are starting to build a spaghetti plate. We can get five metrics from our code:
class coupling, depth of inheritance, cyclomatic complexity, lines of code, and maintainability
index (see Figure 7-21).

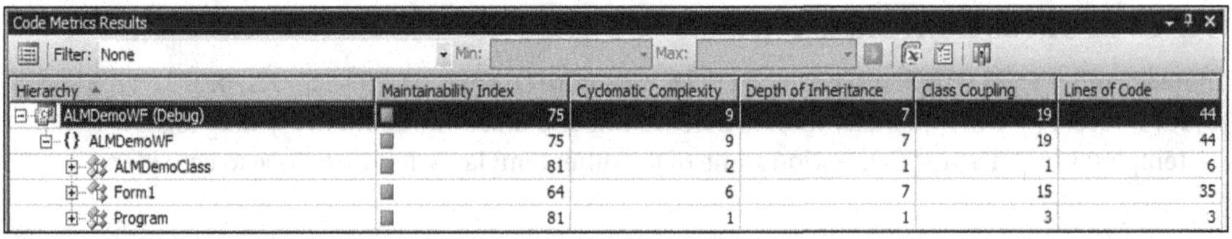

Code Metrics Results

Filter: None Min: Max:

Hierarchy	Maintainability Index	Cyclomatic Complexity	Depth of Inheritance	Class Coupling	Lines of Code
ALMDemoWF (Debug)	75	9	7	19	44
ALMDemoWF	75	9	7	19	44
ALMDemoClass	81	2	1	1	6
Form1	64	6	7	15	35
Program	81	1	1	3	3

Figure 7-21. *Code metrics in VSTS*

Class coupling shows the number of dependencies an item has to other types (excluding built-in types such as Int32, Float, String, and so on), as seen in Figure 7-22. If this number is high, we will probably have difficulties if we perform changes because lots of other items are affected (and the other way around).

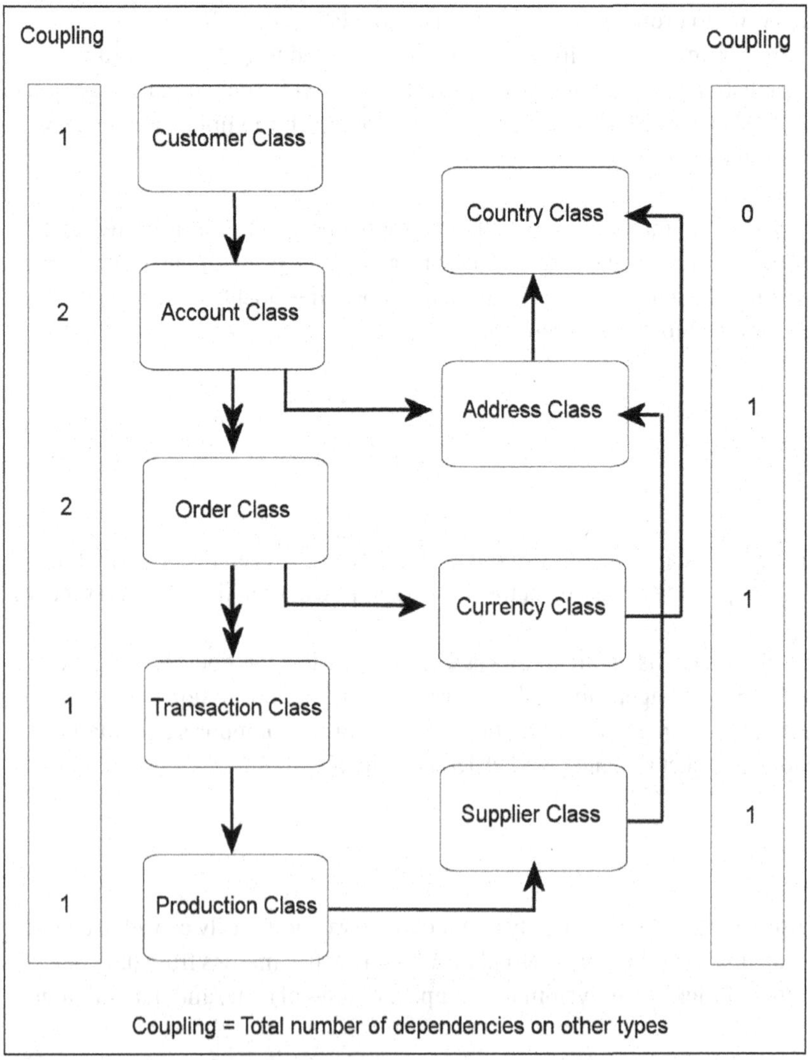

Figure 7-22. *Class coupling (http://blogs.msdn.com/fxcop/archive/2007/10/03/new-for-visual-studio-2008-code-metrics.aspx)*

Depth of inheritance shows us the number of types above the type we calculate metrics from (see Figure 7-23). If this number is high, we might have overengineered our solution to a problem, which will increase the test complexity and also maintainability of the code.

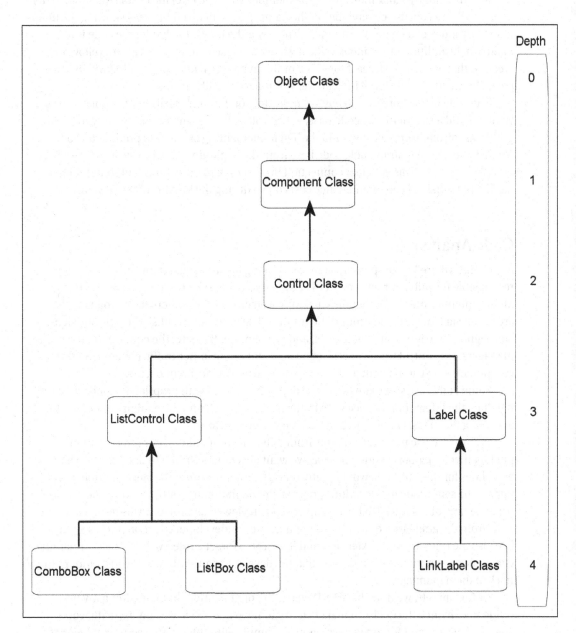

Figure 7-23. *Depth of inheritance (http://blogs.msdn.com/fxcop/archive/2007/10/03/new-for-visual-studio-2008-code-metrics.aspx)*

Cyclomatic complexity measures the number of individual paths through our code. For each decision point in code (for example, an if block or do . . . while loop), we add 1 to this metric. This number will tell us how many unit tests we need to write for our code if we want to achieve full coverage with our unit testing. So a lower value could definitely be better in most cases.

Lines of code tells us the total number of executable lines of code. White spaces, comments in code, or declarations of members, types, and namespaces are not counted. If a simple problem requires many lines of code, something is probably wrong in the logic.

Maintainability index indicates at the member and type level the overall maintainability of our code. We can also get an index at the namespace and assembly level showing the maintainability index of all types within these. The lower the index, the harder the code is to maintain. In addition to the index value itself, we also get an icon showing red, yellow, or green so that we easily will see if there is a problem here. An index of 20 to 100 will indicate green, between 10 and 19 will indicate yellow, and 0 to 9 will indicate red.

The code metrics are nice to have as indicators on the complexity of our code. We do not want to build a spaghetti-like code base, which will be hard to maintain. One way to avoid the problems my mail-order customer had when implementing changes to production code would be to have a maintainable code base from the beginning. Don't make it complex if it doesn't have to be. This is a clear connection from coding to operations and something that has the potential to keep maintenance costs down during the lifetime of the system.

Code Analysis

At the SRA, where I have spent most of my working life as a consultant since 2001, I am responsible for public procurement of IT systems. These systems are used by the Traffic Management Center in Gothenburg to control electronic equipment at the roads in that area, especially within and around the tunnels. The equipment consists of various signs, lane signals, barriers, traffic detectors, and much more. By using the equipment, the traffic managers can control traffic in case of an accident or any other traffic incident. So this equipment is very important and can save lives when an accident occurs.

Some of these systems are run on a Microsoft platform with proprietary applications handling the integration between the traffic managers' GUI and the equipment in the tunnels and along the roads. Others run Linux or some other platform.

Because we use many consultants from different companies in our projects, we have put together a manual covering the way we want developers writing their code. If we had no guidelines for this, the code would pretty quickly turn into a mess, because multiple people update the same code in the various projects. But no matter how strict we try to be, we don't have the time or resources to do a complete code review in all projects. This results in deviations from the guidelines quite often—not because the developers do it on purpose, but because the rules are quite extensive, and it is easy to forget a rule. We have rules for naming conventions, security rules, and so on that the developers must obey, and you cannot keep track of them manually.

Unfortunately, we don't have VSTS yet in the organization, but I am doing my best trying to convince the decision makers to try it. If we had VSTS, we could use the code analysis features and force the developers to comply with the rules by setting policies at the build stage.

The static code analysis feature in VSTS lets us run a number of tests against the source code, checking for compliance with a large number of rules that come with VSTS (see Figure 7-24).

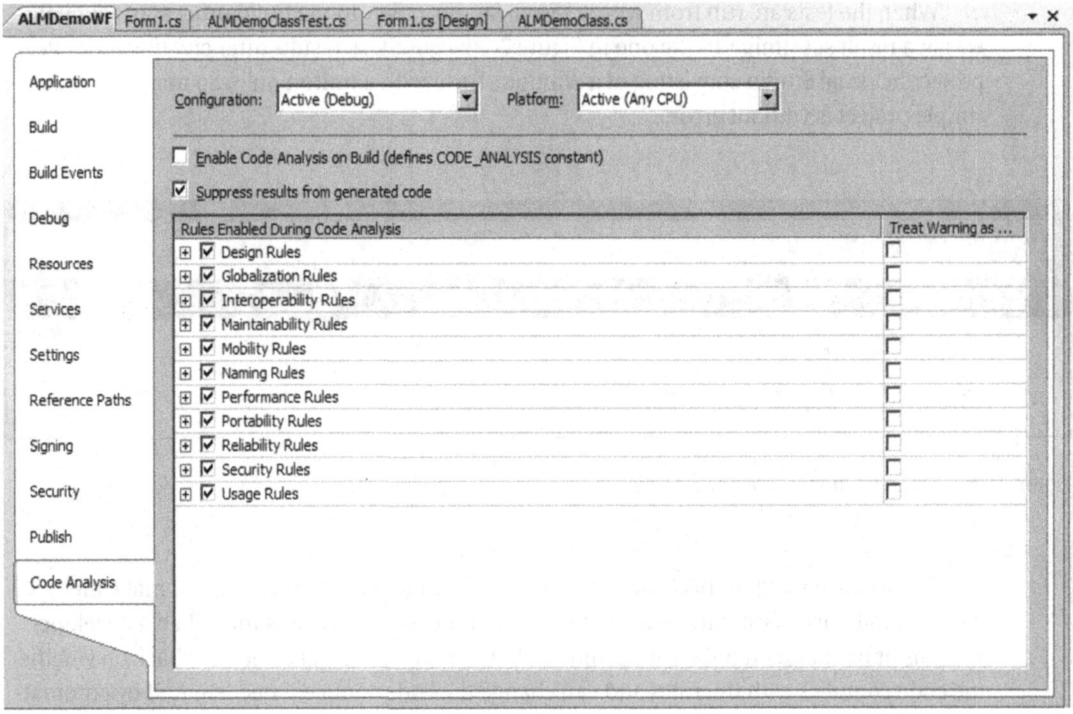

Figure 7-24. *Static code analysis*

In Figure 7-24, you can see the main groups of rules we validate against. If we expand any of these groups, we find the detailed rules, as shown in Figure 7-25. We can easily remove any of these rules by deselecting the check box preceding that rule. We can also add our own rules to this set.

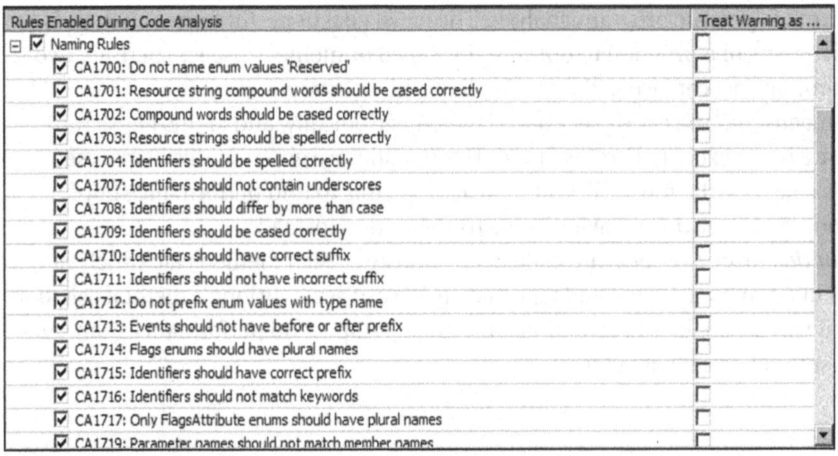

Figure 7-25. *Detailed code analysis*

When the tests are run from within Visual Studio, either in the build process or manually, we get a result set similar to the one in Figure 7-26. I got these results after creating a simple project in Visual Studio consisting of a Windows form with a button on it. So not even such a simple project is without errors.

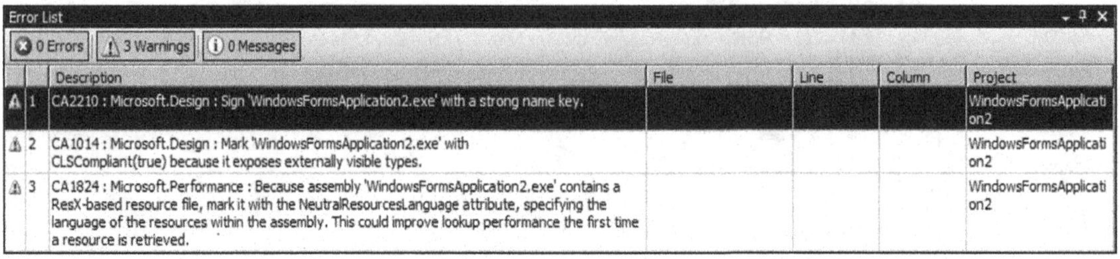

Figure 7-26. *Results from static code analysis*

The whole benefit of this is that we can make our habits into rules. We can make these habits mandatory to validate against at the build process. This means that when a developer runs his or her build on the local computer, that developer will get direct feedback on whether the code complies with the rules and can change the code at once if needed. And by automating the analysis, we know that we will get code the way we want it in the end. For the SRA, these features would be great, because we would know if anybody deviated. We could cut some of the time we spend on doing code reviews, and instead focus on more-important things in the projects.

Code Profiling

In software engineering, performance analysis, more commonly called *profiling*, is the investigation of a program's behavior by using information gathered as the program runs. This means it is a form of dynamic program analysis. The usual goal of performance analysis is to determine which parts of a program to optimize for speed or memory usage. There are two kinds of code profiling we can use in VSTS: sampling and instrumentation.

Sampling means that the code execution is halted periodically, and at this pause the functions that are being executed are recorded. The statistics we get from this help us see which methods consume the most CPU time. We can use this to find performance bottlenecks in our code, and if we do, we switch to instrumentation instead.

Instrumentation inserts probes into code before and after each method call, which allows every code execution to be recorded and reported on. We can see how long a method call took and how often it was called. Instrumentation has a greater impact on performance than sampling, so make sure you use it with care.

Code Coverage

Code coverage is a metric that tells us how much of the code has passed a unit test. The result is given in percent of code covered by the unit tests. The Code Coverage tool records all lines of code executed during a test run and identifies those parts of code that haven't been exercised during the test. We can use these metrics to show that we have tested the code. It will not, however, tell us whether we have implemented the logic correctly. If the developer has misunderstood what he or she should develop, neither the unit test nor the code coverage number will show this. I'm not sure that this will be a problem in real life, but theoretically it can be a problem.

In Figure 7-27, you can see the results of a code coverage test.

Code Coverage Results				
Darren@TFSRTM08 2008-06-26 11:15:54				
Hierarchy	Not Covered (Blocks)	Not Covered (% Blocks)	Covered (Blocks)	Covered (% Block
Darren@TFSRTM08 2008-06-26 11:15:54	69	88,46 %	9	11,54 %
ALMDemoTestProject.dll	8	61,54 %	5	38,46 %
WindowsFormsApplication2.exe	61	93,85 %	4	6,15 %
ALMDemoWF	56	93,33 %	4	6,67 %
ALMDemoClass	2	33,33 %	4	66,67 %
Add(int32,int32)	2	33,33 %	4	66,67 %
Form1	49	100,00 %	0	0,00 %
Program	5	100,00 %	0	0,00 %
ALMDemoWF.Properties	5	100,00 %	0	0,00 %

Figure 7-27. *Code coverage results*

In Figure 7-27, I have used a simple code project that has an Add function. All it does is add two integers and return the result. The project has one Windows form, where we input the two integers and return the result by clicking a button. The results of this code coverage test show that almost 94 percent of our Windows form application has been covered by the unit tests. We can also drill down in the application and see that it is the Add function that hasn't been covered fully by the unit tests. Only 33 percent of the code in it has been exercised. If we double-click the Add function, Visual Studio will take us to the code and show with color markings in blue or red which code has been covered. Blue markings (shown in lighter highlighting) in this extremely simple code mean that we have covered that part of code, and red (shown in darker highlighting) means we have not (see Figure 7-28).

What can we use this information for? I would say that the most benefit comes from the developer quickly seeing whether the unit tests are enough or whether he or she has forgotten to test some aspect of the code. It might be that refactoring has changed the code and the unit tests need to be updated to cover this, and the code coverage would show this very quickly.

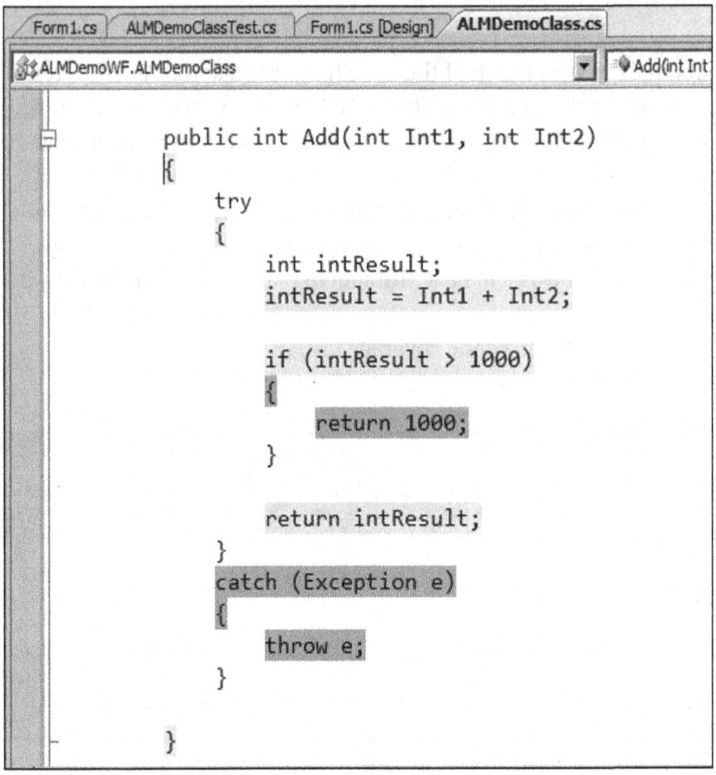

Figure 7-28. *Results from code coverage are color-coded in Visual Studio.*

Is it really realistic to think we could get 100 percent code coverage? I would say no. In easy examples in books such as this, it is fairly easy, but in real life it will be hard, or perhaps not even desirable, to achieve full coverage. My tip is that you somehow divide your system into functional components and then discuss with the team how much is realistic or necessary to have for each component. You should perhaps also set a goal for the whole project and strive for this number. This cuts you some slack for some components and lets you be stricter on others based on their risk and importance. The energy it would take to achieve full code coverage can be better spent on other tasks in the project.

At a project level, the project manager can use a summary of the code coverage results to keep control of how unit tests are carried out and easily get an overview if something sticks out.

Traceability

The work item tracking system provides the core traceability features of VSTS. But using other testing practices that are not so common can greatly improve traceability as well.

Traceability is a very wide topic. This section takes a look at some testing and build practices that can help us enforce traceability in our projects. It covers test-driven development, including unit testing, continuous integration, and some check-in policies. Let's start by taking a look at test-driven development.

Test-Driven Development

In traditional development processes such as RUP or Waterfall, the major part of software testing comes at the end of the development phase. Acceptance tests and user tests are the most common way to perform testing, and most do it manually. The difficult part with having the tests that late in a project is that any bugs found at that stage will be expensive to correct. Even small changes can affect large parts of the system, resulting in new extensive tests just to check a bug fix.

Another problem with this approach has been that if a project is running late, and overrun (time or cost) is expected, testing is usually what takes the largest cut. We simply have not prioritized testing enough over the years.

We can improve our traceability a great deal by changing the way we perform tests. By automating the tests and connecting them to a specific work item (or many work items, for that matter), we can more easily find what requirement is affected by a failed test. When a failure occurs, we can quickly find why we wrote the test by looking at the work item. This will make it easier for us to fix the problem, because we won't have to put as much effort into understanding the code as we would have to if we couldn't see the work item.

Traditionally not many tests are automated. They rely on manual testing, which is costly and complicated, especially if we have no ready test cases for the system. I have seen some customers having no clue as to where the original test specifications were stored when the system had been in production for a few years. So when a change request was implemented, test planning took valuable time from the IT organization.

My customer from the mail-order business I told you about in Chapter 1 had entirely stopped changes and minor bug fixes in their systems just because they had poor traceability of the code and no automated tests for their systems. The testing of changes in the production environment were massive every time they had to perform a change, and the easiest way to prevent this was to stop implementing all but the most serious bug fixes and changes.

If we want our IT systems to be so flexible that they can follow the changes in the business processes, we cannot accept this large test bulk whenever we want to implement a change or a bug fix. We need ways to automate tests so that manual testing is down to a minimum, while still knowing that we test what is important. We also need ways to improve testing during our projects.

In recent years, we have seen a major change in the way we think about testing. New concepts or methodologies concerning testing have emerged, and the most accepted and in my view comes from the agile community and is called *test-driven development (TDD)*. In this methodology, tests are written much earlier in the development process and drive not only validation of software but also specification, analysis, and design.

Unit tests are very common in development. A *unit test* is, to put it simply, a test case written in code that calls, for example, a function or a method, and checks the result. If the result is satisfying, the unit test is successful. If we call a math function named Add and provide two integers such as 2 and 3, we would probably expect the result to be 5 for us to call this unit test successful. Any other result would be a failed unit test.

In TDD, we use similar tests called *programmer tests*. I think we can still use the term *unit test* if we want, but for this discussion we can separate them: whereas unit tests can be written at any time in the development process, programmer tests are written before the code is implemented. This way, the programmer writing the test is not affected by what the code that he or she has written looks like. If he writes the test after the code is done, his judgment might be affected by this, and the test written so that it will cover any problems in the code. It is to find and correct these problems that we write tests in the first place.

Another benefit by writing the test first is that we do not need to write more code than to just satisfy the test case. We do not write unnecessary code, and the whole code base becomes much cleaner and easier to maintain.

This method also forces us to think about testing at the design and planning phases of the project. We can no longer separate these activities from each other and put testing at the end of the development cycle. In TDD, we follow this simple process:

- Write the failing test.

- Write just enough code to pass the test.

- Refactor the code to improve it by removing duplication, and thus making it simpler and easier to maintain.

Note Wikipedia provides this definition of refactoring: "In software engineering, *refactoring* a source code module often means modifying without changing its external behavior, and is sometimes informally referred to as *cleaning it up* . . . Refactoring neither fixes bugs nor adds new functionality. Rather it improves the understandability of the code or changes its internal structure and design, and removes dead code, to make it easier for human maintenance in the future. In particular, adding new behavior to a program might be difficult with the program's given structure, so a developer might refactor it first to make it easier, and then add the new behavior."

TDD is the overall process of developing software by using what the Extreme Programming community calls *test-first programming (TFP)*.[1] This practice is used widely in my own organization with great results. There are two rules in TFP that drive our coding activities:

- We develop new code only when we have a failing automated test.

- We eliminate duplication.

Say that before we start coding, we write a test calling an AddCustomer function. This test will fail because the AddCustomer function does not yet have a body. We then write the function and make the test pass. Then we write a new test for the next functionality we will implement and then write the functionality so that the test succeeds. Then we continue like this until we are satisfied with the AddCustomer function. Between each new test, we look at the code to see whether we can refactor it and thus eliminate duplication.

---

1. Kent Beck and Cynthia Andres, *Extreme Programming Explained* (Addison-Wesley Professional, 2005).

■**Note** A unit test doesn't always have to fail. One of the nice features of TDD is that if we have chosen the order of our tests correctly and refactor as we go, we often find that some tests just pass, not because we specifically coded for them ahead of the test, but because we built up our code in such a way that it's handling more cases than we planned for originally. TDD, done right, should force us to think about the simple cases first and to layer on just enough code for additional complexity in the tests. Often this leads to elegant code that passes more-advanced tests because we thought through things in the right order.

By using this method, we can see that we need to specify the work first and in the end we get a test checking that it has been completed correctly. We write code enough to meet the specification and then stop. The result, as many of my coworkers can validate, is that we write code quicker and testing is also done quicker. This method is a bottom-up process. Instead of having to do the whole big up-front design, the design emerges as coding goes on. Because most big up-front designs never are perfect anyway, the idea of an emerging design appeals to me. It is only when we start implementing the functionality that we can see all aspects of what the design needs to be. This doesn't mean that we shouldn't do any design before starting to code, but we don't need to spend months figuring out every aspect of it, because this will never succeed anyway.

The most attractive benefit with this "test a bit, code a bit, and then design a bit" approach is that we can be much more responsive to changes. We can evolve the working system one small change at a time to converge to requirements changes, making it a different system in the end. We do not have to trash the first design just because of a new requirement or a change in a requirement. This flexibility is what I want in my software projects.

Some of you might at this point argue that if we use the bottom-up approach, don't we have to test the software after each small change? Yes, absolutely. But by using the right tool and the right process. we can automate much of the testing so that this is no longer a show-stopper.

This approach encourages the developer to write only as much code as is needed to fulfill the test. This method is good because the developer will carefully consider what to write, not adding anything unnecessary, and this also makes the developer more responsible for the things he or she develops.

Unit Testing in VSTS

Visual Studio Team System comes with the capability to create unit tests directly from code, enabling us to implement TDD for traceability enhancement. This means that if we have a class with a method, we can simply right-click on the class or the method in our code and select Create Unit Tests from the menu (see Figure 7-29).

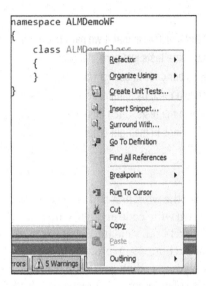

```
namespace ALMDemoWF
{
    class ALMDemoClass
    {                    Refactor              ▶
    }                    Organize Usings       ▶
}
               🔲  Create Unit Tests...
               🔲  Insert Snippet...
               🔲  Surround With...
               🔳  Go To Definition
                   Find All References
                   Breakpoint             ▶
               ⚡  Run To Cursor
               ✂  Cut
               📋  Copy
               📋  Paste
                   Outlining              ▶
rors   ⚠ 5 Warnings
```

Figure 7-29. *An example of how we can create unit tests from within the development GUI in VSTS*

The example I will show you now is very simple, so even if you don't program, you will be able to follow this process. I want to show you this so you can see the benefits we get in VSTS by making it easier for developers to start working in a more test-driven way.

After we click Create Unit Tests, VSTS will ask which part of the code we want to create the unit test for. In Figure 7-30, you can see a class called Service that has a method called AddCustomer that we want to create a unit test for. In this simple example, the AddCustomer function takes an object of the type Customer, which can be used for internal processing. In this example, we check only for a customer name. If this is not provided, we throw an exception to the caller saying that the customer name is missing

```csharp
namespace CustomerService
{
    public class Service
    {
        public Customer AddCustomer(Customer customer)
        {
            if (string.IsNullOrEmpty(customer.Name))
                throw new ArgumentException("Customer name is missing.");
            return customer;
        }

        public Customer UpdateCustomer(Customer customer)
        {
            return customer;
        }
    }
}
```

Figure 7-30. *AddCustomer method*

When we finish with the unit test creation wizard, VSTS will ask whether we want to create a new test project or add the test to an existing test project. This is a very nice feature, which simplifies more than you'd perhaps expect. For this demo, I let VSTS create a new test project called ALMDemoTestProject.

When creation is completed, VSTS opens the new test project, as you can see in Figure 7-31. In this figure, you can also see that all unit tests are actually code. This very simple test creates an object of Customer type and fills in all its values. To evaluate the result of this method, we also initialize an expected value so we can compare the actual result with the expected value. The line Assert.AreEqual (expected, actual); is the line that compares these values. If the values are equal, the test has been successful; and if not, it fails.

```
/// <summary>
///A test for AddCustomer
///</summary>
[TestMethod()]
public void AddCustomerTest()
{
    Service target = new Service();
    Customer customer = new Customer() { Name = "John Doe", Address = "AStreet 1", City = "Unknown", ZipCode =
    Customer actual;
    actual = target.AddCustomer(customer);
    Assert.AreEqual(customer.Name, actual.Name);
}

/// <summary>
///A test for AddCustomer
///</summary>
[TestMethod(), ExpectedException(typeof(System.ArgumentException))]
public void AddInvalidCustomerTest()
{
    Service target = new Service();
    Customer customer = new Customer();
    target.AddCustomer(customer);
}
```

Figure 7-31. *Unit tests are code.*

For this demo, I have also created one more test called AddInvalidCustomerTest, which uses an empty Customer object and sends that as a parameter in the test. This will make the test succeed as well because no customer name is provided and this is controlled by our error control in the code. When we run these tests, we get a nice output showing the result of our unit tests (see Figure 7-32).

	Result	Test Name	Project
✓	Test run completed	Results: 2/2 passed; Item(s) checked: 0	
☐	Passed	AddInvalidCustomerTest	CustomerService.UnitTest
☐	Passed	AddCustomerTest	CustomerService.UnitTest

Figure 7-32. *Unit test results*

The results of these unit tests can be reported upon so we can easily publish unit test results on our web site if we want. We probably don't want individual developers running their own unit tests to display all their test results, but we definitely want to display the results of unit tests connected to a build process.

VSTS also gives us the option to associate a unit test with a specific work item or work items (see Figure 7-33). This is very good for traceability, enabling us to see which tests are connected to which requirements (or any other work item type). If we create a report on this, we can easily make sure that all requirements have associated unit tests. In my example, I have associated my test with a work item ID 543. This is a Bug work item indicating that the outcome of the AddCustomer function was wrong. The developer responsible for fixing the bug associates the test with the correct bug work item, so that we can get it reported upon.

Figure 7-33. *Associating tests with work items enables traceability.*

Another nice feature is that we can let VSTS autogenerate test data if we want. We can also use test data from a database. In that case, we bind the test data to our unit tests and can let the tests run many variations of the same test.

The preceding example shows how easily we can create unit tests in VSTS. But as you saw, the test-first programming practices require us to create the test before we even create the code we will write tests for. VSTS does not support automatic test creation of classes or methods that do not exist. We must at least have the class written before we can create the unit test (or programmer test, if you'd like to call it that). I don't think this is an impediment, really. I can live with the necessity of creating an empty class first and generate the test project from this, or if I want to be strict, I can create the test project manually first.

How will this enable traceability, you might ask? Well, not by itself, but by connecting the unit tests to the build process, we have a different situation. We can do this by using automated builds and a practice called continuous integration.

Automated Build/Continuous Integration

Continuous integration is a software development practice whereby members of a team frequently integrate their work. Each integration is verified by an automated build, which also includes automated tests (created with TFP).

Why do we need to use this practice? The more complex our development projects become, with many team members developing different applications for the software system, the harder it will be to find out that they integrate well. The more developers involved, the more likely that two or more of them will work on the same code at the same time. To make sure the system works as a system, we need to test more than just individual classes and components. It is not enough that we run tests solely on our development PCs anymore; we need to create an automated environment where we can run builds and tests of the whole team's code base.

In some of my recent projects, we have set up a separate build lab doing this work for us (see Figure 7-34).

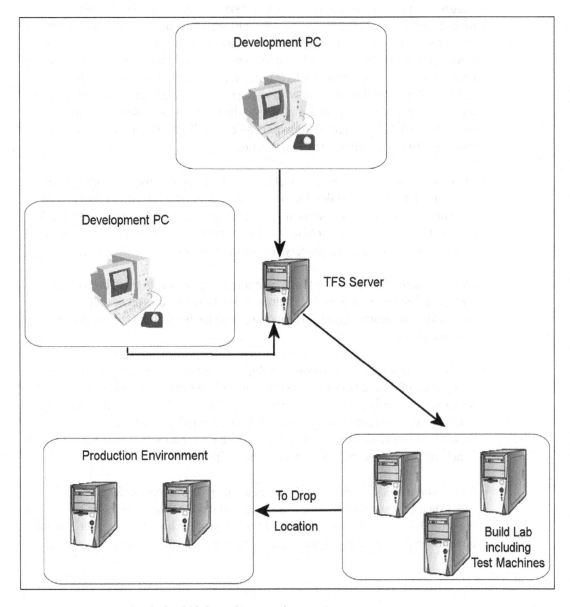

Figure 7-34. *An example of a build lab used in one of my projects*

The benefit of having a separate build lab is that we can run integration tests without disturbing our TFS environment or slowing down our development PCs. We have set up this differently in each project, but we usually start a build process when somebody checks code into the TFS version-control system. This gives us immediate feedback as to whether any check-in breaks the build or fails any of our automated unit tests, and the developer responsible for any code that breaks the build or any of the unit tests can deal with the issue directly, before anybody else has downloaded the faulty code. We have also tried to emulate the production environment so the tests are run in as realistic an environment as possible.

Martin Fowler describes some key practices for successful continuous integration:[2]

- *Maintain a single source repository*: Today the thought of not having a single source code repository using a good version-control system might seem far-fetched. But historically this has not been the case. For the customer I am helping right now, I have found that some of our older projects lack the source code for the applications. For some applications, we have also found that we are in doubt about which version of the code is the one in production. We have one version on disk and another in the source control system, and this has resulted in changes introducing bugs we have already fixed once. But because we have poor control over the code, we have used the wrong version on some changes. Every time we discover something like this, we move the code to source control so we will avoid this in the future.

- *Automate the build*: Manually putting together all things required for running a build can be a tedious task. Most development environments support automation and hence we should let the machines handle the process. Martin Fowler states, "anyone should be able to bring in a virgin machine, check the sources out of the repository, issue a single command, and have a running system on their machine."

- *Make your build self-testing*: As I have mentioned, a good way to catch bugs more quickly and efficiently is to include automated tests in the build process. By doing so, we can directly see whether our recent changes make the old tests fail, and can directly start fixing this.

- *Everyone commits every day*: Having developers committing changes to the mainline source code often makes us find bugs more quickly. Developers should commit at least once every day, preferably more often than that. The more frequently we commit, the smaller pieces our tasks must be broken down to. Fowler suggests that a developer should break down his or her work into chunks of a few hours each, which is supposed to help track progress and also provide a sense of progress.

- *Every commit should build the mainline on an integration machine*: Regular builds should take place on an integration machine, and if this build succeeds, we can say that the commit is done. The developer should never go home before having seen that the build succeeds. If anything breaks, the developer must fix this at once.

---

2. Martin Fowler, "Continuous Integration," (www.martinfowler.com).

- *Keep the build fast*: The point of continuous integration is to get fast feedback. Hence the build process must be as quick as possible. Extreme Programming advocates the ten-minute build practice. This methodology states that within ten minutes after some-one checks something into the source control repository, the latest version of the software should be built and its integration tests run. We cannot solve this manually, so we need to use automated builds. To reduce the time required for a build, the build system should be able to determine which parts have changed since last build, and build only those.

- *Test in a clone of the production environment*: The tests should be done on a clone of the production environment. This is not always possible to comply with, but for several of my projects, we have used a virtual machine setup, using VMware or Microsoft Virtual PC to mimic the production environment as closely as possible. By using virtual machines, we have been able to quickly restore a server, or group of servers, if necessary.

- *Make it easy for anyone to get the latest executable*: Anyone should be able to get the latest version of the system and run it. It could be for demonstrations, exploratory testing, or just to see what's new this week.

- *Everyone can see what is happening*: The whole point of continuous integration is to enhance communication. We must make sure that everyone can easily see the state of the system so they can follow the changes made to it. We can do this by using a web site like the TFS project portal for instance, and displaying the best-suited reports.

- *Automate deployment*: In continuous integration, we move executables between multiple environments. For example, we move from the machine(s) used for commit tests to the machine(s) used for secondary tests. Because we might be doing this several times a day, we need to automate the deployment of our system or application into different environments. When deploying into production, we should also consider having an automated rollback so we can handle things when something goes wrong.

Continuous integration has started to become mainstream in most projects these days. I think this is a good thing, and in my and my coworkers' experience, there is really nothing to hold against it.

The unit tests we have created in a project can be connected to the build process. This means that when we build a version of the system, we can run all unit tests at once, and if any of them fail because of the new code of the build, such as a bug fix or change request, we can easily see which unit test failed and can start correcting the code quickly.

Continuous integration lets us automatically start the build process when we check in new code to the version-control system. If we have connected the unit tests to the build process, they will also be run when the system is built.

We can also schedule the builds to be run at specific times. Many development teams build a new version of the system during the night, so in the morning they have reports on how the build completed. If any unit tests failed or if the build process failed, they will see it and can react to it, at once.

So for traceability, we can use all existing unit tests when doing bug fixes or change requests in production, and quickly see if, and where, the new code broke anything existing. This will not give us good traceability on its own. We need a good way to directly see what requirements (work items) were covered by the failed unit test. This can be done by forcing the developers to associate a work item ID with each check-in and hence with the unit tests that were created for that check-in. When a unit test fails, we can see which work items were the base for the bug fix by using the work item tracking functionality, and more easily find information about the bug fix and the original requirement. Now let's see how this works.

Check-In Policies

When a developer checks code into the version-control system, the team leader can require the developer to add information to the check-in through different check-in policies. One of these policies requires that the developer add information about which work item the check-in is connected with. This way, we can enable traceability as to where in code a work item has been implemented, thus further supporting the ALM process.

As a project manager, I have been in situations where code has been checked in that wasn't ready. This has resulted in build breaks during nightly builds and a lot of hassle for me to get it fixed as soon as possible the day after. This has, of course, caused lot of work for me, but what is more important is that it has the potential to cause problems for the team as well.

One of my worst memories was when a developer checked in some last-minute changes without proper quality tests and then went on vacation. We had some problems the day after when this was discovered in the reports of the nightly build. Nobody really knew which parts of the code he had been working on, and it took some time before we could reach him and get it all sorted out. In the meantime, some of the other developers were unable to work until this was settled.

This experience also taught me a lesson about traceability. If I had had some way of tracing the changes in code to the developer's check-in, we could have expedited the process of fixing what was broken. But at that time we didn't have anything more than check-in notes, and these were of course blank.

When working with TFS version control, we can add check-in policy requirements (see Figure 7-35). These check-in policies require the user to take actions when they perform a check-in to the source control system. If any policy is violated, the user is presented with a warning during the check-in process. The check-in is then prevented. If necessary, the developer can override the policy, but this results in a log entry that I as a project manager will be aware of.

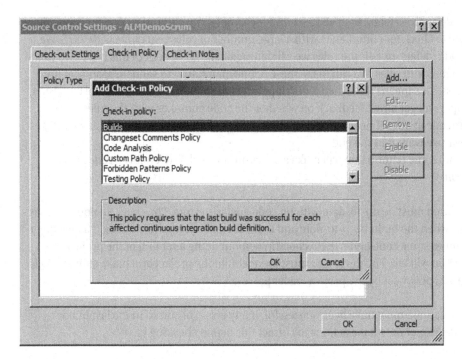

Figure 7-35. *Enabling check-in policies*

One thing that would have helped me in the preceding example would have been the ability for me to require the developers to associate a work item with a changeset in VSTS. This feature is now available in VSTS.

Note A changeset represents a group of versioned files along with their associated metadata such as policy information, timestamps, comments, and similar things.

Out of the box we have a few available types of check-in policy, including these:

- Code analysis

- Testing policy

- Work items

- Check-in notes

The code analysis features in VSTS let us, for example, run a number of tests against the source code to check for compliance with a large number of rules that come with VSTS. We can easily add, delete, or edit the rules we validate against. The benefit of this is that we can make our habits into rules. We can make these habits mandatory to validate against at the build process. This means that when a developer runs his or her build on the local computer, the developer will get direct feedback on whether the code complies with the rules and can change the code at once if needed. And by automating the analysis, we know that we will get code the way we want it in the end.

There are some criteria that will make a check-in succeed if we enable a *code analysis check-in policy*:

- The build must be up-to-date with no code analysis errors. The check-in policy passes code when the build is up-to-date and there are no code analysis errors. If a developer modifies some code and tries to check in without doing a rebuild of the project, the check-in will fail. The developer must then rebuild the project and make sure the code analysis policy set by the project leader passes.

- The last build must have been successful. If any errors occurred in the last build, the developer must take actions to correct this before checking in.

- The check-in can fail if the rules are incorrect. The developer must synchronize the check-in policy from the server to the projects in the active solution.

- A check-in must be done from the GUI, not the command line. This is not supported yet.

- The Visual Studio solution must be open.

- All files must be part of the Visual Studio solution. Project management can set an option that will fail a policy if not all of the files to be checked in are part of the open solution.

A *testing check-in policy* requires that check-in tests must be completed before check-in. If the tests in the provided test list fail, the code is not allowed to be checked in.

In a *work items check-in policy*, work in a VSTS project should always have a corresponding work item associated with it. To allow full traceability from the work items to the checked-in code, we can make it mandatory to supply one or many work item numbers with every check-in.

By using a *check-in notes check-in policy*, we can force developers to add comments to a check-in. This can be information that is not part of the associated work item, for instance.

Microsoft also provides some check-in policies as part of their Visual Studio Team System Team Foundation Server Power Tools, which is a free add-on to TFS (www.microsoft.com/downloads/details.aspx?FamilyID=00DFCD6E-4902-4F42-8E9F-859119C60D6A&displaylang=en). If the default policies and the Power Tools policies are not enough, we can also add our own policies to adjust them even more to our own way of working in the organization. This gives us the capability to enable our own policies in our own custom project template.

In addition to running builds at check-ins and adding work items to a check-in, there are other features of the VSTS version-control system that can help us with traceability. These features are not unique to VSTS but are part of any good version-control system. I am thinking of branching and merging code. The practice of keeping control of your code and the different releases of it is called configuration management, which we covered in Chapter 6.

Extensibility

The whole point of an extensible product such as VSTS is that we are able to customize it to our needs. One of the biggest advantages of VSTS is the capability to customize our process template so that we can realize our ALM process in the tools we use for our projects. Let's take a closer look at how the process template is built up and how it can be changed by using the extensible features of VSTS.

Modifying the Process Template

There are two ways to modify the XML files for the project templates. We can use manual customization or we can use the Process Template Editor, which is a Power Tool from Microsoft.

If we are daring, we can manually edit the XML files. This can be done by exporting the files from the TFS server by using the Process Template Manager that ships with VSTS and updating an existing template (see Figure 7-36). Or if we are even more daring, we can start from scratch. I suggest you use an already-existing process template and modify that.

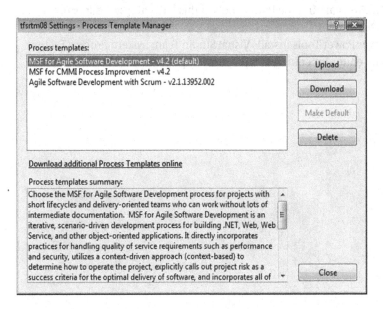

Figure 7-36. *Exporting (Download) a process template from TFS by using the Process Template Manager*

After we have the template in a folder on our computer, we can start modifying all aspects of it. I use XML Spy for this, but you can use whatever tool you want. Why not use VS? In Figure 7-37, you can see an excerpt of what one of the XML files looks like when seen in VS. Then note the nice user interface we get with the Process Template Editor: we do not have to see the pure XML if we don't want to.

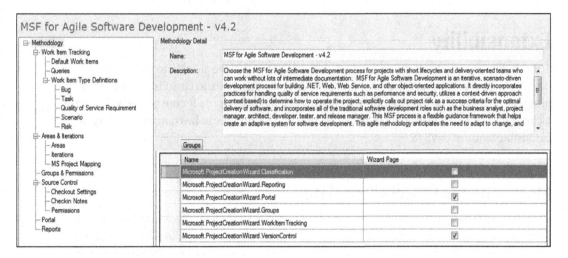

Figure 7-37. *Example of process template XML file in Visual Studio*

The Process Template Editor is a useful tool that Microsoft provides as an integrated part of the Power Tools for VSTS. You can find the Power Tools at this URL: `http://msdn.microsoft.com/en-us/tfs2008/bb980963.aspx`.

Team Foundation Server Power Tools installs Visual Studio Team System Process Editor, which is a process template editor for editing TFS process templates inside the Visual Studio IDE (see Figure 7-38).

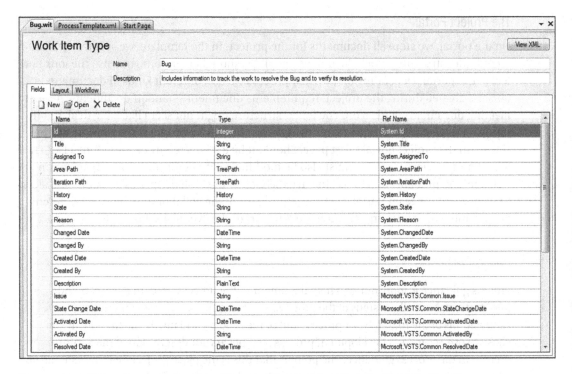

Figure 7-38. *Editing the process template by using the Process Editor inside Visual Studio*

Common Adaptations of the Process Template

What are the most common things people change in the process template? I would say that this depends on your needs and I strongly suggest you consider your needs before starting to customize the templates. You should gather information to help point out these needs by doing an ALM assessment like the one outlined in Chapter 5. Because the process template is a representation of your ALM process, it makes good sense to understand your way of working. What are your organization's needs? Which information is important in your bugs? How do you handle change requests? How do you handle requirements?

Do an assessment, run some workshops about the results, and talk about what your requirements are on the process template(s). Then select one project to use to pilot the process template and see the results. You will probably need to adjust your template after the pilot, but that is quite all right; that's the purpose of a pilot.

The following are the most common parts of the template I usually update when working with my customers.

The Project Portal

On the portal, we store all documents for the project. In the template, we specify the document folder structure, which document templates should be present, and also the look and feel of the portal. Depending on the ALM process we use, different kinds of documents must be created during the project: requirements documents, handoff documents, project meeting documents, and so on. The folder structure might not seem like a big deal, but in my experience it is hard to get teams to agree on this. Also consider which reports will be shown on the project portal's first page. Should it be a status report or something else? The SharePoint Services template must also be modified so that it fits into your organization's web site. You probably don't want to have the look of the MSF templates on your team sites. Consider that the team portal will be a central part of the collaboration between different people and parts of the organization that are part of the overall ALM process.

Process Guidance

Process guidance is more or less a help document to the process used. In it, we can find information about all the steps of the process, all descriptions of the document templates, explanations of the roles in your process and of the reports, and much, much more. If you chose to use Scrum as a development process, you place your description of the Scrum process in the process guidance. The point is that this is the place project members should go first when questions arise about the process. This is important, so don't rush over it.

Work Item Types

You can use the work item types that Microsoft ships with VSTS in the two MSF templates. But as mentioned earlier, I think we should really consider our own needs in the organization and make adjustments to these. Your organization might need more work items or might need to extend the information required for them. If your project managers use Microsoft Office Project, you might want to change the mapping between fields in TFS against fields in Project. Another thing to consider is the workflow of the work items. How is the process in your organization? Which states can a bug transition between? Microsoft supplies a set of default work item instances when a project is created. These represent tasks that need to be done in all projects. Your organization might have different needs for default work items.

Work Item Queries

What information do you need to query about your work items? If you have made many changes to the work items, you might also need to change the queries so they reflect these changes. What queries does your ALM process need? In Figure 7-39, you can see the queries of the MSF for Agile template.

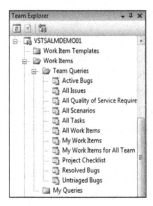

Figure 7-39. *The work item queries in MSF for Agile*

Reports

This is something that most of my customers have modified. The reports in the MSF templates are very good. Figure 7-40 shows one of them, representing how much work is left in a project. This report and some others will be explained in more detail later in this chapter. In choosing which reports and information you need, we once again come back to the fact that this is something that you need to discuss with your project teams and also with stakeholders and managers. What information is important to the various roles in your ALM process? What do the managers need to see? How can we provide great feedback on project status to the team?

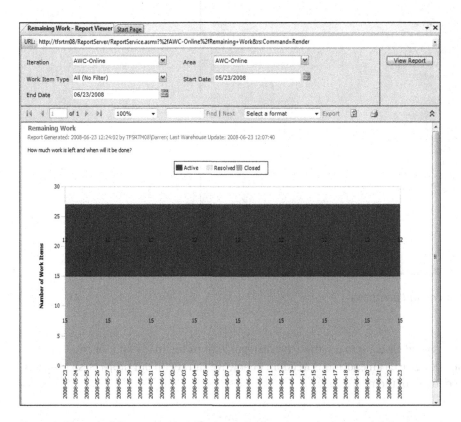

Figure 7-40. *One of the reports in MSF for Agile showing remaining work in the project*

Areas and Iterations

Areas and iterations are interesting concepts. Iterations are what the term sounds like, basically. We use iterations to name the different versions of our project. We can name them anything we want. I have most often used the names Iteration 1, 2, 3, and so on, but that is up to you to decide. We can nest these and build an iteration hierarchy if we want.

Areas are labels we can attach to just about anything. One customer uses labels named after their windows or web forms in their projects. Another uses them for each component in their system. Then they can use areas and iterations to describe which areas (forms) belong to a certain iteration.

What I want to say about this is that we can use areas and iterations to label specific parts of our projects. These concepts are flexible, and we have the freedom to use them as we want. All work items can later be labeled with both an area and an iteration. Depending on your ALM process, you might use this for various reasons. If you run a project using RUP, you might want to use the iterations by naming them after the phases of RUP. Then you can nest iterations below each phase depending on your need. Figure 7-41 shows an example of what this could look like. And if during the project we need more iterations in one phase, we can simply add them.

Figure 7-41. *Areas and iterations*

It is all up to us what we want to use these two categorizations for. In my opinion, they are very useful. They give us an enormous freedom in how we can set up our projects, so I suggest you make good use of them.

Groups and Permissions

In TFS we have a couple of default groups defined after installation (see Figure 7-42). These are something you will probably want to extend or change. To fully use this feature in an effective and secure way, you need to discuss this with your infrastructure team so that the security for TFS matches the security of your Active Directory. Think about which groups of users you need in your projects. They might differ depending on what type of project you are running. What rights does your user group need?

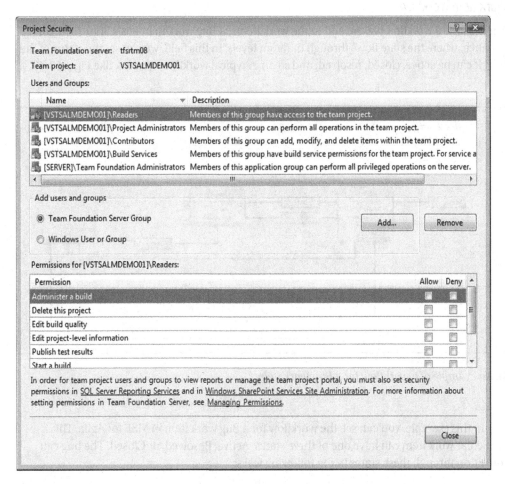

Figure 7-42. *Groups and permissions in TFS using the Project Security form*

Even though I have tried to make this not too technical, you might wonder why you should bother with the details I have presented here. The reason is that I want you to be aware that there are many parts of the process template that are important to adjust to your suit your organization. The standard templates Microsoft provides can get you a bit down the road, but to fully use TFS and VSTS in your ALM process, you should adapt them to fit your organizational needs. And to find out your needs, I suggest you do an ALM assessment and see what areas you need to strengthen and what areas you are strong in. Build a roadmap ahead and then take a look at how your VSTS implementation can help you implement this.

Modifying Work Items

Microsoft encourages us to modify our process template. One important thing I have found worth modifying are the work items. Many organizations I have seen have needed information in their work items that is not available in the two MSF templates. In those cases, we have adjusted the work items to better fit in the organization. This has turned out very successful in all cases. One thing we have changed is the workflow of the work items.

Work Item Workflow

There is also a workflow we can add to the work items. A Bug work item has a State field, for instance, where the state flows through different levels. In this field, we can set the status of the bug. It can be active, closed, resolved, and so on. A typical workflow can look like Figure 7-43.

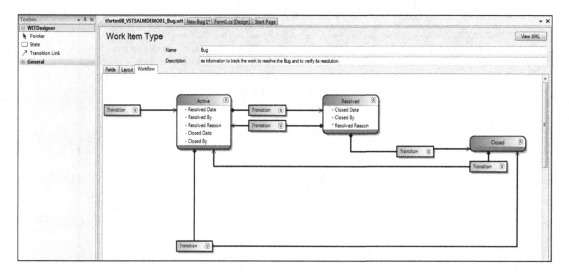

Figure 7-43. *An example of a workflow for a Bug work item*

In this example, you can see the workflow for a Bug work item in MSF for Agile. This particular work item can have one of three states: Active, Resolved, or Closed. The bug can transition through these states in the following ways:

- Active to Resolved

- Resolved to Closed

- Resolved to Active

- Active to Closed

- Closed to Active

We can also let automatic transitions occur in the workflow. Let's say that if a closed bug is reopened because of a new test showing there are still some errors in the code, we can automatically have the bug reassigned to the person who closed it. This way, we can save some work because we don't have to hunt down that person ourselves.

Working with Work Items

After the work items are defined in the process template and we are content with the information in them and the looks of them, we can start using them in our project. When we create a new work item of any kind, we simply create an instance of that work item type and store it in the TFS data tier. When we update the work item during the project, these updates are also stored in the database. We can create work items in several ways:

- From Team Explorer

- From Microsoft Office Excel

- From Microsoft Office Project

- From Web Access

- From Visual Studio Web Access 2008 Power Tool

- From Team Foundation Server API

The most common way for developers to create and modify work items is probably by using Team Explorer (see Figure 7-44). From here we can access all aspects of the work item. The same things apply to Web Access, but this tool is probably most used by people in the project who don't have Visual Studio installed. We can let external project members such as customer representatives from other companies access the Web Access site and add bugs or change requests, for example.

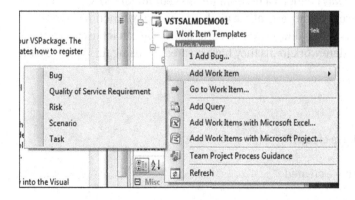

Figure 7-44. *Working with work items in Team Explorer from the Visual Studio GUI*

A project manager will probably not want to use Team Explorer or Visual Studio because most use Excel or Project for this. In Figure 7-45, you can see the Excel interface with the Team System add-in used to access TFS. We can use Excel to add and modify work items and then publish them to TFS. In Project we can also do this and continue working with the work items in the Gantt chart, just as we might be used to doing.

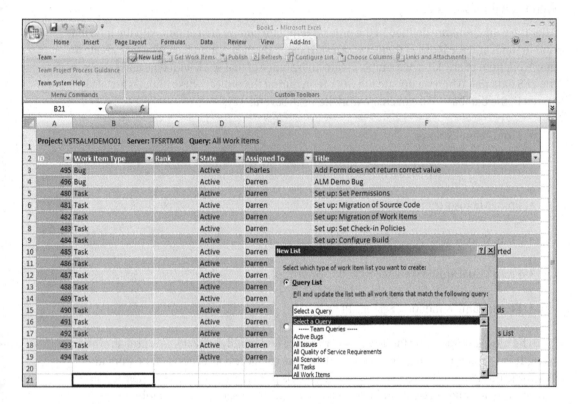

Figure 7-45. *Working with work items in Excel*

In VSTS 2008, the licensing was changed a bit from the first edition of VSTS. Now we can let end users without a CAL access some parts of the work item tracking functionality. By using the Work Item Web Access (a free download from Microsoft), we can let users create new work items and view or update work items they have created. By using this tool, we can do the following:

- Create new work items

- Edit the work items we have created

- View the work items we have created

We cannot do the following:

- See another person's work items

- List, view, or run queries

- Add, edit, or remove work item links (except attachments and hyperlinks)

- Access documents stored on the project portal

- Access reports

- Access source control

- Access the build system

This tool is a welcome addition to the TFS toolset. It is very handy when we have external users from other organizations who need to create work items. I have had cases where we wanted to have external users add work items without having to pay for the CAL. At Know IT, we have in-house projects where we would like our customers to be able to add bugs or change requests to our projects without having a CAL.

Collaboration

There are several ways we can collaborate in a project. Collaboration between the business side and the IT side is, as you have seen, essential. Using the System Designers of Visual Studio Team System Architect Edition, these two organizations can collaborate regarding the architecture of our systems and processes. We can also use these designers to enhance collaboration between operations and IT development.

Architecture with Visual Studio Team System

As you saw earlier, the architect edition of Visual Studio Team Edition comes with four designers we can use for architecting our systems and applications. These designers are great tools for enabling collaboration in our ALM process. By using these designers, we can let the business and IT architects design and evaluate our application systems for deployment by following different workflows (see Figure 7-46).

If we want to design a system but do not want to choose how to implement it just yet, we can use a top-down approach. If this is the case, we start working from the System Designer. We design the system but delay choosing which applications we want to use.

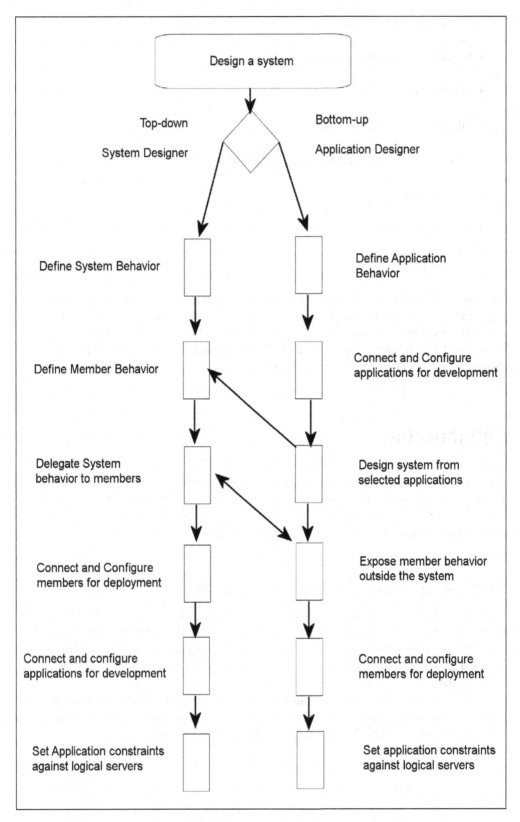

Figure 7-46. *We can work top-down or bottom-up when we design our systems.*

If we know which applications will be a part of our system, we start with the Application Designer and work in a bottom-up workflow. We can also switch between these approaches, as Figure 7-46 shows.

To help you better understand these two approaches, let's look at the four designers to see how they really work. We will do this by following a very simple demonstration of a solution design.

Using the VSTS Architect Edition, we can lay down the architecture of our new system or application. As you know, there are four System Designers that will ease our architecture efforts a great deal.

Application Designer

In the Application Designer, we can define and visualize the applications that can provide services or use these services within the scope of a Visual Studio solution. We can visualize Windows applications, web applications and services, external web services, external systems and applications, as well as databases.

Figure 7-47 shows that this designer has a toolbox to the left of the screen, from where we can drag and drop applications on our canvas to the right. In this case, you can see a solution with one Windows application and one web application. You can also see one web service (the Order Process service), which these two applications connect to. Furthermore, you can see that this web service connects to an internal, already-existing database and one external web service (the Credit Card web service), also existing. In this solution, all applications not already existing will be developed in the project.

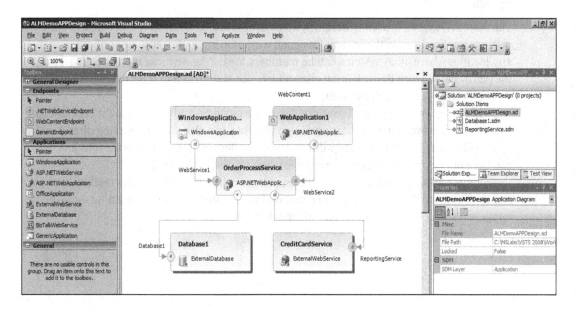

Figure 7-47. *The Application Designer*

There is a Settings and Constraints Editor, which we can use to configure settings in our applications. We can, for instance, say the web service will be built using C# and that the Windows application will be built using VB.NET.

One nice feature with this designer is that we can do many high-level tasks:

- Visualize and define applications

- Reverse-engineer existing solutions

- Define web service and database communication between applications

- Document other types of communication between applications

What I find very exciting about this designer is the potential I see in using this as a discussion base for architects. If we follow the example of Sten and Per Sundblad in Chapter 4, I would say that the business architect and the solution architect could use this designer to map the existing application structure to the new application system we are about to build. If we have an application design already made over our application ecosystem, we can visually see the effects of doing the architecture one way or another. We can see where we already have functionality so we don't build anything redundant, and we can see which services are available so we can reuse them. The two architects can try out different design suggestions and see the result graphically without having to read code.

System Designer

The System Designer is used to design systems of applications. A system can consist of one or many applications. In the System Designer, we define a specific reusable configuration of applications where other systems can be members. We configure these members and describe the pathways between them. We can also validate our system as a unit for deployment by validating it against a logical datacenter.

This designer is the natural continuation of the business and solution architects' discussions that started with the application design. But they can also start by working directly in the System Designer if they use the top-down approach. Because the diagrams are reusable, we can have our environment already available when starting a new project.

Figure 7-48 shows what the System Designer looks like. We still have the toolbox to our left and the canvas to the right. You can see that we have created a system containing the Windows application, the web application, and the web service.

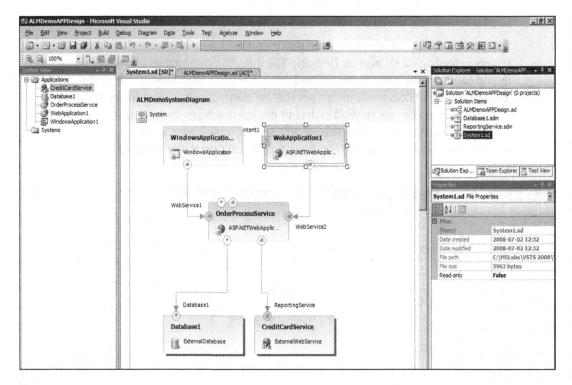

Figure 7-48. *The System Designer*

There are several things we can do in the System Designer:

- Add applications and other systems as a member of a system

- Represent system behavior by adding end-points and define contracts for the behavior

- View the settings, constraints, and definitions of members in a system

- Override the settings of the system members

- Configure communication pathways between system members

- Delegate system behavior and expose member behavior

Logical Datacenter Designer

To represent the logical structure of our datacenter, we create diagrams of the interconnected servers in the Logical Datacenter Designer. The infrastructure architect uses this tool to specify and configure the types of servers available in the physical datacenter. He or she can add information about communication types that are allowed, communication pathways, and what kinds of services are enabled in the infrastructure environment. By using this tool, the solution architect and the infrastructure architect can collaborate about how we can implement the new system(s). Figure 7-49 shows the Logical Datacenter Designer.

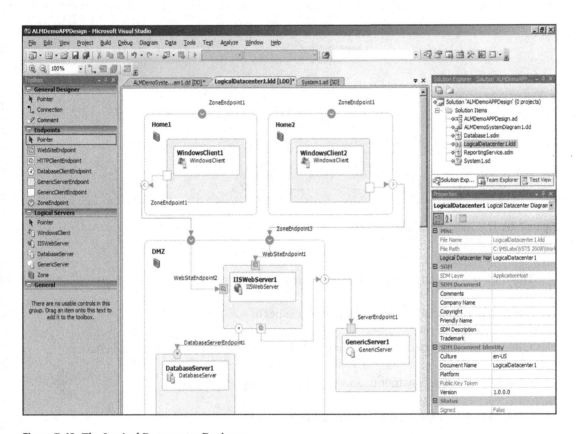

Figure 7-49. *The Logical Datacenter Designer*

It is important to know that the logical infrastructure diagrams do not represent the physical implementation on servers. If we have a server running Windows Server 2008, SQL Server 2005, and Internet Information Services (IIS), this will be represented as three logical servers and not as the one physical server it really is. (Keep in mind that a web server or application cluster, for instance, is represented as only one logical server.)

We can define something called *zones* in our logical datacenter diagrams as well. A zone is, simplified, an area separated from its surroundings by a firewall. For instance, we can represent the demilitarized zone (DMZ) where our web servers are deployed as one zone, our application servers (if applicable) as another zone, and our data storage as another, and so on. A zone can be constrained by specifying the communication that can travel in and out of the zone.

These diagrams can be created independently of the development process so we can create these for use in many projects. This is very useful in architecture discussions between the various architect roles.

We can do the following in the Logical Datacenter Designer:

- Describe the types of application servers and the types of applications they can host

- Describe the application server configuration settings on the host environment

- Describe dependent service configuration

- Describe available protocols

- Describe communication boundaries

- Describe authentication requirements on applications

- Describe application configuration constraints

In the simple demo shown in Figure 7-49, you can now see that we have placed the Windows application in one zone, the web server in another, and the database in a third.

Deployment Designer

The last designer is the Deployment Designer (see Figure 7-50). Here we take our application system and create the deployment configuration. This is then validated against the logical datacenter representation created in the Logical Datacenter Designer. In the validation process, I think it is essential for the solution architect and the infrastructure architect to collaborate so together they can resolve any conflicts or errors we get.

We validate on different levels. For example, we ensure that the required communication pathways exist and that the correct communication protocols are present, and of course are compatible between applications and the servers hosting them.

We can create deployment diagrams from either the System or the Application Designer. If we choose to use only the Application Designer, VSTS creates a default system diagram for us from which we start the Deployment Designer. What we do when creating a deployment diagram is to take one logical datacenter diagram and describe how the applications will be deployed in the logical datacenter. The deployment diagram mirrors the logical datacenter but also tells us where each application will be deployed. In our example, you can see that the Windows application is deployed on a client computer, the web service on a web server, and so on.

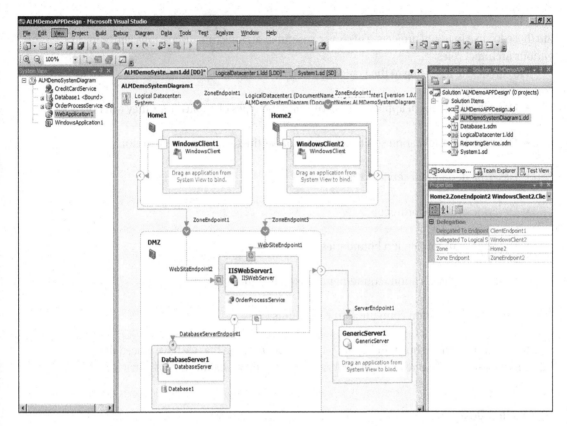

Figure 7-50. *The Deployment Designer*

When we are happy with our deployment diagram, we create the deployment report. We find a lot of information in the deployment report useful for both developers and infrastructure staff. We also get great documentation of our intended system. The following things can be found in the deployment report:

- Settings that need to be updated in application configuration files.

- IIS metabase settings required by ASP.NET applications for deployment.

- IIS metabase settings for IIS web servers that need validation on the target servers.

- Paths to deployment output files.

- Connection information for applications, logical servers, and zones.

- Relationships between applications and the logical servers that host those applications.

- Absolute URIs for web service and web content provider endpoints. (The URI can be said to be the deployment location.)

Figure 7-51 shows how these four designers are connected under the hood. The Application Designer creates some application definitions that are used as an input to the System Designer. The System Designer in turn creates system definitions as input to the Deployment Designer. From the Logical Datacenter Designer we get logical server definitions, which are incorporated into the deployment diagram together with the system definitions. The end result will be our initial complete architecture.

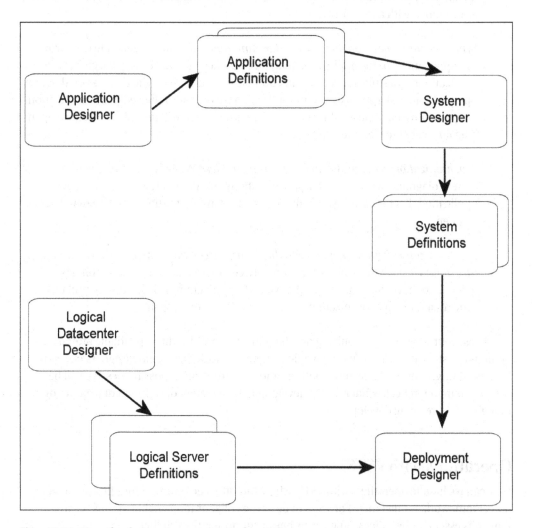

Figure 7-51. *How the designers are connected in TFS*

Synchronizing System Diagrams

Remember what I said about Visio earlier? I don't like Visio because its output always seems to remain static; nobody goes back and changes architecture descriptions after they are created and the project has started. I know this is not Visio's fault, but still. In VS we have synchronization across the distributed system diagrams we have just talked about.

There are four ways in which diagrams are synchronized:

- *Synchronization between application diagrams and system diagrams*: Most changes we make to an application diagram are synchronized with the system diagram, as long as both are open. If we close one, the synchronization will not take place until the system diagram is opened. But at least it will occur. There is one exception to this: if we delete an application, VS will not remove it from the system diagram. Instead it will be marked as orphaned with a red dashed outline.

- *Synchronization between application diagrams and code*: We can generate code from our applications in the application diagram. VS will create the basic projects for the applications and stubs for communication. As long as we have the application diagram open, we can make changes in code and see those changes reflected in the application diagram. If we have closed the diagram, synchronization will take place when we open it again—very nice feature.

- *Synchronization between system diagrams themselves*: When we work with several system diagrams, we have synchronization between them the same way as between application diagrams and system diagrams. The same restriction applies when deleting a system.

- *Synchronization between deployment diagrams, system diagrams, and logical datacenter diagrams*: We have full synchronization between these diagrams. If something is deleted, we have this synchronized as well. If any diagram is closed during updates to other diagrams, synchronization occurs when it is opened again.

These four ways of synchronizing our diagrams make Visio a bit expendable after development has started, in my opinion. I would rather work with the system designers instead because they give me so many more options and synchronization possibilities. We will have a living system that reflects what is being developed, not a system description of what we once thought we were going develop.

Operations with VSTS

How can we handle operations with VSTS? Microsoft offers no template for Microsoft Operations Framework, for instance. For VSTS to be a true collaboration enabler in this regard, I think it is essential that Microsoft gives us better support in the product.

Operations are an important part of any ALM process. When I talked to some of the Microsoft employees in Redmond, they told me that that the vision was that operations could use Microsoft System Center to gather information about the systems in production. When an issue occurs, the operator can use a custom-made integration to report a bug or perhaps a change request into TFS.

This makes sense, but we still have to make our own template for how we want to use TFS with operations. How will a change request or a bug be handled after it is sent to TFS? We are pretty much left to our own devices here, and so far Microsoft offers little help in this matter.

I would like to see an ITIL template or a MOF template, just to mention two. If we want to use VSTS to support the whole ALM process, this is an essential part of that. In my opinion, we need to spend some time on this matter and figure out how we want to use TFS in operations.

Operations should probably be the longest-running process of an application lifecycle and I am a bit surprised that Microsoft has not offered any insights into how they look at this matter. This is a bit typical perhaps, because we often make the mistake of overlooking operations in our projects.

Requirements Specifications

One thing I would like to be improved in VSTS is the handling of requirements specifications. I am not sure how this should be implemented, but support is poor in VSTS today. Basically, the only way we have to solve this is to create a new work item for each requirement and then work from there. Maybe there should be a tool that even business people could use to input requirements early in the process. This tool could then connect to VSTS and save the requirements as work items. By using the workflow and work item tracking features, we could build a very nice workflow for requirements. I know that Microsoft is working with this issue, but so far I am not sure how they will act on this topic.

User Experience and User Experience Requirements

User experience, or UX as it is referred to, is a very important area in system development projects aimed at a human end user. Often this task is left to the developers to accomplish. I have seen this myself in many projects, where the managers downgrade this in regards to other development tasks. I really don't know why we treat UX in such a way so often. Developing software involves many factors: visual appearance, interactions, appropriate content, responsiveness, and so on, at least if we want the software to be really useful to the end user.

This also means that we need different skills in a project. We need a graphics designer to create the visual experience. We probably need someone who can organize, prioritize, and interrelate the content. Then we need some developer(s) who can integrate the visual experience with the content and any back-end systems we might need. I think that a single person who could master all of these different skills is uncommon and hard to find. Yet this is often one of the most common ways we handle this.

The latest example I saw was when I made an ALM assessment at a large European travel company in early 2008. They have a great web site for booking flights, hotels, and much more. The user experience should be very important to them, but somehow they did not have a good grip on it. They had marketing people doing research about what users wanted on the site, but no good way to communicate it to the developers. Most often they sent JPGs or BMPs explaining what they wanted it to look like, and then they dropped it until they could see a demo or mock-up of the web site.

On the development team, only one person—let's call him Peter—was interested in UX, but the role itself didn't exist. Peter took the role in all projects he could, just because he liked the area and saw it as important. In the projects he couldn't participate in, developers handled UX. What's more was that Peter wanted the collaboration between the marketing/web people and the development team to be better. The way it was handled in the organization made it unnecessarily complicated and expensive, leading to a user experience that was not as good as it could have been.

The result of the ALM assessment also showed that the UX team was not included in the projects and that they scored very low on all UX questions. Management knew that the area was a bit downgraded, but not that they actually were pretty bad at it. In the end, UX was one of the issues we started working on improving.

I think that this company is not unique, and that these problems exist in many other companies. UX teams, like web developers and marketing people, are often separated from the rest of the development team, and communication between the two is pretty poor. So what can we do about it?

Microsoft has created a new markup language to represent user interfaces that will help us improve collaboration between these areas; this language is called Extensible Application Markup Language (XAML). This new language is a part of Microsoft Expression Studio, which is a toolset aimed at web designers and other graphic designers. What is even more interesting is that Visual Studio can handle this language as well. And both can even work with the same project at the same time. Talk about collaboration.

If a UX expert produces the GUI for the application in XAML, with all buttons and text boxes and so on, the developer can produce all code behind these objects. When the UX person updates a file, VS will tell the developer this and we can easily refresh the GUI.

XAML almost vaporizes the barrier between designers and developers, and they are no longer forced to work with a hard design freeze, which they usually do otherwise. As long as the basic visual language is there, the rest can remain pretty loose until the last minute with little or even no impact on the work the developer is doing.

The potential for improving collaboration by using Expression Studio and Visual Studio for these different roles in the same project is great. We now have a great opportunity to integrate the work created by these people, and not leave the UX to the developer. Much of the user interface work that traditionally fell into the hands of the developer may now be in the hands of the designer. This can free the developer to focus on other aspects of system.

What Microsoft has done here is definitely something that will simplify the development process. Now I'm just waiting for an integration of Expression Studio with TFS so that the UX experts can access this functionality, including work items, reports, and so on. This is something that has to come in place for it to be as useful as possible.

Extensibility

Collaboration can also be improved by using the VSTS extensibility. Many projects have to solve problems on different platforms. Most of my customers do not have a pure .NET/Microsoft environment. They have Java development, mainframe development, and so on, because much of their business logic and information is spread across these platforms. Teamprise will run on operating systems that support a Java Runtime Environment (JRE) 1.4 or newer, which enables us to better collaborate in projects doing development on multiple platforms.

Summary

This chapter has focused on some deeper features of VSTS. You have seen many of the benefits it offers us in solving the ALM issues of Chapter 2.

There are features for collaboration, traceability, roles, and much, much more in this product from Microsoft. The next chapter provides an example of how I have helped companies by introducing an ALM process using VSTS as a tool.

CHAPTER 8

■■■

Real-Life Example

This final chapter shows a real-life example of how I have helped a customer implement an ALM solution on VSTS. The example does not show implementation of all the ALM practices, but illustrates how you can use the assessment tools to implement an ALM process on VSTS.

This example is compiled from a collection of experiences from several projects. The events described here are an amalgam of those from several real enterprises. Although this chapter's example is real, some of the reports are not from actual projects, because I needed to maintain client confidentiality. In those cases, I have used screenshots from a demo setup at Know IT and also some provided to me by Conchango, makers of the Scrum for Team System process template.

Customer Case

The company has most of its development in Sweden, with about 50 people in the development department. Furthermore, they have a department focused on usability and web site design. Most of their new systems are running on a Windows platform with development on the .NET platform, but some systems remain on mainframes with development in Common Business-Oriented Language (COBOL). VSTS is available in the organization, but employees had used little more than some version-control features when the company contacted me.

The CIO was interested in running the IT development in a more-effective manner. She wanted to see if there could be improvements that would lead to better management of IT resources. The CIO wanted to spend less on operations and more on development, without losing the quality the company had.

As she described all this, I started to consider my options for helping them. This could be one of my first opportunities to try the ALM assessment workshop that my coworker and I had come up with. I put together a plan and presented it to the company's decision makers. In short, the plan looked like this:

- Perform the ALM assessment I described in Chapter 5

- Perform workshops to prioritize the results

- Choose low-hanging fruit

- Select pilot project(s)

- Use Assessment Builder to make a rough plan

- Go through with a pilot

- Measure the effects six months later

Before starting any work, we talked about the importance of obtaining a commitment from the company's management. In this case, getting a commitment was not so hard, because the company had contacted me in the first place. Still, I think it is important to talk about the commitment anyway. It is essential for management to know that a workshop will take place and that the result might very well lead to (development) process changes in the organization. After all, the company is paying for it and therefore should have final say in things like this. It is also management who is responsible for the outcome of the projects and the business value they provide.

We also agreed that if the assessment and workshops showed a need to carry out a pilot project, I or another project manager from Know IT should lead that change project. After all was agreed, we started planning for the performance of the assessment phase.

ALM Assessment

We chose to use the setup from Chapter 5, which includes three workshop gatherings. We sat down with management and discussed which people should be included in the process. We wanted at least one person—and preferably several people—from each area to be involved in the assessments. We agreed that management should be part of the process, so that their input could be obtained. We ended up with nearly 20 people participating.

We selected three dates, with two weeks between each date, so that my coworker and I would have enough time to go through all the material. We didn't want to rush any of the process. We also carefully set up interview slots for all participants in an effort to complete as many interviews as possible in one day. Table 8-1 summarizes what we (from Know IT) wanted to achieve for each of these meetings and also what we delivered to the customer.

Table 8-1. *Summary of Goals and Deliverables for Each ALM Assessment Meeting*

	Goal	Deliverable	Key Participants
Meeting 1	Get to know the organization and the people in it Get some early indications of the organization's status	Results from assessment Report of findings (including our own observations)	Management (business and IT) All ALM roles (developers, business analysts, project managers, testers, and so on)
Meeting 2	Deep knowledge of the organization for as correct an assessment as possible	Results of assessment Report of findings (including our own observations) Report of our suggested way to find the lowest-hanging fruits for the organization	Management (business and IT) during introduction All ALM roles (developers, business analysts, project managers, testers, and so on)
Meeting 3	An awareness from the organization that change is (or is not) necessary Understanding of strengths and weaknesses in the organization	Prioritization of the steps necessary to enhance the organization's weak areas Roadmap indicating prioritized steps	Management (business and IT) Key persons from each ALM role (developers, business analysts, project managers, testers, and so on)

Meeting 1

When the first day came, we started with an introduction to the whole process by describing what we were going to do and why. We also gave a brief overview of ALM and why it is important to the participants and their business. This led to interesting discussions as many participants had differing views on ALM. When we finally agreed on the definition that we would use for this assessment, we started with the interviews.

The interviews were time-boxed to one hour, but we easily could have used an hour and a half in many cases. So if you are trying this yourself, please make sure you have plenty of time.

The first assessment covered the following areas, as described in Chapter 5:

- Development

- Data management

- SOA and business processes

- Business intelligence

We discussed all of the assessment questions with each participant. It was also essential for us to take notes during the interviews so we could record information that the questions did not cover. As a result, there was a lot of material for us to process after that day.

My coworker and I spent days going over the material. Then we used the APO assessment from the Microsoft web site (described in Chapter 5) to enter our answers. We could soon see that our results were more accurate than they would have been if the CIO had answered the questions alone. This was as we suspected, but was good to have confirmed, because it strengthened our belief in the method we chose.

The results from day 1 are presented in Table 8-2.

Table 8-2. *The Results of the APO Assessment*

Practice	Score	Capability Summary
Development	Standardized	The organization has only lightweight development methodologies and some nonintegrated lifecycle tools. The development is done on both legacy and modern platforms. This brings down efficiency and drives up costs.
Service-Oriented Architecture and Business Process Management	Basic	The organization does not have SOA; instead there are hard-coded integrations across systems. Standardization has not been implemented except for perhaps XML. The organization is dependent on much manual work. This makes integration between systems harder and seen as costly and difficult to implement.
Data Management	Standardized	The systems benefit from protected and recoverable data services that are also integrated and flexible. Continuous data availability helps reduce both planned and unplanned downtime, driving up responsiveness and productivity. The organization has the potential to gain higher levels of security, responsiveness, and productivity by moving to the advanced level.
Business Intelligence	Standardized	The business intelligence (BI) capabilities are more evolved than the basic level, but the organization still uses data marts as the only method of storage. The BI infrastructure is ready to move forward to provide not only user-driven and centrally managed reporting and analysis, but also enterprise-wide business alignment.

The results also offered some advice on how to move the organization to the next level for each of these four areas. We realized that even though the questions sometimes seemed a little odd and at times were a bit hard to understand, the results generally agreed with our own opinions of the organization's status based on our interviews.

We found that the organization could benefit a great deal from advancing at least one level in all areas. The company had started using VSTS and some processes for development, but had not taken control of the entire ALM process. The SOA and Business Process Management (BPM) areas could definitely gain from advancing at least two levels. The company used some services but had no strategy for combining SOA and BPM. At this point, IT was seen as a cost center and not as a possibility center ready to support the business.

We also clearly saw that the organization lacked a good testing methodology, and that VSTS could help greatly with this. And because VSTS was already in place, most issues were "just" a question of taking control of the process.

We produced a report of our findings, added some information that we had discovered ourselves, and prepared to present this to the company at the next meeting. We also sent the report to the managers so they could read it and reflect on it until we met again. We also planned time slots for interviews that we should conduct on day 2, but this time we extended the time by a half-hour so we wouldn't have to rush.

Meeting 2

Day 2 was started with a summary of the results from day 1. We allowed plenty of time for discussions of the findings. These discussions were very good to have, especially for me as an observer. We realized that the discussions enabled people to come up with new ideas, and this energized the participants in a way that readied them to move on and take the next steps.

The interviews this time were focused on eight areas, as described in Chapter 5:

- Requirements Engineering and User Experience

- Testing and Quality Assurance

- Code Quality

- Architecture and Design

- Project Planning and Management

- Software Configuration Management

- Deployment and Operations

- Data Management

We didn't ask each person all the assessment questions this time. Instead we focused on those questions that were more closely related to the specific role that each person usually performed in the projects. Because we had so many questions this time, our notes were far more extensive than they were the first time. We soon discovered the benefits of holding the first meeting because my coworker and I now knew much more about the organization and could use this knowledge to dive deeper into all areas and to ask better and more-relevant follow-up questions.

After summarizing the questions, we entered them into the assessment form on the Microsoft web site and got the results. The overall score for this organization was 3.07, which put the organization at an advanced level.

At an advanced level, IT is truly seen as a business enabler and partner. Infrastructure and systems are more easily managed throughout their lifecycles. The business processes are well-defined and well-known. The business side has begun to truly take advantage of IT and can rely on the IT department to quickly make adjustments when changes in the business occur. Such a company has standardized a robust and flexible application platform for the most critical systems and processes.

The score of 3.07 meant that the organization just barely reached the advanced level, so there was still some work to do, for them to become truly advanced.

Table 8-3 presents the scores for each separate area.

Table 8-3. *The Results of the Application Platform Capability Assessment*

Area	Score	Maturity
User Experience	1.67	Basic
Requirements Engineering	2.94	Standardized
Testing and Quality Assurance	3.09	Advanced
Code quality	2.36	Standardized
Architecture and Design	2.76	Standardized
Project Planning and Management	3.54	Advanced
Software Configuration Management	4.17	Dynamic
Deployment and Operations	3.80	Advanced
Data Management	3.32	Advanced

The results were mostly as my coworker and I expected. However, we were surprised by the score in one area: Testing and Quality Assurance, which rated advanced. We didn't agree with this score because our interviews indicated that this area had great room for improvement. People on the development teams said they often had a test plan, but only on paper. The plan was never followed up or updated.

In addition, the company did not use unit testing, code reviews, or continuous integration, which I think are more or less required for a good testing strategy. We could also see that there was no test leader in place for most projects. Most testing was acceptance testing at the end of a project. All in all, this told us that the company would score lower than it did. We would have expected a "standardized" score on this, especially because code quality scored only 2.36.

Our own summary from the day could be described in five main points:

1. Both development and operations could benefit from better structuring the process, from requirements to tested executable code. This structuring could be achieved by enforcing better and more-automated processes, traceability, and structured requirements specifications. The organization had started looking into different development processes and had purchased VSTS, but was not using these processes optimally. The participants needed to decide which way they wanted to work, what their ALM process should look like—and then use VSTS to implement it. They also needed to address traceability, especially by starting to use the work item tracking system in VSTS. By enforcing a test-driven development approach, we could also attain better traceability. Documentation could also be improved, because most documents never were updated after they were written.

2. Roles in the projects were often confusing. Sometimes the project manager, the requirements manager, and the tester were the same person. This is quite unsuitable in my opinion because tests might be (subconsciously) structured so that they don't show the bugs or flaws that really exist. By better separating these roles, projects would improve. Other roles in the company were often handled in a good way, so it was mostly these roles that were the problem.

3. The user experience could use improvements, especially by better integrating this role in the projects. As it was now, the only interaction between the UX team and the development team occurred when the UX team sent figures to the development team, and the development team showed some mock-up in return. The company really needed to start involving the UX team in its projects, so that at least one representative was included every time.

4. The interface between projects and the operations team was unclear. Deployment could be improved by better integrating the operations team in the projects. This was evident when it was time to deploy an application or system. The operations team had not been part of the project and suddenly found themselves with a new system that should run on their infrastructure. Often this led to some delay in deployment, because the operations team needed to prepare servers and the network for the new system.

5. Testing, especially during coding, could improve. There was no good strategy for testing, no unit testing (unless an individual developer took this initiative), and no automation of testing. The company also did not use code reviews or continuous integration. We could also see that there was no test leader in place for most projects, and most testing was acceptance testing at the end of a project. With a test-driven approach, the company had much to gain.

We then created our own review of how these five points could be implemented by assessing them on a scale that indicated how complex they were to implement and the benefit they could give the organization once implemented. This review showed the lowest-hanging fruits and also gave us arguments as to how the organization could move forward. These results are shown in Figure 8-1. Each of the numbered points corresponds to a number in each circle.

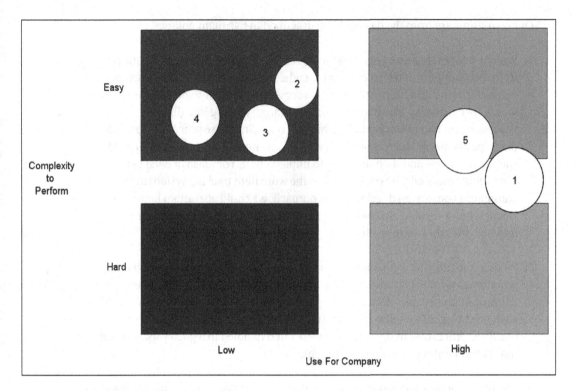

Figure 8-1. *Finding the lowest-hanging fruit*

As you can see, none of these would be especially hard to implement, but two of them could definitely provide great benefits to the organization: automated processes and traceability (1) and testing (5).

The suggestions we came up with for this organization to move forward were the following:

- Better quality

  - Working in a structured manner with automated processes makes the process less error-prone and less bound to particular people.

  - A better-structured process from requirements to tested executable code enhances traceability.

- Better efficiency

  - Better traceability helps in evaluating and implementing changes in a more structured and faster way.

  - Implement test-driven development. This will increase productivity, because fewer errors will be transferred into system and acceptance testing.

Table 8-4 summarizes how we could achieve these changes by taking a few necessary steps. Each step could of course improve both efficiency and quality, but I have chosen to mark only one or the other, depending on where the most impact would be seen.

Table 8-4. *Our Suggestions for Implementation Steps and What They Would Achieve*

Step	Efficiency	Quality
Use TFS work item tracking to introduce traceability	X	
Start using a well-defined ALM process		X
Use the TFS capability to automate the ALM process		X
Start using automated unit testing	X	
Start using continuous integration to build several times a day	X	
Start using a model such as ITIL for operations		X

Taking these steps would provide the following benefits for the company:

- Working in a more structured way by automating processes and providing traceability will lower costs for development as well as for operations. This improvement might affect the operations team especially, because they had an ad hoc way of doing things.

- Project members will have better and earlier control over the consequences of their decisions.

- Automated unit testing and continuous integration will lower the cost for fixing errors because fewer errors will be found late in the project timelines.

- More resources can be spent on new development and on improvements to existing applications and systems because the cost of operations will be lower (without loss of quality).

- The benefit of every invested dollar will be higher.

We put together the report for day 3 but chose not to send it over before the meeting. We wanted to hear the participants' first impressions this time because we realized that sending over the report before meeting 2 made the customer reflect on topics before we had a chance to explain and discuss them first. This led to some unnecessary discussions that took time from the other agenda items. We then started to produce the agenda for day 3 (which in fact took two days this time, as we found much we wanted to discuss).

Meeting 3

The agenda for day 3 was as follows:

- Summary of day 2, with discussions

- Introduction to traceability in TFS

- Introduction to process templates in TFS

- Introduction to MSF and Scrum

- Introduction to test-driven development and continuous integration

- Introduction to ITIL

- Workshop about lowest-hanging fruits

- Workshop on how to move forward

The results from day 2 were somewhat surprising to the CIO. She probably expected the scores to be a bit higher in some areas. These areas were her babies, so to speak, and she cared for them deeply. It is always harder to be objective and reflect on something that you invest a lot of time and effort into, and the CIO drove much of the work in regard to these areas. But during discussions with other members of her team, we agreed that the scores and our own reflections were probably right on in most cases. This is one of the reasons I suggest that an independent party perform the assessment based on interviews with several team members.

The introductions to several topics, which you can see in the preceding agenda, were a direct result of our findings. We chose to gather specialists from Know IT who came and gave short presentations followed by discussions on each subject. Participants greatly appreciated the discussions, both during the results and the presentations, and these gave birth to new thoughts on how to improve the ALM process. This was our intention: we wanted the participants to start thinking in a fresh, new way.

Workshop with Priorities (Lowest-Hanging Fruits)

We then carried on by having a workshop focusing on the priorities for how to continue. This was a traditional workshop with Post-it notes and whiteboards, but it worked very well because we got everybody focused. During these workshops, we met with the CIO; the CIO's closest coworker, who was IT manager of the Swedish part of the company; and a few of the most experienced developers. We did not meet with all of the nearly 20 people involved in previous presentations. Six representatives from the company and two from Know IT were present. Having too many people at the workshop would have prevented us from reaching good decisions within the three-hour timeframe that we had set aside for this activity.

My coworker and I knew how we wanted the company to proceed, but it was the company's decision on how to move forward. We had already planted a seed, so to speak, through the presentation of our findings, but at this point the company would guide us in outlining the next steps in their ALM process improvement plan:

1. *Automated processes, traceability, and structured requirements specifications*: This clearly was one of the most important issues we found. We realized that we had to start working on this at once, but that it would take some time to accomplish. This was a clear candidate for a pilot project.

2. *Project roles*: The company representatives agreed with us that the way they handled the roles in projects sometimes conflicted. We decided to better separate the roles. This did not mean that one person always should play one role. Each person could very well play several roles, as long as these roles did not conflict in a project. This was something that we could start with immediately, without too much effort.

3. *User experience*: For a company so focused on doing business with customers through the interface of web pages, it was peculiar that this area wasn't more of a company priority. We decided that this could be corrected quite easily, with minimum effort. We all agreed that making a move from the company's Adobe web suite to Microsoft Expression Studio was out of the question. The designers and web experts would never allow such a large switch in their work process. We, however, agreed that we should try to get a few people to try Expression Studio so they could get a feel for it. This activity was not given a high priority, though. Instead we decided that representatives from the user experience group would become active members of all development projects from now on, and that regular meetings between the development and user experience groups would be scheduled. So a group that was not necessarily seen as part of the ALM process in this organization turned out to be important in the process.

4. *The interface between projects and operations*: This unclear interface was another easy thing to correct. We decided to start integrating the operations team in development projects earlier, even during planning. We decided to try to see whether having the designers use the architect edition of VSTS could provide benefits. This meant that we needed some time for preparation, but that we quite soon could try it out. We decided to include this in the pilot project we had started forming in our heads.

5. *Testing*: This was an essential and important issue. Not many of the developers had looked into test-driven development or continuous integration, so in order for this to be an integral part of development, we realized that we had to start educating the team. This was something that we wanted to include in the pilot as well, especially because this was part of the development process that we would formalize anyway as a result of the first point in this list.

We then used the Assessment Builder (formerly called Roadmap Builder) available in the assessment tool to plan the implementation process. We decided to have a startup project first that would take care of all preparations for running the pilot(s). We included education and training in this, as well as some evaluations of the process and the tools in VSTS.

This startup project would prepare the organization for the changes they were going to implement. We wanted to train the people involved, let them evaluate processes and tools, let them consider their way of working so they could see that this way was actually built into the automated process in VSTS in the end, and also select a pilot project. During the startup project, we would also do the implementation of the process in VSTS. This means that we would change the process template (if necessary) and make it available for all new projects in VSTS. We also wanted to use this phase to enable better communication between the business, IT, and operations groups within the company. We estimated that this process would be a three-iteration project, with each iteration lasting a maximum of four weeks.

After this startup phase, we decided to have a pilot project during which we would evaluate the process template and then make adjustments if necessary.

After these two days of workshops and presentations, everyone was quite happy and excited to take the next steps to improve their processes. The participants realized it would take some effort, but they were convinced that they would get so much back that the effort would be worth it.

Implementation

Figure 8-2 shows the iteration plan for the startup project. Note that I cannot show you any direct screenshots from the Assessment Builder because they contain specific customer information that I am not allowed to reveal.

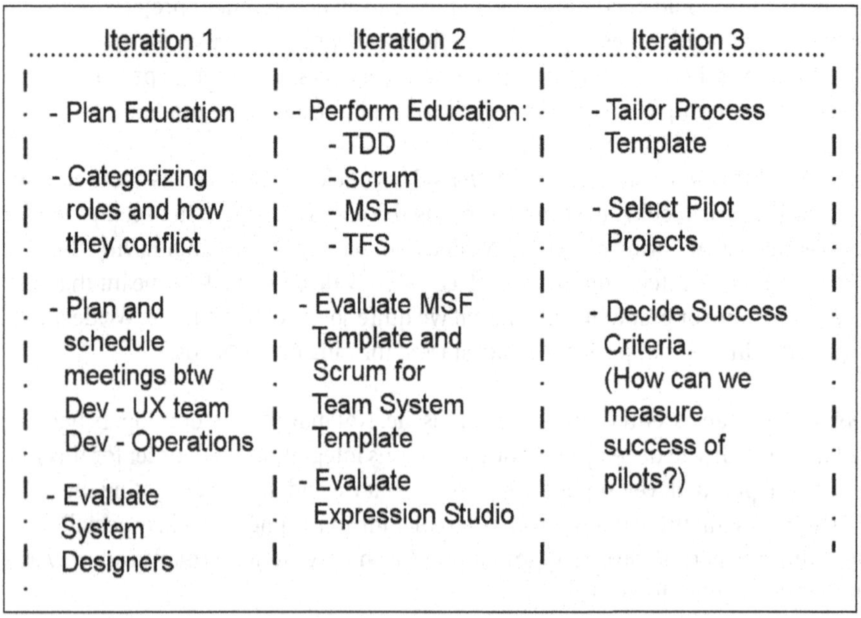

Iteration 1	Iteration 2	Iteration 3
- Plan Education	- Perform Education:	- Tailor Process
	- TDD	Template
- Categorizing	- Scrum	
roles and how	- MSF	- Select Pilot
they conflict	- TFS	Projects
- Plan and	- Evaluate MSF	- Decide Success
schedule	Template and	Criteria.
meetings btw	Scrum for	(How can we
Dev - UX team	Team System	measure
Dev - Operations	Template	success of
- Evaluate	- Evaluate	pilots?)
System	Expression Studio	
Designers		

Figure 8-2. *Iterations of the startup project*

The first (startup) project was scheduled to last up to 12 weeks and would have three iterations.

Startup Project

The following activities were performed during this project.

Iteration 1

The overall goal of iteration 1 was to prepare everything for the coming iterations. We also wanted to start evaluating VSTS in those areas where the participants (for example, the system designers) had not used it before.

Planning the education meant that we selected the trainers for the TDD, Scrum, MSF, and TFS training we were going to have. We also scheduled these training sessions so that as many attendants as possible could participate during iteration 2.

We also started categorizing the roles now existing in their company and discussed which were conflicting. The roles we used are the ones described in Chapter 2:

- Business manager

- Project manager

- Business analyst

- Architect

- User experience team

- DBA

- Developers

- Testers

- Operations and maintenance staff

Regular meetings between the development team and user experience team as well as between the development team and operations were scheduled. We wanted the team members to get to know each other and learn more about each other's skills. We decided to start the whole thing by having a kickoff meeting during which all groups presented themselves and their skill sets.

We also scheduled recurring meetings between stakeholders and project managers of the development team. If the project was to be successful, we needed to get these people better acquainted because the stakeholders should act as product owners and be a part of the coming projects.

We also decided to let one person from the development team get together with one person from operations and evaluate the system designers in Visual Studio Team Edition for Architects. They should then present their findings in the kickoff meeting.

Iteration 2

The goal of iteration 2 was to educate the team members so they were prepared for the change implementations later. We also wanted to continue our evaluation of tools and processes.

The trainers we selected in iteration 1 came to the company and provided training on site. Project managers and some experienced developers were trained to become certified scrum masters. Some of the stakeholders were trained in the product owner role of Scrum, so they would know what Scrum was all about and could improve their requirements specifications. We also let managers from operations go through some ITIL training.

After training was done, we let some of the more experienced developers/architects and project managers start looking into the process templates. We looked at MSF for Agile and Scrum for Team System. We soon realized that we wanted to do a pilot of each process, to determine whether one was most suitable or whether we should have both installed in the TFS. We also decided on which information we wanted in the work items, which document templates were important to have in the process, and what the test and build strategy would look like. This information would be used during process adjustments in iteration 3.

The operations representatives started looking at how to implement ITIL or at least a more formalized operations process in TFS. In the end, we chose to move this activity to a separate project following the pilot projects. Recent findings in Swedish articles at www.idg.se showed that using an agile approach to improve the operations process could be a benefit, and that companies implementing Scrum for operations had cut costs. The CIO wanted to investigate this further before implementing changes to the operations department and their processes. We couldn't manage this task at the same time as the others, so it was moved from the pilot.

During this iteration, two user experience experts evaluated Expression Studio. They saw the benefits of integrating this with Visual Studio, but chose to use their existing tools because switching would require too much training. We didn't abandon the idea, however; we just postponed it.

Iteration 3

The goal of iteration 3 was to start the implementation of the company's new ALM process. We also needed to start thinking about how to evaluate the result of the pilot.

In this iteration, we adjusted the process templates as we had determined was necessary in iteration 2. We spent about a week and a half making the initial adjustments. After that, we let developers and other team members reflect on the changes and then we implemented their comments as well. The project portal was adjusted as were the web access pages. Some work item templates were extended. Some reports were reviewed and changed as well. Scrum for Team System was chosen as our Scrum template, with no adjustments. MSF for Agile was extended a bit, as some information on the work items needed to be included. We also decided to evaluate the information in the work items at the end of each sprint/iteration. We finally rewrote the process guidelines so they would better suit the organization.

Keep in mind that we still had not tested any of these changes in a real project. We had selected a pilot to start immediately after this iteration. The pilot would use the new processes, and it was during this pilot that we would start seeing the benefits of them.

One important thing we wanted to enable was code analysis. We decided to try the default rules set by Microsoft and evaluate them during each sprint/iteration and remove or adjust as we moved along.

We decided on a continuous integration strategy, which meant that we would set up a build and test lab (see Figure 8-3). The lab used one server for the build process, and virtual PC images for the test machines. This way, we could easily reset the test machines after tests were done. We enabled automated unit tests with the builds to be run with every integration.

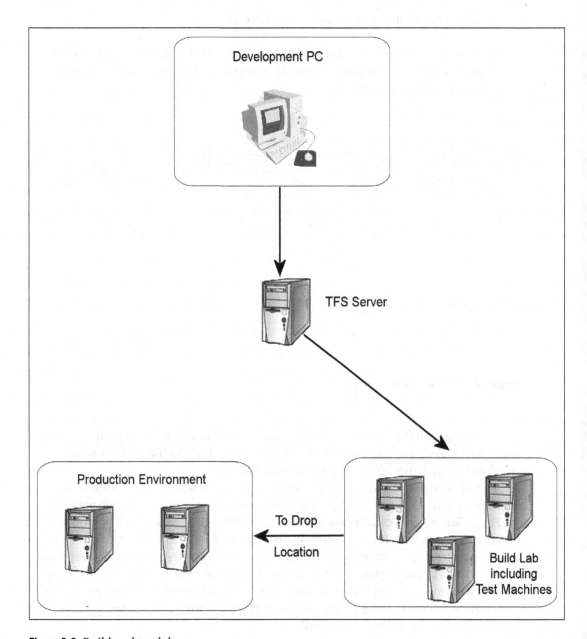

Figure 8-3. *Build and test lab*

We also made sure to enable the following check-in policies (see Figure 8-4):

- **Work item for traceability.** Everyone should include a work item ID so we can enable traceability from requirements to executable code.

- **Code analysis for improving code quality.** We wanted to enforce a better way of writing code and of complying with coding practices in the organization.

- **Test policy** for running unit tests at each check-in.

- **Check-in notes.** We wanted the developer to write a short description of what he had done so that we could easily see what the changeset included and not have to read through one or more work items.

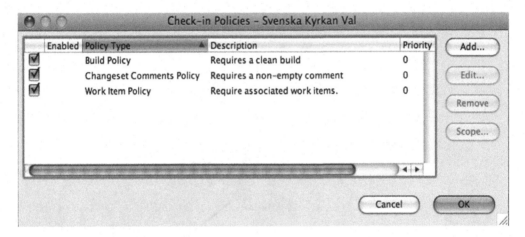

Figure 8-4. *Enabled check-in policies*

The company had two new projects that could be used as pilot projects. Both were web application projects and thought to be of reasonable project size for the pilots. They were scheduled to start in late 2007, which suited us just fine.

Project managers and scrum masters were able to choose whether they wanted to use Microsoft Project or Excel. The company had no Project server in place, so we did not go for the Project Server Connector. Microsoft Office Project Server is Microsoft's server product for resource management between projects. Microsoft Office Project is the client tool for Project Server, enabling project managers to work on their individual projects while still updating the server database so that all project managers have updated resource information. Project can be used as a stand-alone application without Project Server if a project manager wants, or if the organization does not have a Project server. If that is the case, resource management must be handled manually or from another tool.

The Project Server Connector makes it possible to integrate VSTS with Project Server for better resource management, and in this organization they had no Project server. We choose to let project managers use either Project as a stand-alone application or Excel, and to synchronize their work directly from them instead. That way, we could still benefit from letting project managers use their familiar tool (Excel or Project), but lacked the resource management features. This enabled the managers to use one of these tools for gathering requirements and adding work items to the TFS.

A lot of discussions took place when we started to talk about how to measure success. In the end, we agreed that we should perform a new assessment three to six months after the pilots were completed. The criteria for success was an increase of one maturity level in the following areas:

- User experience

- Requirements engineering

- Testing

- Code quality

If we could manage to attain the one-level increases with the efforts we put in now, the CIO and the other stakeholders would be satisfied.

Pilot of MSF for Agile and Scrum for Team System

The company wanted to evaluate both Scrum and MSF for Agile, and then compare the experiences of both processes.

There were two separate teams for the pilots. One team was seated on the premises (the Scrum pilot) and the other (MSF) had some members on the premises as well as at a remote location. The setup for this was done as in Figure 8-5. The Scrum team consisted of seven team members, and the MSF team had nine.

■**Note** Unfortunately, I am not allowed to reveal the original setup or original information from work items and reports here, so I am using a demo project instead. Also note that Know IT provided support for the scrum master and product owner during the process, because the company was so new to Scrum.

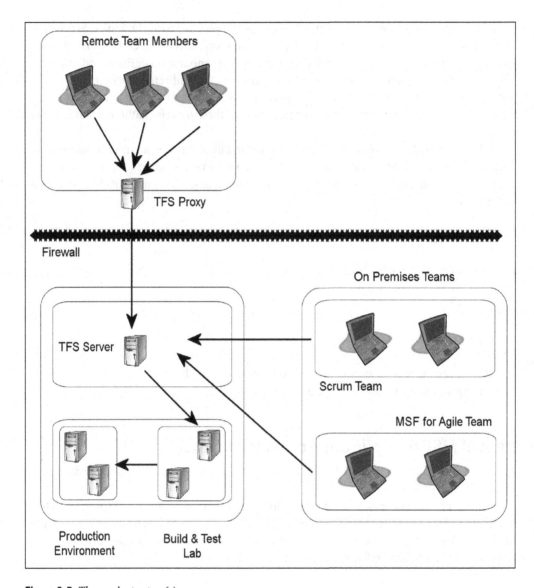

Figure 8-5. *The project setup(s)*

Scrum Team

The Scrum team used Conchango's Scrum for Team System template. They used the Product Backlog work item type to enter all product backlog items. The product owner handled this together with the scrum master. The team then selected the product backlog items for the first sprint. At the first sprint planning meeting, team members discussed each item with the product owner and then started breaking them down to Sprint Backlog items.

The Scrum team had its daily scrum at 9 AM in an office at the company. The team used the Impediments work item type (see Figure 8-6) to enter things that would arise during the sprints and also the Impediments query to keep track of the impediments.

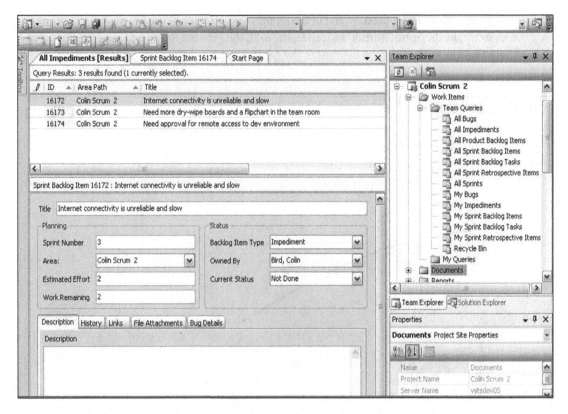

Figure 8-6. *Impediments in the Scrum team*

During the sprint retrospectives, the team used the corresponding work item type in the process template (see Figure 8-7).

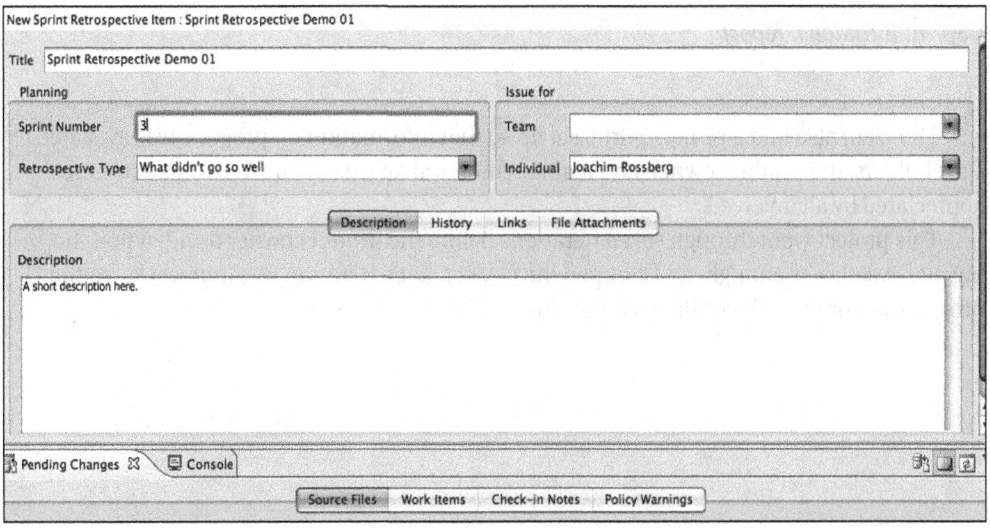

Figure 8-7. *Sprint retrospective*

The scrum master used several of the reports to keep track of the progress of the project—
for example, the Sprint Burndown (see Figure 8-8), the Product Burndown, and the Bug Found
and Fixed reports.

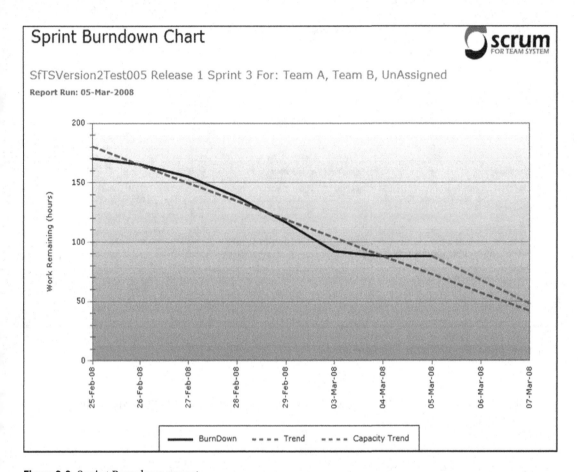

Figure 8-8. *Sprint Burndown report*

The team also had a project portal set up so that information on progress was available to
stakeholders, the product owner, and team members alike (see Figure 8-9). This was much
appreciated by all involved.

This project went through seven iterations before the product owner decided that the
business value was enough, and stopped the project. Each iteration was four weeks, so the
project was completed within seven months.

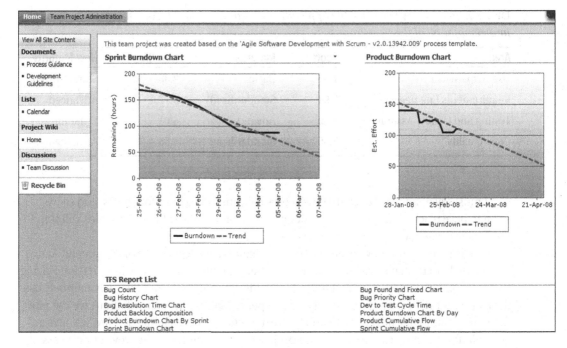

Figure 8-9. *The project portal*

MSF Team

The MSF team pretty much adopted an agile approach and did not use MSF as a process all the way. They chose to have an iterative approach much like the Scrum team did, with the same kind of handling of work items and team meetings. What differed most was the use of reports and queries that came with the MSF for Agile process template.

This project was a little more extensive and is still in progress as I write this. The team is on its ninth four-week sprint. This is the last sprint, and the project will soon end.

Follow-Up

One of the pilots is not finished, so we have not carried out the follow-up assessment yet. But because I wanted to get the teams' opinions anyway, especially for this book, I selected the scrum master, product owner, and project manager from the teams and let them do the assessment again. So remember, these results are not final in any way; things can very well change when we do the assessment with all participants.

Table 8-5 shows the preliminary results of the assessment.

Table 8-5. *Preliminary Results of the Application Platform Capability Assessment After Implementation of the New Process*

Area	Score	Maturity	New Score	New Maturity
User Experience	1.67	Basic	2.88	Standardized
Requirements Engineering	2.94	Standardized	3.77	Advanced
Testing and Quality Assurance	3.09	Advanced	4.01	Dynamic
Code Quality	2.36	Standardized	3.56	Advanced

I must say that I am excited that the scores have improved in all four areas, and so we seem to have reached the goals of the pilot projects. I am confident that the scores will stand the final test when we do the final assessment.

The team members have been very positive about using test-driven development. At first it was a bit hard to change their mindsets, but after that initial phase, they liked it a lot. Having the traceability from the requirements to built code amazed them, and they will definitely use the features of VSTS in coming projects. As one person said: "Why on earth didn't we use more than the version-control system before? This experience has been fantastic. Now we have a great platform that we can use to run our project on, and continue to improve our process with. The work item features are very useful."

The stakeholders and product owners praised the collaboration possibilities and information flow that they got with the team portal and web access. To have such information at their disposal at any time helped them get more involved in the progress of the projects. They knew at once if anything was beginning to be a problem.

Summary

In this chapter, you have seen one way of using the ALM assessment for implementing a better ALM process. A well-thought-out ALM process could help an organization in delivering more-successful IT projects that in the end better fulfill the business requirements through achieving better business value. I do want to stress that an organization adjusts VSTS to the needs of the organization, and not the other way around. Use the ALM assessment tool to evaluate the present situation, and then take the steps necessary based on these results.

This book has tried to show my vision of how we can use the ALM assessments to evaluate the maturity of an organization. The primary goal for this is that we can better implement an effective collaborative ALM process, which will deliver better business value to the organization. By using a tool such as Visual Studio Team System, we can automate this process, which will make it easier for all development project participants to follow the process.

The three pillars of ALM—traceability, process automation, and visibility—are all important for any organization to have. Visual Studio Team System is a great foundation for building our ALM solutions. The company described here benefited a lot even in the early stages of implementation, just by taking some smaller steps toward a better process. Because the evaluation has not been completed as I write this, the full benefits have not yet been revealed. Still, indications point in the right direction.

Keep in mind that VSTS is so much more than a version-control system. It has great power, and great flexibility, to help us improve our organization's ALM process. I cannot stress enough the importance of doing an ALM assessment before starting your VSTS implementation, so that you focus your improvement efforts on the most beneficial aspects first. If a small step can show good return on investment quickly, it is easier to continue the change process with full support in the organization.

Tools will not get us all the way, however, so I have also discussed the use of SOA and the importance of redefining the architect roles in order to fully improve the ALM process. Collaboration is important, and much of this is done between people. Architecture and architects are important in bringing together the business and IT side of an organization.

Index

You Need the Companion eBook

Your purchase of this book entitles you to buy the companion PDF-version eBook for only $10. Take the weightless companion with you anywhere.

We believe this Apress title will prove so indispensable that you'll want to carry it with you everywhere, which is why we are offering the companion eBook (in PDF format) for $10 to customers who purchase this book now. Convenient and fully searchable, the PDF version of any content-rich, page-heavy Apress book makes a valuable addition to your programming library. You can easily find and copy code—or perform examples by quickly toggling between instructions and the application. Even simultaneously tackling a donut, diet soda, and complex code becomes simplified with hands-free eBooks!

Once you purchase your book, getting the $10 companion eBook is simple:

❶ Visit **www.apress.com/promo/tendollars/**.

❷ Complete a basic registration form to receive a randomly generated question about this title.

❸ Answer the question correctly in 60 seconds, and you will receive a promotional code to redeem for the $10.00 eBook.

2855 TELEGRAPH AVENUE | SUITE 600 | BERKELEY, CA 94705

Offer valid through 4/20/09.

Printed in the United States
By Bookmasters